CALIFORNIA NATURAL HISTORY GUIDES

NATURAL HISTORY OF
SAN FRANCISCO BAY

California Natural History Guides

Phyllis M. Faber and Bruce M. Pavlik, General Editors

Natural History of
SAN FRANCISCO BAY

Ariel Rubissow Okamoto
Kathleen M. Wong

UNIVERSITY OF CALIFORNIA PRESS
Berkeley   Los Angeles   London

University of California Press, one of the most distinguished university presses in the United States, enriches lives around the world by advancing scholarship in the humanities, social sciences, and natural sciences. Its activities are supported by the UC Press Foundation and by philanthropic contributions from individuals and institutions. For more information, visit www.ucpress.edu.

California Natural History Guide Series, No. 102

University of California Press
Berkeley and Los Angeles, California

University of California Press, Ltd.
London, England

© 2011 by The Regents of the University of California

Library of Congress Cataloging-in-Publication Data
Rubissow Okamoto, Ariel.
    Natural history of San Francisco Bay / Ariel Rubissow Okamoto, Kathleen M. Wong.
        p.   cm. — (California natural history guide series ; no. 102)
    Includes bibliographical references and index.
    ISBN 978-0-520-26825-8 (cloth : alk. paper) — ISBN 978-0-520-26826-5 (pbk. : alk. paper)
    1. Estuarine ecology—California—San Francisco Bay.   2. Endangered ecosystems—California—San Francisco Bay.   3. Restoration ecology—California—San Francisco Bay.   I. Wong, Kathleen M. (Kathleen Michelle)   II. Title.

    QH105.C2R83 2011
    508.794′6—dc22   2010046564

Manufactured in Singapore
19 18 17 16 15 14 13 12 11
10 9 8 7 6 5 4 3 2 1

The paper used in this publication meets the minimum requirements of ANSI/NISO Z39.48-1992 (R 1997) (*Permanence of Paper*).

Cover photographs: large photo, author Ariel Okamoto and scientist Katharyn Boyer explore herring egg deposits on an eelgrass bed off Keller Beach in Richmond (John Karachewski); left photo, container ships (Port of Oakland); middle photo, pickleweed (Kathleen M. Wong); right photo, juvenile Black-crowned Night Heron (Edward M. Nguyen).

The publisher and authors gratefully acknowledge
the generous contributions toward the publication of this book
provided by

the California Coastal Conservancy,
the Moore Family Foundation,
Friends of the Estuary,
the San Francisco Bay Joint Venture,
U.S. Fish & Wildlife Service, Coastal Program,
San Francisco Bay Initiative,
Bay Area Clean Water Agencies,

and

the General Endowment Fund
of the University of California Press Foundation.

CONTENTS

PROLOGUE

This book is unusual among the California Natural History Guides. It explores not only the natural history of San Francisco Bay but also its human history and how each affects the other. It may be the first in the series to describe a place so urbanized and to focus on a body of water rather than a piece of land, though land and water here are inextricably linked in their destiny.

This guide may also be the first to have so many voices in it. As a journalist who has researched and reported on water issues for over 20 years, I have come to know dozens of scientists, agency staffers, activists, teachers, engineers, and businesspeople with a passion for the bay and its watershed. By including so many quotes and memories from diverse people, I hope I've captured here the intensity with which people view the bay and the amount of energy they pour into studying it, understanding it, and caring for it.

Something else that may be different in this guide, in comparison to others, is the way in which I explore my own particular interest in science and scientists, and the extraordinary ways in which they test their theories in a medium—water, waves, tides, mud—that is relatively challenging for humans to work in. I am personally fascinated by the lengths to which humans will go to learn, and I marvel at the inventions they create to enable them to measure and track the subtle changes in the estuarine environment and all that lives in it.

As I observe our millennial battle for control of nature, I am encouraged that we humans continue to seek our proper place within it. I am heartened that we can not only build a dam but also take it down, as well as by the fact that we can spend hours counting weeds, sifting bay mud for tiny forms of life, following a plastic drifter downriver, or trying to mimic nature so that we can better balance our relationship with the ecosystem.

Perhaps the human race is destined to find the meaning of life onscreen, but I, for one, am all for getting hands dirty and feet wet.

Ariel Rubissow Okamoto

ACKNOWLEDGMENTS

Ariel Rubissow Okamoto

In the two decades that I have been writing about the waters that run down from the Sierra into San Francisco Bay and the Pacific, three people in particular helped me find my voice as an environmental writer: Marcia Brockbank, Tim Ramirez, and Kim Taylor. As they worked to push the envelopes of estuarine science and ecosystem management—often within cumbersome bureaucracies steeped in convoluted water politics—they remained unfailingly inspiring and supportive of my work and my voice.

Thanks also to those who have consistently helped me to think big across disciplines and see the connections: Gary Bobker, Jim Cloern, Bruce Herbold, and Phil Williams. They were critical to my being able to pull together a book of such broad scope.

I also appreciate those who always return my calls and emails, and who have made the time to explain complicated science and politics to me throughout my water-writing life: Jon Burau, Jay Davis, Kathy Heib, Rainer Hoenicke, Jim Kuwabara, Wim Kimmerer, Sam Luoma, Peggy Olofson, Steve Ritchie, Dave Schoellhamer, Stuart Siegel, Tina Swanson, Jan Thompson, and Will Travis.

In addition, much of my work over the last few decades has involved writing documents conveying the work of government science to stakeholders and the interested public. I drew heavily in this book on my earlier work on the annual San Francisco Estuary Project *State of the Estuary* reports, the project's *ESTUARY* newsletter, and CALFED *Science Action* publications. I also found invaluable such bibles as Andy Cohen's *An Introduction to the San Francisco Estuary*, The Bay Institute's *From the Sierra to the Sea* report, the *Baylands Ecosystem Habitat Goals* report and *Species Profiles*, and the annual *Pulse of the Estuary* from the San Francisco Estuary Institute. To remind me how to tell a good bay story, I used Harold Gilliam's *San Francisco Bay*. And I will always be grateful to my professor, Annie Dillard, who told me I was no good, which made me work to prove her wrong.

Thanks also to my wonderful cowriter, Kathleen Wong, and the other writers who helped me complete the book: Cariad Hayes, Lisa Owens Viani, and Susan Zakin.

Particular thanks to everyone whom I interviewed for the book (see the References); to those who read the book back to front for me: Bruce Herbold, Rainer Hoenicke, Jim McGrath, and Peter Moyle; and to my editors, Phyllis Faber and Jenny Wapner, for engaging me in such a unique project. I also was enchanted by how the book communicated a whole new level of information about the bay via the wonderful photography donated by Max Eissler, Francis Parchaso, and Jude Stalker, among others.

Special thanks to the Bay Area Clean Water Agencies for providing critical gap funding for the book's production. BACWA is a joint powers agency whose members own and operate municipal sewer systems in the nine county San Francisco Bay Area. BACWA and its members are public agencies governed by elected officials and managed by professionals charged with and committed to protecting public health and the San Francisco Bay environment.

Last, I could not have written this book without the faith and love of my family—Paul, Tira, Mikki, and my mother, Joyce Carlyle. Thank you for sticking with me through my werewolf moments.

Kathleen M. Wong

First and foremost, I am indebted to my coauthor, Ariel Rubissow Okamoto, for making my long-standing dream to write a book come true. Her strong relationships with bay scientists and broad knowledge of California water issues have shaped my reporting and sparked a whole new appreciation for the wonders of the bay.

I am also grateful to the many researchers, engineers, activists, and photographers I interviewed for this book. They were generous with their time and professional expertise. In particular, I would like to thank Peter Baye, Laurel Collins, Robin Grossinger, John Largier, Marilyn Latta, Jeff Miller, Tim Ramirez, Christopher Richard, and Sarah Warnock.

The one I have leaned upon most during this journey, however, is my husband, Max Eissler. His enthusiasm for exploring strange corners of the bay and his zeal to capture better photos for the book never waned. I couldn't ask for a better companion in life or love.

One day when I was at the 1939 World's Fair I watched the sun going down from Treasure Island, reflected in all the windows in Berkeley and Oakland, a blaze of fire over there. The Bay Bridge was new at that time, and I looked up at this bridge in the sky, and the bay reflecting the sunset light, and I thought, "Wow, what a place, I've got to live here someday."

HAROLD GILLIAM, JOURNALIST & WRITER

EMMA MACCHIARINI SWAM before she walked. On the morning of July 12, 1989, she got up early, dressed in a sparkly swimsuit with a pink bow, smeared herself with Vaseline, and stepped into the bay. Swimming from Fort Point under the southern tower of the Golden Gate Bridge to Lime Point on the opposite shore, she aimed to cross a coastal opening where currents surge with all the force of an entire ocean on one side and the state's mightiest rivers on the other. She recalls thinking while in the water that they'd got the tides all wrong. The swim was much more work, and took much longer, than she'd imagined.

At one point during her swim, Emma feared she wasn't going to make it. But she kept lifting her arms and kicking her feet in the freezing grey water, accompanied by her father swimming beside her and her mother paddling a boogie board. At another point, a container ship cut across her path, and the two bar pilots shadowing her in a Zodiac signaled wildly to both the towering vessel and the slip of a girl to watch out. Eventually she was able to see the beach ahead, but never seemed to get there. Then she remembers her father saying, "Stand up, Emma," as she found her footing on the Marin County shore.

The headline in the *San Francisco Chronicle* the next day read: "Girl, 8, Conquers Gate." The black-and-white photo hid the green algae on her face. Macchiarini was one of the youngest people ever to swim the mile-wide channel under the red bridge. She got fan mail, and television coverage of her feat.

On that foggy day decades ago, Macchiarini swam across the deepest part of San Francisco Bay, where the bottom lies 330 feet below sea level.

Girl dives into the bay in the early 1900s. (Courtesy of The Dolphin Club, Shirley Coleman Collection)

But most of the bay, which encompasses 470 square miles of open water between the narrows of the Golden Gate and the Carquinez Strait, is less than 12 feet deep. From one end to the other, the bay is about 42 miles in length and ranges from 5 to 13 miles in width. Before radar and sonar, ships regularly hit the fog-obscured rocks at its entrance. And gold-seekers abandoned so many vessels off the tiny town of San Francisco that new residents built right on top of them. These opportunists became the first in a long line of Bay fillers who saw more dollar signs along the waterfront than up in the mother lode.

Today, 7 million people live on the shores and hills surrounding San Francisco Bay. Around this extraordinary natural harbor, they and their predecessors have built 46 cities, 6 ports, 4 airports, and 275 marinas, not to mention myriad industrial centers, oil refineries, and military bases. They have also set aside miles of bayshore for recreation and wildlife in the form of 135 parks, refuges, and reserves.

To locals, the bay is a breathing space, a blue prairie of water outside their windows and beside their communities. To tourists, it's the water under the Golden Gate Bridge, the rippling backdrop to one of the engineering marvels of the West.

An Ever-Changing Environment

San Francisco Bay is an estuary where rivers draining 40 percent of California's landscape meet and mix with the Pacific Ocean; where coastal and inland ecosystems overlap; where seabirds and songbirds ply the skies; where sharks swim with sardines; and where species both native and alien compete for space and food alongside some equally competitive primates.

Here at the edge of the North American continent, cool ocean water and air encounter their warmer inland counterparts, shaping an environment in constant flux. One minute the sun may blaze down from above, whereas the next is wet with fog drip. Tides coming in may suddenly go out; wave trains may collide, encountering a shifting breeze or a change of current; and brown plumes of sediment-laden fresh water from the rivers upstream may dissolve into the bluer bay just west of the Carquinez Bridge or drive a muddy arrow through the Golden Gate and out to the Farallon Islands.

In this coastal zone, the continental and oceanic plates of the planet can shift against one another at any moment, sending a bridge or levee collapsing into the water. It can grow hot and dry enough for fire to consume most of Angel Island in one night, and cold enough for snow to stick on Mount Tamalpais. El Niño and La Niña rearrange the water layers

A scientist samples a square meter of the estuary for invasive plants. White plastic quadrats provide measuring tools for diverse organisms and bay conditions. Some of the longest standing records of bay conditions reside with the U.S. Geological Survey, which set up the very first tide gauge at the Golden Gate more than 100 years ago. (Francis Parchaso)

every two to seven years, and every few decades the whole North Pacific experiences a change so profound that entirely different types of fish take up residence in the bay.

"The bay is not a static thing," says aquatic ecologist Jim Cloern of the U.S. Geological Survey. Cloern had been studying the bay for over 20 years when he saw plankton growing in places and at times they had never been seen before. His state colleagues surveying fish began pulling in more sole than halibut and seeing unusual surges in bottom-dwellers. "In terms of these biological communities, it's almost like the bay flipped from one state to another state. Ecologists call these 'regime shifts' or 'crossing a threshold,' " he says.

To survive in such a changeable place, local fish and wildlife must be unusually resilient—able to endure winter floods and summer droughts, as well as times of scarce food between times of plenty. Lately, however, more than a few species have been having a tough time adapting to the most dramatic changes of all: the arrival of people. During the past 150 years, entrepreneurs and engineers have straightened rivers, culverted creeks, drained marshes, and paved coastlines. They have also rerouted the flow of water from land to sea, directing the lion's share into reservoirs, faucets, and irrigation pipes.

"We have plumbed more of our system and diverted more of our fresh

TABLE 1. San Francisco Bay through History

	1700	TODAY
Bay surface area	~800	~580 square miles
Bay Area human population	10,000	8 million
Tidal marsh	190,000	45,000 acres
Freshwater flows through Bay	~30	~20 million acre-feet/year
Salmon returning to spawn	>2 million	<150,000 (only 1/5 wild origin)
Spring shorebird count	millions	hundreds of thousands

Sources: Data from Bay Conservation and Development Commission; Margolin 1978; *Habitat Goals*; Department of Water Resources; California Department of Fish and Game.

water for longer than anyone, anywhere, on the West Coast," says the U.S. Geological Survey's Jan Thompson. Though Thompson has spent most of the last two decades studying an alien clam decimating the bay food web, she remains optimistic. "What better system to prove that you can turn something around than one that has been so manipulated, and one we can still manipulate?"

Saving the Bay

Californians are as changeable as the bay itself. Many come to the Golden State expressly to escape their former lives or to experience something new. People arrive ready to fight for a dream, whether gold or freedom or tolerance or redwood trees. And one of the dreams they've fought hardest for is a healthy bay.

By the 1950s, the bay was more stinky and ugly than healthy. For years, locals had been dumping their garbage at shoreline landfills, draining their sewage into creeks and tidelands, and banishing their industries, refineries, and canneries to the waterfront. Fish kills, oil spills, and bay fills—the dumping of dirt into the shallows to create new real estate—were considered a normal part of doing business. The shore was not a place to go for recreation and exercise, as it is for many Bay Area residents today, but a place to avoid.

In 1961, Berkeley's plan to fill several thousand acres of the bay lit a fire under three of its residents. Kay Kerr, Esther Gulick, and Sylvia McLaughlin could see the muddying of the waters and the changes to the shore from their living room windows up in the hills. Investigating the matter, the women heard city council members discussing the removal of all of the coves to achieve tidy waterfronts, and saw an Army Corps of Engineers map in which the wide waters of the bay had been confined to a narrow channel in the name of progress. The women sent a flyer out to a thousand neighbors and fellow citizens, emblazoned with the words, "Bay or River?" The response was disbelief.

"[Most local citizens] thought the bay belonged to everybody," one of the women, the elegant Esther Gulick, recalled in a 1987 oral history. "Then, when they found out that a good part of it along the edge belonged to corporations like Sante Fe [railroad], they just couldn't believe it, and they couldn't do enough . . . to help."

The women proved adept at channeling citizens' outrage through a new organization they founded called the Save San Francisco Bay Association. That first flyer garnered about 2,500 memberships at $1 a piece—the founders wanted saving the bay to be affordable. By 1970 they had 18,000 members and activist cells in the East Bay, on the peninsula, and in Marin. Known today as Save the Bay, the group was one of the first citizens' organizations formed to save a body of water rather than a rare bird or pretty canyon. With a lot of persuasion and considerable political clout, the association soon legislated stewardship of the bay through the creation of the San Francisco Bay Conservation and Development Commission (BCDC)—a first in regional governance.

Over the years, many other Bay Area residents have taken up that torch, working to protect the wetlands, clean the water, cap the landfills, and preserve the salmon. Today, more than 200 environmental groups have their headquarters in the San Francisco Bay Area; many focus in

Fishers on a shore of concrete riprap. (Max Eissler)

some way on the health of the bay. Natural resource managers arriving here from jobs in other parts of the country are always amazed at the forest of hands raised, number of speeches made, and degree of passion expressed at public meetings.

"The [Bay Area] contains a fortuitous assemblage of citizens with a special culture and style of life, a special environmental awareness and appreciation. There is a heady mixture of international cosmopolitanism, of varied shorelines with the flavor of ships and water, of the free spirit of the frontier, and of youthful and harmonious living," wrote Rice Odell in a 1972 Conservation Foundation booklet about saving the bay. His words are every bit as valid today.

Inside and Out

Most people living in the 46 cities that ring the bay know a nearby place for a bayside barbecue, a Sunday stroll through the marshes, an afternoon fishing expedition, or a salty swim. Many run and pedal the trails now gracing the levee-tops and waterfronts, or take their city dogs to romp along the wide open spaces of a bay beach.

But the bay attracts more than those in search of exercise or family time. People leap from the Golden Gate in their hour of despair, or sip champagne on a bay cruise in their hour of celebration. Blue Angels zoom over the bay during Fleet Week, fireworks burst over the water on the Fourth of July, and fireboats spew fountains into a crowd of sailboats during April's Opening Day on the Bay.

Equally riveting can be the natural wonders that appear on San Francisco's watery doorstep. In 1985, a 36-ton Humpback Whale dubbed "Humphrey" wandered delta waterways for over a month. It took a flotilla of boats banging on steel pipes to make enough noise—a Japanese fishing technique known as *oikami*—to drive him back to sea. In May 2007, the

Avocets showing off the orange plumage of breeding season. (Robert M. Chilvers)

Central Bay kiteboarders. (Max Eissler)

Sacramento River once again beckoned to whales, this time an injured mother and her calf.

Signs of nature abound in the bay for those ready to see them. Most locals have admired flocks of ducks paddling air as they lift off the water and the glistening domes of seal heads noodling offshore. Tourists come to marvel at the sea lion colony lolling on San Francisco's Pier 39 and to visit the Aquarium of the Bay. Here, a walk through an underwater tube reveals the Armored Sturgeon, Skew-eyed Halibut, and flashing schools of herring that live below the bay's blue surface. In the region's shoreline parks, visitors can see curlews and peeps poke their beaks into the mud for goodies, and pelicans and terns dive-bomb for fish.

Of course there are many more up-close and personal ways to experience the bay. Emma Macchiarini's father belongs to the South End Rowing Club, one of several thousand residents who have joined open water swimming clubs in San Francisco. Just as many enjoy catching bay waves and winds with kiteboards, ketches, catamarans, and boogie boards, or indulging in the age-old pastime of fishing.

Jim McGrath races formula boards, the latest and lightest type of windsurfing rig. In a good race under the right conditions, this retired port environmental manager can skim from Berkeley to San Francisco and back again in an hour and a half. He has raced in the confines of Washington's Columbia River and through what he calls the "organized" waves off Hawaii, as well as in the big warm swells off Florida. To him, the bay is rougher, bigger, more unpredictable than those locales. Experienced though he is, McGrath has lost his gear and had to be rescued more than once from bay waters.

Anthony Mirkovich likes working in an urban fishery. "You can eat a fancy lunch in the best restaurant on the Wharf and be out fishing that night," he says. Mirkovich fishes for herring in the bay, helps a friend crab outside the Golden Gate, and heads to Alaska for salmon. Doing all three jobs is the only way to make a living fishing on this coast now, he says. Yet in the 1900s, every Bay town had a fisherman's wharf, and every other a sardine cannery; the shallows grew oysters, and the coves teemed with shrimp.

Mirkovich's grandfather used to fish out of Seattle, but Anthony didn't inherit his boat and gear from family. His pride and joy is a 32-foot bow-picker called the *Masterpiece*—a herring boat. Most years the herring fleet is not allowed to bring in more than a few thousand tons of the tiny, silvery bait fish. It's a quota set by the state to protect the fishery. In 2007, Mirkovich brought in 72 tons, his most recent big catch.

Mirkovich started fishing when he was 12 years old, when 130 herring boats worked the bay. Today, the local fleet numbers around 30. But the handful of guys Mirkovich fishes and barbecues with all help each other out, and he enjoys the camaraderie. "In the early morning, there's the smell of diesel on the docks, with the boats warming up, the guys slinging

Herring fishery research vessel tied up on San Francisco's Embarcadero. Seagulls often follow fishing expeditions looking for easy pickings. (Ryan Bartling)

gear back and forth, seagulls cawing, radio chatter. That's when bay fishing comes alive," he says.

Apart from the last few fishermen, some residents still know the ways of the bay with the intimacy of the past, when more of the local populace relied on the bay for food, transport, and a living. Bar pilots guide the wallowing tankers and top-heavy container ships in and out of the Golden Gate. Miners claw and suck sand from the bay bottom to fill freeway beds, and dredgers do the same to keep shipping lanes and port berths safe for marine navigation. Ferry operators still zip to and fro in busy white boats, powered by the jet engines that have replaced the early paddlewheels. Their wake is so powerful it sometimes erodes the mud from bayshore marshes. Engineers still make salt by trapping sheets of bay water in the sun. And builders still negotiate with the shifting elements to raise bridges and anchor waterfront seafood joints over and around the water.

But most people only cross the bay or admire it from afar. They may not know the bay intimately, but its bridges and freeways keep them apprised of its moods and colors. Almost everyone smiles at the sight.

"The bay gives our region its name and creates a sense of place which defines the community where we live," says Will Travis, 20-year leader of BCDC, the government agency in charge of preserving this watery regional treasure. "The bay is our Eiffel Tower, our El Capitan, our Big Ben. It is a visual icon which gives our region its identity as a place different from everywhere else."

But to all those who live or visit here, perhaps the most amazing quality of the bay is its proximity. "To me, the bay is direct access to wild nature—unmanaged, unmanicured nature," says swimmer Emma Macchiarini.

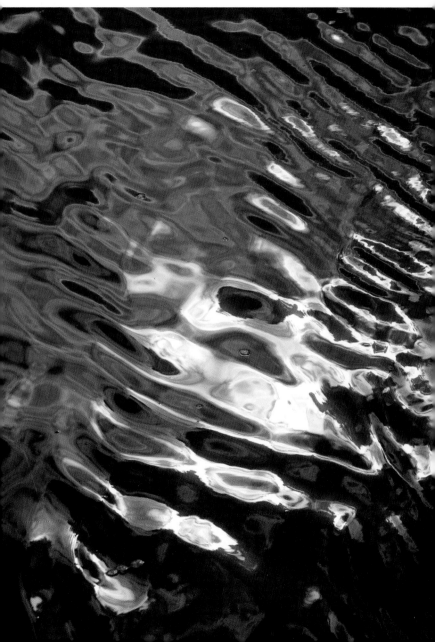

At a recent game at AT&T Park during the national anthem, I was looking out at the Bay, and what a show I got. I could see brown water from the north flooding in from left field to right field, and green water to the south, with a foamy front a few feet wide in between. That's what I do when I go to baseball games: look at the tide going in and out. It's a curse.

DAVID SCHOELLHAMER, HYDROLOGIST, U.S. GEOLOGICAL SURVEY

AT FIRST GLANCE the bay may look like a big lake full of blue water, but look again. Most days a closer inspection might reveal some white caps crawling east, or a finger of green or brown water meeting blue, or sloops with full sails that nonetheless seem to be going nowhere. These are all clues that the bay is neither a lake (a landlocked pool of water) nor a simple inlet of the sea, but an estuary.

In a 1967 article in *Estuaries,* oceanographer Donald Pritchard defines an estuary as "a semi-enclosed coastal body of water which has a free connection with the open sea, within which seawater mixes and usually is measurably diluted with fresh water from land runoff."

San Francisco Bay is the lower part of an estuary that extends up into the heart of the Central Valley, embracing in its upper reaches a web of 700 miles of waterways and sloughs and 57 islands that form the delta of the Sacramento and San Joaquin rivers (see Map 1). In addition to these big rivers and their watershed, 70 to 80 creeks flow into the bay itself. The water flowing down these rivers and creeks connects the ecology of the uplands to the tidally influenced estuary.

"At the landscape scale, the most far-reaching effect of inter-ecosystem interaction is related to the natural movement of water and all that is carried within it—sediments, nutrients, drifting organisms," according to The Bay Institute's *From the Sierra to the Sea* report.

Windsurfers and whitecaps on the San Francisco shore. (Jude Stalker)

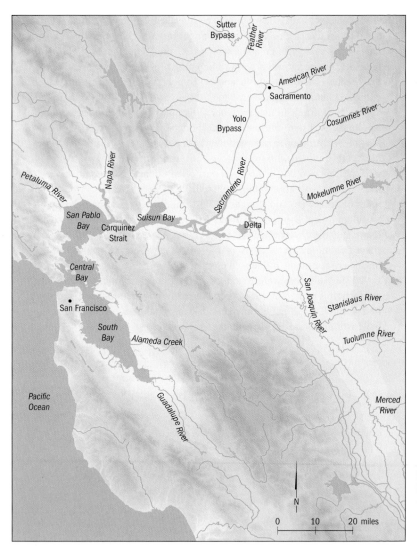

Map 1. Major rivers and sub-bays of the estuary encompassing the Sacramento–
San Joaquin River Delta and San Francisco Bay. (S.F. Estuary Institute)

Below the cobweb of islands and canals in the delta and the confluence
of the two largest rivers, the bay assumes the geography of a series of
smaller bays (or sub-bays), each with different hydrodynamics and conditions. Most of these corners of the larger bay can be described as wide

shallows of murky water spread over a muddy bottom, but in a few spots such as the Central Bay—bounded by the Richmond, Bay, and Golden Gate bridges—the water clears and deepens over a sandy and rocky bottom.

Moving these waters are visible forces on the surface like winds and storms, as well as subsurface forces like tides, currents, and differences in salinity that interact with bottom topography, also known as bathymetry. In general, water moves in one direction down rivers and creeks, and back and forth in the lower bays due to ocean tides. Beyond these underlying basics, scientists have found that the water—not to mention everything in it—can move in any number of directions, because so many forces are at work in this complex estuary.

In the last century, humans have greatly changed the estuary's natural hydrodynamics and bathymetry, straightened and dammed its rivers and creeks, and filled and diked its shores. More recently, however, those in charge of protecting California's water supply and fisheries have learned that the naturally variable hydrodynamics of the bay and its watershed remain key to the health of the larger ecosystem.

As estuarine science veteran Bruce Herbold of the U.S. Environmental Protection Agency once put it, "The system is much more complex than a bunch of blue lines and blobs on a map."

Geography and Geology

Most rivers get wider and deeper the closer they are to the mouth of their estuaries. This is the geography of a big river like the Mississippi, which widens and deepens before dumping its water and mud into a vast triangular delta extending out into the sea.

The San Francisco estuary looks nothing like the Mississippi. The bay empties into the Pacific not through a vast delta hundreds of miles wide, but via a one-and-a-half-mile-wide keyhole break in the coastal mountain range, leading *Wikipedia* to label it "an inverted river delta." The bay itself, meanwhile, consists of several smaller interior bays rather than one big curve in the coast.

From downstream to upstream, the estuary looks more like one of those long balloons sold by sidewalk vendors, twisted and turned at various points: open in the ocean, narrow at the Golden Gate, open again into the Central and San Pablo bays, narrow again at Carquinez Strait, open yet again into Suisun Bay, then finally narrowing into a labyrinth of river channels and an inland "delta" miles from the ocean. At each narrowing

Above: The shape of San
Francisco Bay is different
from that of other major
bays. Nearby Monterey Bay,
and Santa Monica Bay far-
ther south, are both much
more open ended. Neither
has San Francisco Bay's
multiple sub-bays, nor its
headlands reaching rocky
arms around the water so
tight they nearly cut off the
bay from the Pacific.
At right: Maryland's Chesapeake Bay is a long, nar-
row finger poking into the
continent with jigsaw-puzzle
coastlines. *Facing page:*
And no bays at all define
where the 2,340-mile-long
Mississippi River meets
the Gulf of Mexico; rather,
long fingers of sediment
spread silt from the

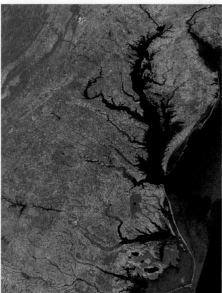

nation's interior out into the sea. Only in San Francisco Bay did the power of flowing river water and rising seas cut gaps in the hard rock of coastal ridges. (NASA Goddard Space Flight Center)

the water gets deeper and faster; at each opening it shallows, slows, and warms.

"It's a really weird estuary," says Herbold. "These two rivers cut down and form a big delta, and then they come back together into one little bottleneck out into the bay. Shapewise from the air, it looks like it should be flowing the other way."

The forces that created the estuary's unusual geography thrust mountains up from the seafloor and warmed or cooled the climate enough to cause a change in sea level. The estuary has only been around for about 5,000 years in its current shape. But geologists trace the building blocks back much further. Rock and soil profiles under the bay and in the coastal cliffs reveal at least three periods during which the sea level rose and fell across the landscape in step with glacial changes over the past million years. The most recent rise occurred about 15,000 to 18,000 years ago. At that time, Pacific waves didn't crash as far east as they do today. The shore extended out to the rocks of the Farallon Islands, and river waters emptying out of the valley and through the Carquinez and Golden Gate straits still had 20 miles to go west of today's gate before meeting the sea.

Geologist Doris Sloan paints a picture of this time in *Geology of the San Francisco Bay Region*: "On a sunny weekend you could have hiked out across the broad, gently sloping continental shelf for a picnic on the Farallon Ridge overlooking the Pacific Ocean to the west. Or you could have stood on the headlands above the Golden Gate and watched the mighty flow of the river as it poured through the valley, tumbling over great cascades or waterfalls. A roar would have filled the air as the melt-water from faraway glaciers sent floods through the Golden Gate to the ocean. The river cut deep channels into the bedrock at the Carquinez and Raccoon Straits, turning the tip of the Tiburon Peninsula into an island that became Angel Island. The river also carved a canyon through the Golden Gate."

The series of bedrock ridges thrust up between the Pacific and the Central Valley bestowed upon the estuary its unusual hourglass curves. They also gave it a unique river delta, many miles inland from the sea. Before the watershed's rivers cut the Carquinez Strait, the sediments they carried had been backing up for thousands of years behind the Carquinez Hills. The material accumulated at the confluence of the Sacramento and San Joaquin rivers and eventually formed the 540-square-mile marsh of the historic delta.

According to Sloan, "Until about three million years ago, rivers that drained into the Central Valley flowed southward to an ocean outlet down near the San Joaquin Valley's Kettleman Hills. As the valley slowly emerged from the sea and movement along the San Andreas fault closed off this southern outlet, a lake formed in the Central Valley." The lake swelled and shrank with the ice ages, but eventually it broke through the coastal hills at

15,000 years ago
End of last Ice Age—sea level approximately 400 feet below present level; rivers not shown

10,000 years ago
Formation of Farallon Islands and intrusion into the "Golden Gate"

5,000 years ago
Formation of Bay and Delta Basins

125 years ago
Landward edge of undiked tidal marsh

Today
Includes changes due to hydraulic mining sediment deposition, land reclamation, and filling of wetland areas

Figure 1. Marine water intrusion into the Central Valley created today's bay and delta. (The Bay Institute, Courtesy of CALFED)

Carquinez and formed the Carquinez Strait. A clue to the timing of this breakthrough can be found in the bay mud, where layers of volcanic ash from a Mount Lassen eruption about 579,000 years ago suggest the time when the Central Valley began draining through the Golden Gate.

It wasn't until much more recently that the bay itself was formed. Sloan writes: "About 10,000 years ago, the rising ocean entered the Golden Gate and began to fill the Estuary basin—advancing at first at a rapid rate of 100 feet per year, and then slowing about 5,000 years ago when glaciers reached their present size." Sea level has since been slowly rising, and climate change promises to accelerate this inland advance very soon. Scientists say global warming will create new bays farther inland, and perhaps one day a new inland lake like the one that once filled the Central Valley (see p. 285, "Climate Change and the Bay's Future").

Regardless of sea level rise and fall, the bay has remained relatively shallow over the last few centuries. As part of the United States' earliest attempt to define its navigable waters, the Coastal Geodetic Survey first mapped the bay floor in the 1850s using a boat, lines, and a sextant. Surveyors would pick points on the shoreline, and sight through the sextant for positioning, using this highly accurate instrument and three points to triangulate their location. They'd throw a lead-weighted line out in front of the boat, catch up to it, and take a reading when vertical. Then they'd pull it up and do it again. In shallower areas of the bay, surveyors would stick poles in the water and measure to the quarter foot.

These 1800s depth measurements were actually more accurate than those gleaned today. Early surveyors reviewed their data every night, and if they saw a discrepancy between two independent readings, they'd go back the next day and redo their work. Scientists today tow a sidescan sonar device behind a boat that bounces multiple beams of sound off the bay floor. The data produced go straight into a computer and don't get checked until months later, when the surveyors are more likely back in the lab than on the boat. As such, historic bathymetric maps can be more accurate than modern ones.

Fresh and Salt Mix

Beneath the surface, the bay today is a blend of unusual topography and marine and riverine waters. But its most defining feature is that it is an estuary. The most telltale sign of the presence of estuarine conditions is the change in salinity as the water flows from inland out to the ocean. Upstream in headwater rivers and creeks, the water is fresh, with the amount of salt in the water measuring about 0.5 parts per thousand (ppt). By the

The Sacramento River winds its way through the warm, flat Central Valley. Farther upstream, below Shasta Dam, boaters often bring cushions to sit on because the water can be cold enough to be felt through fiberglass. (Francis Parchaso)

time the Sacramento River flows past the town of Rio Vista, the salinity is around 2 ppt. A little farther downstream, in San Pablo Bay, the salinity more than doubles to around 7 ppt. The water is about 30 ppt—nearly as salty as straight seawater—beneath the Golden Gate. In other words, the salinity is greatest near the ocean and smallest near the rivers.

The rivers—two large ones and nearly a dozen tributaries—deliver most of the fresh water in the estuary. These rivers, in turn, gather their water from the runoff of rain and the melting of snow into creeks, streams, drains, and culverts from a watershed that encompasses 40 percent of the state of California. Nearly half the land area of the state drains into San Francisco Bay.

The drainage itself is significant. Between 1921 and 1990, flows into the bay from upstream ranged from six million acre feet (maf) to more than 69 maf, depending on whether California was experiencing drought or deluge, and on how much was diverted for human use. Currently, an average of about 24 maf arrives per year, an amount about five times the volume of the bay, making this freshwater inflow one of the most powerful hydrodynamic forces in the system. It rained so hard in 1997 that the resulting flood of fresh water (16 maf in three months) changed the bay as a whole from 79 percent to 27 percent seawater.

The freshness of the water at any given point in the estuary was once determined by natural climate changes. Now, it is decided by water managers, who control how much snowmelt and runoff flows out to sea through the bay. The upper estuary is one of the most managed water systems in the country, with over half the natural flows diverted into reservoirs, aqueducts, and pipelines for human use. What's left to flow downstream and mix with seawater is important to many estuarine species.

Little of the fresh water from upstream rivers has made its way down to the South Bay in recent decades. There the water is so shallow and the circulation so sluggish that scientists consider the conditions "lagoonlike." Only winter and spring storms send enough fresh water downstream from the Central Valley to influence South Bay salinities. In fact, apart from the ocean tides and the occasional storm surge from a local creek or river, the biggest flows into the South Bay come from the plant that treats all of San Jose's sewage and wastewater.

Rivers

The two largest rivers delivering fresh water to the bay are the Sacramento and the San Joaquin. The Sacramento River flows north to south, springing out of rugged mountain ridges dominated by two active volcanoes: Lassen and Shasta. The Sacramento's headwaters join the Pit and McCloud rivers before backing up behind the 602-foot-high plug of concrete in the river that is Shasta Dam. Below the dam, the Sacramento slows and widens, meandering across the flats of the great Central Valley and gathering water from Butte, Battle, and Cache creeks, among others. At Marysville it merges with the Feather River, and at the state capital with the American River, before joining the San Joaquin and flowing out to sea. The river plain in this valley is so flat that natural winter and spring flooding once lasted for months on end.

The San Joaquin River follows a 742-mile-long bed in the opposite direction from the Sacramento River, flowing south to north. Eight tributary rivers and 22 streams drain into the San Joaquin, the largest of which are the Tuolumne, Merced, and Stanislaus rivers. About 20 miles north of Fresno in the foothills, the flows of the upper San Joaquin are trapped behind Friant Dam, leaving the lower reaches dry until the Merced joins and rewaters it.

Confluence of the Sacramento and San Joaquin rivers in the delta below Rio Vista, before they flow together into San Francisco Bay. (Dr. William Bowen, California Geographical Survey, Northridge)

The confluence of the Sacramento and San Joaquin rivers is located near the town of Rio Vista. It's such a wide, flat place that the meeting point of these two waterways is difficult to see from a boat or the shore. A few tule islands poke out of the shallows here and there, hinting at the enormous freshwater marsh that once filled the delta. Below this indistinct confluence the North Bay receives waters from the Napa and Petaluma rivers, both of which are strongly influenced by tides. In the South Bay, the only major freshwater input is from the Guadalupe River, which, unlike all the other rivers, flows from west to east out of the coastal ridgelands.

All of these rivers are dammed save one. The Cosumnes flows for a mere 80 miles from 8,000 feet above sea level to its confluence with the Mokelumne River between Sacramento and Stockton. As the last free-flowing river in the bay watershed, it's one of the few places where scientists can get an unfettered sense of the natural water flow pattern, or hydrograph.

Most of the rivers in the bay watershed also no longer spread out over their banks onto floodplains. The natural seasonal flooding throughout the watershed that once created valley topography, imported new soil, spread tree seeds, and engulfed fields—spurring the growth of fish food in the warm shallows—is now constrained by levees and walls.

Humans now treat most of the watershed's rivers like pipes, instead of allowing them to be the agents of variability that nature created, according to Tim Ramirez, a river rat and former assistant secretary of water policy with the state's Resources Agency. "We still talk about building new dams because water is being 'wasted' by letting it spill from full reservoirs and run down the river out to sea. But these 'spills,' the closest thing we have to the small seasonal floods natural rivers once had, aren't a waste, but a great benefit to the ecosystem and the fish," says Ramirez.

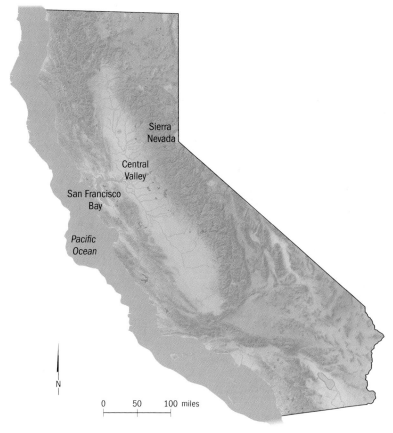

Map 2. Watershed of San Francisco Bay, encompassing 40 percent of the state. (S.F. Estuary Institute)

FIELDWORK: TESTING BAY CONDITIONS

The captain of the *Polaris* pulls back on the throttle, hits a red button, checks the numbers on a GPS screen, and speaks into an intercom in a firm, even tone: "Station 36, 25." A voice from the other end of the 96-foot-long science research yacht says, "thank you," back through the intercom, noting the location and the depth. The two voices will repeat their exchange 36 times in the course of the next 12 hours as the *Polaris* tests how salty, cloudy, and deep the bay water is at set stations between Alviso in the far South Bay and Rio Vista on the Sacramento River. The *Polaris* has been taking this two-day trip—passing under six bridges and traveling 80 nautical miles upstream the first day and retracing its route downstream the next—once every month since 1988. It is from the data gathered by the USGS and other scientists on board that we've glimpsed a small part of the action beneath the 470-square-mile surface of San Francisco Bay.

Polaris crew in action. (Francis Parchaso)

The sun is just backlighting the South Bay hills with flamingo pink when the captain hits that red button at Station 36, our first sampling spot. It is 6:30 a.m. A scientist in jeans and Keds steps out into the dark dawn and onto the teak deck to unclip an instrument dangling from a pole so that it swings freely over the water. This is actually not one instrument, but many. To me, it looks like a diver's oxygen tank encrusted with gadgets. This conductivity, temperature, and depth gauge, or CTD, measures physical conditions in the bay and feeds the information back into the *Polaris*'s lab computers. The instrument can take 25 samples per meter, per second.

As the instrument descends to just short of the bottom and then rises back up again, the crew works the keyboards and watches the incoming measurements pop up on two screens. On one screen, blue, red, green, and black lines snake their way down a graph as the instrument sends back a vertical profile of everything going on in the water column. On another screen, numbers flash in white boxes indicating GPS position, time, depth, salinity, temperature, turbidity, dissolved oxygen, and wind direction. When the instrument comes up dripping, the crew leader presses the intercom and tells the captain, "Good to go."

We repeat the same drill at a number of stations as the *Polaris* works its way out of the southern backwaters and nears the Bay Bridge. Our top speed between stations is about 10 knots. Our captain listens to the maritime traffic chatter on the radio and watches a bunch of yellow dots (ships) on an on-screen nautical chart move in and out of port. A click of a keyboard reveals the names of all other Class A vessels over 65 feet long operating or parked in the bay at this precise moment. This is no virtual harbor traffic game.

Past the Bay Bridge, the *Polaris* follows long trains of small white caps headed east. I step out on deck and hold onto my hat to watch the crew undertake a special set of experiments with a charcoal-grey PVC canister called the Niskin bottle— a canister with a spring-loaded stopper on either end designed to "grab" water

USGS scientist deploying a Niskin bottle (right) and CTD (left), instruments used to measure physical conditions in the bay. (Ariel Rubissow Okamoto)

samples from the bottom of the bay. Once the sample is grabbed, the crew compares the water from the bottom with that from the surface of the bay back in the yacht's lab.

Heading north under the Richmond Bridge, we pass Red Rock, where three counties meet in the middle of the bay: San Francisco, Marin, and Contra Costa. The turbo-charged Vallejo ferry streaks past us. On-screen, captains can distinguish ferries from other vessels by the high speed of the yellow dots. The Vallejo ferry sends a wake the size of a small tsunami under the *Polaris*, and she rolls.

The *Polaris* follows the ferry out into the open waters of San Pablo Bay, where suddenly the shorelines seem less distinct. Our video sounder flashes a sonar reading of less than six feet—the average depth of most of San Pablo Bay. The water is a browner hue here: it's easier for the wind tickling the surface to reach the shallow bottom and stir up sediments. The crew checks the water samples for suspended sediments by flushing them through quarter-sized paper filters.

Soon the *Polaris* reaches the narrowest spot in the entire estuary—the Carquinez Strait. Four crewmates climb into red waterproof suits and prep a small Boston whaler for some specialized sampling in the shallows. The captain soon has the whaler winched up and suspended from three ropes in mid-air. Then he lowers the small boat over the side.

Steaming into the strait, the captain describes making this trip in both fair weather and foul. During floods, this estuary bottleneck can be clogged with dead cows, torn-up trees, refrigerators, and, most hazardous, propane tanks from flooded households, ready to explode on impact.

Past the strait the estuary opens out again into Suisun Bay, which at this time of year is as placid and glassy as a bathtub. It suddenly gets hot. We pass the mothball fleet of decommissioned naval vessels and watch a sea lion circle a red buoy, stick its nose in the air, then heave its 800-pound body up onto a small ledge. The buoy swings madly.

Farther along, as dusk gathers, small fishing boats appear here and there, harking back to older, quieter pastimes than watching CNN and TV autopsies. Two men near the marshy edge sit in a rowboat staring at us, unblinking, holding two beers and two rods.

Out on deck at Station 5 it's so still I can hear the radar and GPS gear—three black cups and three white wings spinning on the cabin top—move the air. We pass the confluence of the largest rivers in the state, the San Joaquin and Sacramento. It doesn't look like much: wide waters, an island, a few trees on a levee.

At Station 2 we winch the whaler back up onto the deck of the *Polaris* and its crew begins sifting muddy bay-floor samples through a screen in search of small life forms. Around sunset, we reach the delta town of Rio Vista. We have come through four bays and into the central delta, seen the path of water from land to sea, and measured the water's physical condition at each of 36 stations along the way. We batten down hatches and wash coffee cups. ARO

Creeks and Drainages

Dozens of creeks tumble from the steep slopes of the Coast Ranges onto the flatlands before merging with the bay. The water that flows between their banks is a highway that connects the ecology of the uplands to the tidal estuary. From the leaves and sediments that drift from hilltops and valleys; to the animals that travel between the ocean, marshes, and land; to the fresh water itself that helps shape the aquatic habitats of the estuary, creeks are an integral part of the estuary's anatomy.

In the Bay Area, creeks typically begin within creases in the steep slopes of foothills and coastal mountain ranges. These headwater zones collect water from natural springs or ephemeral runoff from storms. Farther downhill, beneath the shady limbs of tanoak and bay trees, creeks gather seasonal trickles, then coalesce into true streams punctuated with still pools, gravel riffles, and sandbars. As the land flattens, streams may peter out into alluvial fans or pool into freshwater marshes filled with sedges and touched by the brackish fingers of the tide. "The ecosystem doesn't draw a sharp line between creek, baylands, and bay. There's a continuum where these blend into each other," says Phil Stevens, director of the Urban Creeks Council. Every individual watershed recapitulates the design of the larger estuary, with the tidal marsh at the foot of each creek acting as its own miniature delta, and each creek mouth serving as a mixing area for salt and fresh water.

Colma Creek near San Francisco's airport. (Jude Stalker)

At least 85 watersheds, defined as having a mouth connected to the bay, border the bay proper, and have a total drainage area of about 3,500 square miles within the nine-county Bay Area. A region roughly equal to the size of Puerto Rico, this represents just 6 percent of the drainage of the total Sacramento–San Joaquin river system. The largest stream in the area by far is Alameda Creek, which drains 700 square miles of the Diablo Range and the East Bay hills. Its watershed alone comprises 20 percent of the bay's total drainage. Second in size is the Napa River in the North Bay, and the third is Coyote Creek in the south, which drains out the Diablo Range.

Bays within the Bay

Scientists divide San Francisco Bay into four basic sub-embayments (sub-bays for short), using bridges as the most convenient borders on a fluid surface (see Map 1, p. 16). Distinct hydrological conditions and geography are what define these smaller bays, not the bridges themselves.

At the southernmost end of the estuary, between the San Mateo Bridge and the city of San Jose, lies the lagoon of the South Bay. The Central Bay is what most people see from their hilltop homes or San Francisco office towers, or from the three main commuter routes across the water: the Golden Gate Bridge, the Bay Bridge, and the Richmond Bridge. It's much deeper and colder in the Central Bay than in other sub-bays, because ocean tides surge back and forth and big pulses of fresh water roll down from the mountains.

The waters under the Golden Gate itself are the deepest part of the bay—they form an underwater canyon dropping 330 feet below sea level. Here, high-speed tidal currents continually sweep the bay floor clean of sand and mud, leaving boulders and rock exposed. Down in these dark, cold, fast-moving waters, few things can linger. The exceptions may be the engine blocks of historic shipwrecks, Before the advent of modern-day navigation tools, more than 90 ships crashed into the rocks and sank in

Sidescan sonar of the bay floor under the Golden Gate. (Patrick Barnard)

and around the Golden Gate headlands—testimony to the narrowness and frequent obscurity of this opening into the world's greatest natural harbor. Indeed, annual averages indicate that fog obscures the Golden Gate for several hours a day, especially in summer.

In the middle of the Central Bay, however, the bottom warps into a field of underwater sand dunes. These are not like the diminutive ripples in the sand often seen on the beach. Central Bay sand dunes can reach 25 feet in height and hundreds of feet in length. And they aren't static: they move, much like tractor treads, says U.S. Geological Survey (USGS) scientist Bruce Jaffe, who spends a lot of time following sediments around the bay floor. Depending on the strength of tidal currents and the size of the sediment, sand grains hop a certain distance along the bottom and then build up over a slight bump. Once formed, they keep moving back and forth, like the waves above.

Up on the surface, the Central Bay contains several visible islands—Alcatraz, Angel, Yerba Buena, and Treasure—and more invisible ones. Four large rocks—Shag, Harding, Arch, and Blossom—have all been dynamited over the years to keep them from pricking the hulls of supertankers and container ships.

The third sub-bay lies to the north between the long span of the Richmond Bridge and the short span of the Carquinez Bridge. Called San Pablo Bay, or sometimes the North Bay, this compartment empties two small rivers, the Petaluma and the Napa. Here, the city skylines and dramatic topography of the Central Bay fade, and horizons grow more distant and rural. San Pablo Bay opens wide into shallows created by the

Suisun Bay's quiet shallows. (Francis Parchaso)

deposition of tons of sediment swept downstream during the gold-mining era.

Between San Pablo Bay and Suisun Bay—the fourth sub-bay—the flow of water up and down the bay must squeeze through the half-mile-wide Carquinez Strait. The dictionary defines a *strait* as "a narrow passage between two seas," though in this case the passage links two bays. Suisun is deeper than San Pablo, and lies at the mouth of the official confluence of the Sacramento and San Joaquin rivers. It's ringed on the north shore by golden hills, windmills, and the region's largest brackish marsh, and on the south shore it's encircled by oil refineries, industry, and small towns. The strait and Suisun Bay are the primary mixing zone of fresh river and salty ocean waters.

In hydrological terms, the Suisun, San Pablo, and Central bays all join together in a larger single system that is a classic estuary, with rivers flowing out to sea and tides coming in and out; the South Bay, however, has become an estuarine backwater.

Tides, Offshore Currents, and Upwelling

Bay waters are in constant motion. The most massive of these water movements are caused by ocean tides. Ocean water pours into the bay and pushes upstream during *flood tides*. The surge subsides again, pulling water out of the bay, on *ebb tides*.

Tides are caused by the gravitational pull of the sun and moon on the ocean. Two high tides and two low tides occur each day. The largest tide, a *spring tide*, occurs at the full and new moons year-round, not only in spring. At these times, the moon, sun, and earth align so that each reinforces the gravitational pull of the others, creating a tide powerful enough to move nearly a quarter of the water volume of the bay. The smallest tide, a *neap tide*, occurs in-between times, when the moon waxes or wanes to a quarter, and when the gravitational pull of the sun and moon are not aligned. The movements of the sun and moon across the seasons also influence tidal strength. Extreme high and low tides take place in the bay from May through June, and from November through December.

As the tides turn, most of the water goes in and out, over and over; only a relatively small portion is "new" water each time. "It's like a concertina—you can squash it up and stretch it out again, and while things are moving they're not really going anywhere," says John Largier, an oceanographer with UC Davis's Bodega Marine Lab.

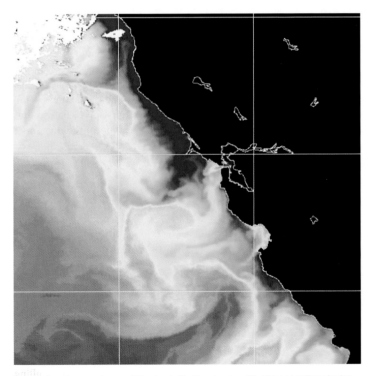

Sea surface temperatures off the bay's Pacific shores, with red and yellow depicting the warmest waters, blue the coldest, and green in-between. San Francisco Bay often shoots a jet of warm, fresh surface water through the Golden Gate. At the same time, local winds push California current waters in an arc (the yellow swirl), west past the Farallon Islands, south toward Half Moon Bay, then north again toward the Golden Gate. Cooler upwelled waters appear off Point Arena and Point Reyes. (John Largier)

Once through the Golden Gate and in the bay, the average parcel of water can travel up to nine miles with the tides, touching the shore of the South Bay in about two hours and reaching the banks of the state capital in about eight hours. At the Golden Gate, a flood tide can raise the water level by up to five and a half feet, which gradually diminishes to about three feet upriver near Sacramento. In contrast, tides flowing into the South Bay are amplified. With no major river inlets in this semienclosed system, tides tend to slosh back and forth. Water can linger in these backwaters for a month or more. The exchange happens more rapidly in the vicinity of the Central Bay, where tides and currents may drive a ribbon of seawater from the Gulf of the Farallones to the Bay Bridge and back in one tidal cycle.

To seasoned bay captains, the tides feel as familiar underfoot as the topography of dry land. Says Byron Richards, the retired captain of the science research vessel *Polaris,* "When you're fighting the tide, it feels like the boat's going uphill."

San Francisco Bay exhibits much stronger, more pronounced, changes in the spring/neap tidal cycle than do East Coast estuaries. A spring tide can bring 30 percent more water into and out of the bay than a neap tide. "All of the mixing and circulation of the water—including the transport of anything in the water like sediments, salt, and organisms—changes dramatically over a 14-day cycle, with a pretty big ecosystem response," says

The USGS research vessel *Polaris* was originally built for pleasure, not science. When insurance tycoon and delta marshland developer Lee Allen Phillips built the 96-foot-long yacht in 1927, he named it *Pasada Mañana* (which translates from Spanish as "maybe tomorrow"). Phillips took her into the ocean to troll for marlin and swordfish, sailed her up to the delta to visit farmers on his properties, and used her as a floating hotel to entertain the likes of Winston Churchill and Herbert Hoover. During Prohibition, he even sailed her to Canada and brought back whiskey in two copper tanks hidden behind a secret wall panel. (Francis Parchaso)

Jon Burau of the USGS, who may know more about how and where water flows within the bay than anyone else.

Offshore currents dictate the type of water that tides push into the bay from the ocean. Local wind patterns exert the strongest influence on what enters the Golden Gate. Water heading south from Alaska along the California Current tends to get pushed offshore by Point Reyes. Local winds force that water in an arc past the Farallon Islands and toward Half Moon Bay, then northward again in front of San Francisco Bay. This current may on occasion deliver southerly plankton species and tar balls from seeps in the Santa Barbara Channel, but more frequently it mixes with cold, upwelled water from off Point Arena.

Coastal upwelling, a phenomenon that occurs outside the Golden Gate, influences not only bay hydrodynamics but also the coastal and estuarine food supply. During upwelling, winds and the California current drive a giant river of warmer coastal surface water to the southeast. The rotation of the earth deflects this water offshore as it travels, and colder, deeper waters rise up to replace it. These upwelled waters are rich in both nutrients and oxygen, spurring a flurry of photosynthesis and plankton production. Local ocean upwelling occurs largely in late spring and summer (from March through August) between Point Arena and Point Reyes. Upwelling can depress sea level by six to nine inches, forcing the bay to empty by a proportional amount. When the winds that drive upwelling stop blowing, the flow reverses and a large surge of water enters the Golden Gate on the next tide (see p. 66, "The Power of Upwelling").

Water Layers and Flows

The water on the surface of the bay is not always the same as the water on the bottom. It doesn't all flow out to sea, either, or simply slosh back and forth with the tides. Scientists had to do quite a bit of work to figure this out.

They started their experiments back in the 1970s, when most people assumed that everything in the bay—water, sediment, sewage, trash, dead bodies—eventually ended up out in the Pacific. But early USGS scientists suspected the bay's hydrodynamics were more complicated than that, and set out to prove it.

A team led by John Conomos, the godfather of bay hydrodynamic studies, climbed aboard their research vessels and airplanes, headed out into and over the water, and dropped 1,345 drifters into San Francisco Bay. Half of these yellow plastic disks, each shaped like a saucer and trailing a

An early drifter, circa 1970s, called a "sea daisy." Text on one side offers a 50-cent reward for reporting the date and location where the sea daisy was found, as well as the serial number, to the USGS. (Francis Parchaso)

tail, were intended to stay on the surface, and half were supposed to sink to the bottom. Researchers bunched the latter together in groups and attached them to a ring of salt. The salt weight carried them down to the bottom, then dissolved—releasing these "seabed" drifters to go with the bottom currents. To keep them from floating back up again, their tails carried a five-gram brass ring. Scientists called the yellow disks with tails "sea daisies."

Like messages in a bottle, the drifters went out bearing a return address and the promise of a reward for information on where and when they were found. The light ones, floating on the surface like any piece of plastic trash, ended up among Pacific swells or washed up on ocean beaches. But the heavy ones all turned up in the bay.

The police heard about the scientists' work. One day, they gave Conomos a call. The police had found a body on an East Bay beach and wanted him to speculate about where it might have been dumped in the first place. Those were the days of the gang wars in San Francisco. The gangs assumed, like most casual observers, that anything they tossed off the Golden Gate would disappear out to sea. But the bodies, heavier than any drifter, sank; they then hitched a ride on bay floor currents that flow landward, then bloated and popped up in Berkeley. Conomos pointed the police to the red bridge.

"I'm always amazed at the shear at the Golden Gate: what's on the surface goes 20 miles offshore; what's at the bottom goes in. The sucking power is enormous," says venerable USGS oceanographer David Peterson, who worked with Conomos on the early drifter experiments.

Scientists have been tossing similar drifters in the bay and upper estuary ever since, and their results fill in some of the details about why bottom and surface waters behave differently from one another and often flow in different directions. In some cases, salinity differences in water masses are responsible; in others, the bathymetry of the bay floor is the deciding factor.

Fresh water is lighter than salt water. Though the two mix in shallower portions of the bay, in deeper areas they often flow in opposite directions. In other words, regardless of tides, a two-layer flow called *gravitational circulation* occurs: fresh water on the surface flows toward the sea, and salty water flows underneath upstream, as shown in the sea daisy studies. As the fresh water flows downstream, gathering ocean waters along the way, deeper ocean waters move upstream to replace it.

In the upper bays and straits, the fresh water coming down on top and the salt water coming up along the bottom encounter each other in much more confined and bumpy conditions than those in the Central Bay. Studies using current meters conducted by Jon Burau of the USGS in the 1990s showed that the strength of this two-layer flow is highly dependent on the shape of the bottom of the estuary. In particular, sills and shoals (bumps on the bottom) effectively shut down this two-layer flow, creating localized "entrapment zones," where sediments and organisms concentrate.

San Francisco Bay has a sequence of these zones associated with sills, whereas most other estuaries only have one zone where fresh water and salt water meet. This difference is entirely due to San Francisco Bay's unique shape and bathymetry, according to Burau. Scientists call their resulting concept of how water moves through the estuary a "sills and cells" model, with sills being bumps such as the Pinole Shoal and cells being areas between sills where the two-layer flow is strongest, such as in Carquinez Strait (see Figure 2).

Burau developed his concepts by deploying current meters and by chasing drifters around most of the critical bottlenecks and confluences in the northern estuary and delta. He is the modern-day Conomos, but the water movements he's studying are finer than the gross to and fro of water under the Golden Gate. Burau's drifters look nothing like the sea daisies. Instead of waiting for someone else to return them, Burau follows the devices in a boat.

Burau's first drifters comprised a plastic dish carrying an early GPS chip, a big underwater sail, and a tiny flag above the water. "You want min-

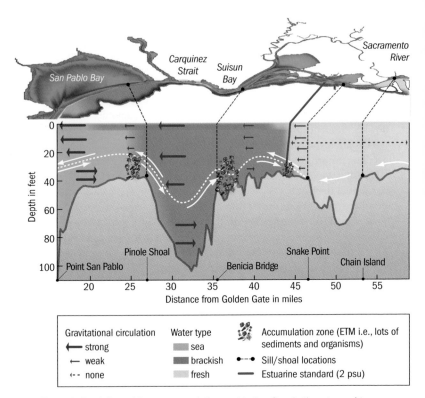

Figure 2. North Bay mixing zones are influenced by bay floor bathymetry and two-layer flows as salt water and fresh water meet. (Data from Jon Burau; redrawn by Jeanne Dileo, USGS)

imal footprint in the air and maximal footprint in the water; otherwise, the drifter will be more influenced by winds than flows," Burau explains.

Releasing even a dozen drifters in Suisun Bay used to mean chasing them all over the place. If he dropped the drifters in a clump by the navy's old mothball fleet, they'd be everywhere after two tidal cycles, he says. Burau calls this the "mixmaster" effect of tides and flows, whose technical term is *dispersion*. The drifters also have an unfailing propensity to get snagged under submerged logs, challenging their retrieval.

Burau has since hit upon the perfect drifter. He tucked a cell phone inside a Campbell's soup thermos and strapped a sail to the top. He then programmed the cell phone to transmit its exact location in the water at regular intervals, making the drifter much easier to track. The package costs less than $100—cheap for science equipment so easily lost. Back in the engineering lab, Burau's colleagues have been designing a fully auton-

Drifters used to track which way water is flowing are designed with a large sail under the water (to catch prevailing currents or tides) and a smaller flag on the surface (to reveal its location while minimizing exposure to wind). This drifter combines everyday materials including a cell phone encased in a waterproof thermos to collect sophisticated science data. (Jon Burau)

omous "smart" drifter that can even be programmed to stay away from the perils of the river bank, and won't need an expensive 24-hour vessel escort.

All this effort was aimed, of course, at finding out how the estuary's mixing zones work. Other research, by scientists like Wim Kimmerer of San Francisco State's Romberg Tiburon Center for Environmental Studies, has shown that the exact location where the mixing occurs is critical to ecosystem health. Estuarine species benefit from these specific conditions, in specific places, at specific times of year.

Juvenile clams and fishes in this part of the bay use the complex interactions among river flows, bathymetry, and tides to control their position, because they are too small to swim against the current. Their goal is to stay close to the mixing zones, which is where the food is (see p. 56, "Living Conditions"). Many estuarine organisms ride the high-velocity near-surface currents of flood tides upstream, then drop down to the lower velocity layers on the ebb—to remain within range of the mixing zones.

Jon Burau had a tougher time maintaining his position in the Carquinez Strait one day back in 1996. As he remembers it, he was out sampling zooplankton with a small crew on the 53-foot USGS research vessel *The Turning Tide*. They had strapped a submersible pump to the side of the boat. The pump included a long tube that could be lowered to various depths in the water column to gather plankton samples. On that trip, he remembers a freshwater pulse coming down the river, resulting in dramatic two-layer flows. On the surface, the water was flowing at the fast clip of more than two feet per second; on the bottom, it was also speeding by at two feet per second—but in the opposite direction.

The sampling started out smoothly enough. As the scientists dropped the pump in the upper part of the water column, it moved along with the vessel and surface currents. But the minute the pump dropped into the lower part of the water column, disaster struck. "The pump went one way and the boat went another, and the tube suddenly took off, straight into our props," says Burau. "The props usually chew things up, but this was a big tube, 4–5 inches in diameter. Things did not look good."

The captain threw the anchor in response. Just about then, Burau looked up and noticed a huge ship coming around the bend. "It seemed like a 15-story building was headed straight for us," he recalls. The two captains had a rapid radio exchange, with one warning of restricted maneuverability, and the other responding, "looks like you're right in the center of the shipping channel." The ship started turning, but continued bearing down on them sideways with the tide. Burau's crew retrieved their life vests and got ready to jump, but at the last minute the ship just missed them. "That's the kind of trouble you can get in because the estuary can flow in different directions at the same time," he says.

Wind, Waves, and Erosion

Anyone who has ever stood on the Golden Gate Bridge in a T-shirt and wished for a down jacket knows that the wind blows hardest through the narrowest parts of the estuary. Strong winds also brew in spring and summer due to temperature differences between the warm valley inland and the cool ocean offshore. Northerly winds drive surface waters out of the estuary, and southerly winds drive water into it.

Wherever the wind blows, it pushes the water into waves. A moderate summer wind can generate a wave half a meter high and two seconds long; a wave whipped up by a winter storm can last as many as five seconds. These waves reverberate down to water depths of about 10 feet but often don't affect deeper parts of the bay.

The readings from the 1850s Coast Geodetic Survey for San Pablo Bay suggest that it was not always so uniformly shallow and wide. The survey found two big, deep channels: one leading up into the Petaluma River and one into the Carquinez Strait. Myriad smaller channels extended the paths of local streams and tributaries beneath the surface of the bay. All of this changed after the California Gold Rush, whose miners washed away entire hillsides in search of the yellow ore. Bruce Jaffe's research shows that sediment pouring down from the gold mines over three decades (1856–1887) filled up the Petaluma River channel, more than doubled the acreage of surrounding mudflats, and smothered San Pablo Bay with 230 million cubic yards of soil from the Coast Ranges and Sierra uplands (see Figure 3).

The USGS's Jaffe notes that all of this deposition on the floor of the bay 100 years ago stopped around 1950. Then erosion began. As farmers around the bay and river banks built dikes to drain land for agriculture and to control flooding, and others upstream diverted river flows for human uses, these waters were cut off from sediment supplies upstream and along shores. Ninety acres of San Pablo Bay mudflats—those flat buffer lands between bay and shore—disappeared every year between 1951 and 1983, says Jaffe.

Today's bay shallows remain at the mercy of the wind. When it's shallow, it's easier for the antics of the wind on the surface to roil the bottom. In shallow parts of the bay, winds create waves that loop water up, down, around, and back again—from surface to bay floor. And since these wind-waves reach all the way down to the bottom, they also pick up and move things on the bottom, like mud.

Sediment

For many people, brown water is a red flag. Water quality managers receive frequent reports of brown water from concerned locals who assume it's a sewage leak or pollutant spill. San Francisco Bay is certainly more brown and turbid (cloudy) than most estuaries. Even if the water is very brown, it's generally not dirty or polluted, but filled with sediment. Indeed, whatever the color—brown, green, grey, blue—most hues come from suspended sediments and how they absorb and reflect light. Even a small amount of sediment can reflect a lot of light. On the muddiest days (usually in spring, when runoff volume is greatest), the amount of sediment in the water is well below 1 percent. USGS scientist David Schoellhamer, who has studied sediment transport in the bay, says if you flooded an island with 10 feet of chocolate-hued water from the bay and let it settle out, you'd wind up with less than a tenth of an inch of deposition on the bottom.

Sediment is an important part of the bay's physical condition. The largest concentrations appear on the surface with freshwater runoff in spring and summer. By fall and winter, most of it has sunk down to the bottom or

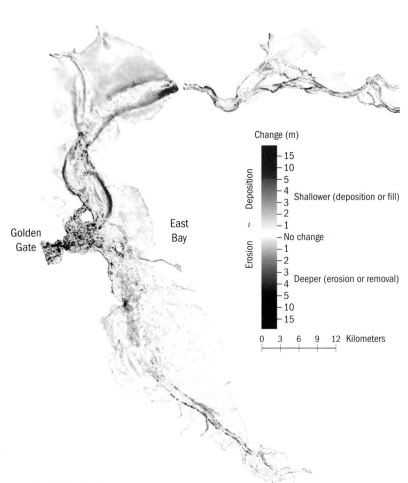

Change (m)

15
10
5
4
3
2
1
No change
1
2
3
4
5
10
15

Deposition

Erosion

Shallower (deposition or fill)

Deeper (erosion or removal)

Golden
Gate

East
Bay

0   3   6   9   12 Kilometers

1850s to 1890s

Figure 3. Changes in sediment deposition and erosion patterns in the bay between the 1850s and 1980s, largely as a result of hydraulic gold mining. (Bruce Jaffe)

settled out on a shoreline. "Rocks want to sink, because that's what rocks do in water. They're 'negatively buoyant,' " says Schoellhamer. "If the rock had a life jacket on, it would be 'positively buoyant.' " He goes on to explain how two primary forcing mechanisms keep the rocks up in the water column instead of allowing them to sink down: tidal currents and wind-waves.

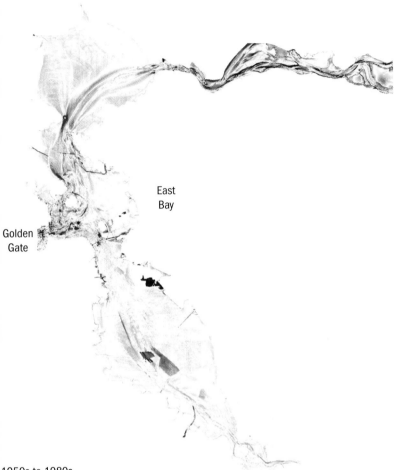

East
Bay

Golden
Gate

1950s to 1980s

Sediments hitching a ride on river flows can take months to find their way to a final settling place. Many go through a repetitive cycle of movement with the tides, depositing on a slack tide when water stops moving for a few minutes, then getting picked up again when the tides change. Wind-driven waves also pick up and put down sediments intermittently. Once in the water, these specks of rock, sand, and silt can move dozens of times before settling out. Multiply that by the billions of specks suspended in the bay at any given moment and it's clear just how solid the liquids are in this estuary.

"Typically in estuaries the finest material is up near the rivers," explains Schoellhamer. "Things like the two-layer flows and the asymmetry of tides generally move the finer material preferentially toward the land, and the coarser material out toward the ocean. In this estuary, we have the large sandbars out on the continental shelf, and those may act as a source of sand moving into Central Bay. Also, near the mouth of the estuary at the Golden Gate, we have generally the biggest tides and biggest water velocity, which again applies the most force, so the smaller rocks are not going to settle, as they are constantly picked up and moved somewhere else with every tide. Only the heavier stuff—the sand—can actually stay down there. That's why it's clearer down at the bottom of the Central Bay than in the shallower bays."

Sediments are good for the bay in several ways. First, the bay's natural turbidity protects it from the harmful algae blooms that plague other estuaries. Not enough sunlight penetrates into the water to drive phytoplankton growth. Second, contaminants introduced into the water often attach themselves to sediments and settle out, thereby getting removed either temporarily or permanently from circulation. Third, the estuary's wetlands and beaches need a steady supply of sediments to sustain places for

Erosion of the San Pablo baylands shoreline. (Jude Stalker)

Imagine three rocks sitting on the sunny slope of a Sierra foothill in the 1850s: one a speck of quartz, one a particle of clay, and one a skipping stone–sized pebble. A miner aims a hose at the hill and blasts all three rocks off the slope and down into a sluice box, where they are all separated from their gold-bearing peers and dropped on the bank of a creek. The pebble is too large and heavy to move far, and it ends up stuck on the bank for centuries, until a major storm carries it down to a sandbar a few miles downriver, where it spends more centuries. The speck, however, soon gets carried away and joins the swell of spring rainwater rushing downstream. Being very small and fine, the speck moves as fast as the water, surfing the surface flows right through the bay and out the Golden Gate within a matter of days. The heavier clay particle, meanwhile, follows the speck but makes a few stops along the way downstream until it settles on a channel bank at the bottom of San Pablo Bay. Here it soon gets a lot of company, as a blanket of other particles of clay, mud, and silt slowly builds over it until it's buried under six feet of other solids. Several decades later the clay particle might be scooped up and deposited on a dike by a dredger or scoured out by a 100-year flood, resuspended, and grabbed by a scientist in a bay-floor sample.

shoreline jaunts and barbecue spots, and for egrets, rails, and sandpipers probing the mud for goodies.

The bay may not be murky forever. Between 1957 and 2001, the amount of sediment coming down the Sacramento River decreased by 50 percent. But the supply will never dwindle away to nothing. Sediments will always be eroded off banks and shores by water and will move downstream.

Weather and Ocean Cycles

Climate often dictates the state of bay waters. It drives winds, currents, and waves, and it alters the temperature of air and water. Central California experiences a Mediterranean climate pattern with two distinct seasons: a warm, dry period from April to October, followed by a cool, rainy period from November to March. As the rainy season ends, snowmelt fortified by the season's final storms swells the banks of streams and lowers the salinity of estuary waters. This runoff wanes with summer, reducing many creeks to a trickle.

Westerly winds that began in spring intensify in summer, forcing ocean waters shoreward. Near land, the rotation of the earth deflects currents to

Fog creeping into the bay from offshore. (Francis Parchaso)

the south. Warmer surface waters get pushed away, to be replaced by deeper waters that are colder by as much as 15 degrees Fahrenheit. This phenomenon gives rise to the fog so characteristic of Bay Area summers, as evaporation from the ocean condenses above cold, upwelled waters. The higher pressure of this cold air mass pushes a river of fog through the Golden Gate and other Coast Range gaps toward the warmer, lower pressure region of the Central Valley. As air over the Central Valley cools, marine air retreats, returning hot weather to the region again in a repeating cycle.

When fall arrives, shorter days prevent Central Valley temperatures from rising to summertime peaks. Diminishing temperature differences between land and sea cause a series of new changes. The westerly winds weaken, the fog machine stutters to a stop, and a period of warm, clear days follows. This is why, for the Bay Area, September to November tend to be the balmiest months of the year.

All too soon, Indian summer fades. The jet stream moves into California's latitudes, bringing with it cold polar air masses. Encounters with the warmer southerly air above the Pacific often give birth to cyclonic storms that drop rain over the Bay Area all winter long. In fact, about 80 percent of the watershed's annual precipitation falls from November to March. The heights of Mount Tamalpais ensure that the North Bay receives the lion's

share of rain, up to 52 inches on average, compared to the 14-inch average
for San Jose.

Several large ocean cycles inject variety into seasonal weather patterns.
The best known of these is the El Niño Southern Oscillation (ENSO).
During an El Niño year, waters in the eastern tropical Pacific grow unusually warm. Normal upwelling currents get reversed. Meanwhile, the jet
stream often diverts storms that fall over the Pacific Northwest to California, drenching the Bay Area. Because water expands as it warms, the tides
swell beyond their normal reach. Now and then, instead of El Niño, the
region can come under the influence of La Niña conditions, which are
marked by cooler-than-average tropical waters and extraordinarily strong
upwelling. Each phase tends to last between 6 and 18 months, but one
round of the cycle may take three to four years to complete.

Two other major ocean cycles operate closer to home. The first to be
discovered was the Pacific Decadal Oscillation (PDO) in the early 1990s.
Reviewing salmon catch numbers in the North Pacific for the past century,
fisheries biologist Steven Hare noticed a distinct pattern. When nets were
full in Alaskan waters, those off Washington and Oregon would be empty.
Intrigued, Hare and oceanographer Bob Francis of the University of
Washington dug through more ocean records and found an oscillation
that in essence regulates the thermostat of the North Pacific. It keeps temperatures around the Gulf of Alaska cool when the west coast of North
America is warm, and vice versa. It swings average sea surface temperatures in each region up and down by about 12 degrees Fahrenheit, repeating the exchange every 20 to 30 years.

Scientists didn't discover the second ocean cycle for another 15 years.
While studying computer models of the North Pacific, climate scientist
Emanuele DiLorenzo of the Georgia Institute of Technology noticed a

distinct correlation among salinity, chlorophyll and nutrient cycles, and weather conditions. In 2007, he dubbed this phenomenon the North Pacific Gyre Oscillation (NPGO). The gyre itself is a circulatory pattern affecting 10 million square miles of the North Pacific.

With the oscillation in the gyre come strong north-to-south winds that favor upwelling off the northern and central California coast. This brings a heavy dose of salt and nutrients to the surface, fertilizing big phytoplankton blooms, whereas opposite conditions of lower salinity and weaker upwelling reign in coastal portions of the Gulf of Alaska. These states reverse when the NPGO cycle flips.

Scientists make several distinctions between the PDO and the NPGO. Though both cycles last 20 to 30 years and affect the North Pacific, they influence different conditions. Whereas the PDO modulates sea temperatures, the NPGO affects just about everything else: salinity, upwelling intensity, and plankton levels.

The discovery of the NPGO has given scientists a new perspective on how the ocean affects an estuary. "For a long time, we have believed that what happens in watersheds, and is delivered by rivers, is a primary source of variability in estuaries. That's the overarching theme of estuarine science. But the more we learn and observe, the more we're realizing that climate-driven change in oceans can be just as powerful a driver of change in estuaries as processes in the watershed," says USGS scientist Jim Cloern.

An understanding of the NPGO might have helped prevent the historic sardine crash in Monterey Bay 50 years ago. Says UC Berkeley plankton scientist Zack Powell, "If this picture is correct, then right when we were harvesting that sardine population the hardest in Monterey, the natural oscillation was bringing those fish down. The coincidence of harvesting with oscillations like this may be the reason why that fishery has not recovered."

The NPGO may be an even stronger influence on the bay in the near future. Satellite data suggest certain aspects of the oscillation have been strengthening in recent decades as earth temperatures rise.

Climate over Millennia

Ever since people have used instruments to measure state temperatures and rainfall, conditions around the estuary have been mild compared to most other regions of the country. Yet these written records do not begin to hint at the extreme weather California has experienced in millennia past—extremes such as mega-droughts, torrential rains, and dizzying temperature swings.

By analyzing natural records of climate in the form of tree rings and sediment deposits, scientists have pieced together a chronicle of state climate extending back 10,000 years. Trees lay down a new ring of wood in their trunks with each year; these rings are wider in wetter, warmer years. Pollen trapped in mud can reveal which plant species grew there. Sediment cores can show how big and wide streams were in decades past, and diatoms can indicate inundation by fresh versus salt water. Each of these records provides a different snapshot of climate conditions. Overall, they point to how lucky modern settlers in California have been—and how much change may be in store.

About 10,000 years ago, the ice ages that had frozen much of North America beneath glaciers began to thaw. A warmer, drier climate melted polar ice and raised sea levels until the ocean could enter the Golden Gate. Conditions warmed so much that by 6,000 years ago, bristlecone pines and other mountaintop species had retreated to the highest peaks, and the

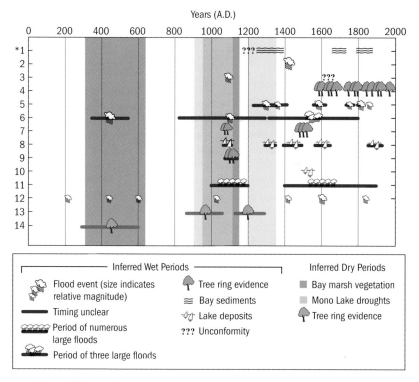

Figure 4. Extreme climate events in California over the last 2,000 years. *Numbers refer to references provided in the original research paper. (Frances Malamud-Roam, redrawn by UC Press)

sea had filled the bay to its modern shorelines. Conditions cooled suddenly again about 3,600 years ago; large cobbles in estuary cores suggest a devastating flood had poured into the bay, helping to build marshes and support oyster beds. Though the state then entered a cooler, drier time, the climate of the most recent millennium has been more erratic. Two "epic" droughts parched the state for about 150 years each, followed by a 300-year cold period known as the "Little Ice Age."

The last 150 years have been among the most welcoming in California's known climatic history. In fact, the twentieth century was the third wettest in 1,000 years. This spate of good weather supported a burgeoning human population and a strong state economy, "providing us with a limited, somewhat optimistic perspective on the carrying capacities of California's landscapes and resources, including our water supply and flood control structure," writes UC Berkeley climate scientist Frances Malamud-Roam and colleagues. Such skewed expectations are due for a jarring adjustment. The warmer years projected for the next century, resulting in earlier snowmelts and floods, are expected to bring a harsher future.

Conclusion

Under the bay's temperate skies and surface lie more than islands, dunes, and plain water. The water can be cold or hot, salty or sweet. It can come from far away or near at hand, from a spring in the Sierra or the middle of the Pacific Ocean. It can move straight or sideways, or it can sink to the bottom or be whipped into a wave by wind. In the water can drift bits of sand and silt, shreds of plants, fish, and even monsters of Jaws proportions. No human can fully grasp what it's like beneath the bay's mirrored surface.

Those who have put their minds to it have learned, however, a number of attributes of the bay and its watershed that escape initial notice. One insight has been that the rivers, delta, bay, and ocean cannot be subdivided into distinct ecosystems. The water has a way of connecting all corners, seeping through the boundaries erected by human perceptions of the landscape.

"It's a whole different ballgame thinking of our water and fish as moving through a mixing bowl, rather than through a series of one-way canals," says Kim Taylor, a USGS manager who oversaw some of the most interdisciplinary science research ever done concerning the estuary.

Not so long ago, scientists believed rivers dominated the estuary between the Sierra and the sea. Now they know tides may be an even bigger influence. Recent grand-scale changes in the Pacific have in turn suggested that ocean conditions don't just occur outside the Golden Gate. Instead, the ocean influences almost every element of the estuary—the weight and temperature of the air and water, the types of marine species to be found in the bay—from year to year and decade to decade.

In March 2007, a five-year-old boy playing on Marin's McNear's Beach found one of Conomos's drifters more than thirty years after it was released under the Golden Gate. Though a bit beaten up, it still looked very much like a yellow plastic sea daisy with a red stem. The boy's mother tracked down the local USGS office in Menlo Park and found a couple of scientists who still remembered the experiment. Soon afterward young Leaf Allen received the long-promised 50-cent reward, as well as a packet of USGS pencils and postcards.

VISIBLE AND INVISIBLE LIFE
Fish, Birds, and Other Wildlife

One winter day we were out collecting fish for the bay study, and I came up from below to find our technician trying to extract himself from an octopus. It was a big one, with about a four-foot reach. He'd picked up a pile of debris that came up with the net, and the octopus had immediately crawled up the sleeve of his raincoat and onto his shoulder. So he's lifting one tentacle off, then two, and runs out of hands. I went back there and started lifting them off too, but we didn't have enough hands between the two of us to compete with the octopus's eight. In the end, we had to take the tech's raincoat off and drop the whole tangle in the water until the octopus let go.

RANDY BAXTER, FISHERIES BIOLOGIST,
CALIFORNIA DEPARTMENT OF FISH AND GAME

GLANCING AT THE BAY from a speeding auto or at the edge of the pier, it's difficult to tell that it teems with a dazzling variety of life. With time and patience, however, signs of life always materialize. For most observers, birds are the first to move into sight: white gulls circling overhead, sanderlings poking beaks into the smear of shoreline mud, or a black-and-white Western Grebe, long neck arched for a fishing expedition.

Those who scramble down to the water's edge encounter an even broader slice of estuary organisms. Empty crab carapaces, fish vertebrae, and bottle-green strands of eelgrass offer a taste of what resides beneath the opaque chop. Mudflats at low tide reveal the telltale breathing holes of clams, worms, and invertebrates.

Observing fish requires more effort. Flatfish, crabs, sharks, and rays can be seen wriggling within plastic buckets near anglers, or staring from atop mountains of ice at Fisherman's Wharf.

Willets gather in the shallows of former salt production ponds at the Coyote Hills Regional Shoreline. This decrepit pipeline and pilings still poke out above the high tide line, but a recent survey found 33,000 abandoned pilings lie invisible beneath the bay's surface. Some offer important hard substrates for aquatic creatures to latch on to— a rare habitat in a largely soft-bottomed bay. Many old pilings contain creosote, however, a wood preservative that can be harmful enough to marine life that biologists would like to see all abandoned pilings removed.
(Kathleen M. Wong)

The extraordinary diversity of species found in the bay mirrors the broad range of available environments. As a place where fresh and salt water mix, and liquid ocean and dry land overlap, its waters and shores embrace an ever-shifting blend of salinities, temperatures, substrates, and currents. The resulting profusion of habitats draws a mix of coastal and aquatic species to live side by side. The physical processes at work in the water bring order to the locations and arrivals of bay species.

This chapter describes a number of representative invertebrates, fish, birds, and mammals found in the ecosystem of the estuary. All are native except for the clams (which hail from Asia) and the introduced Striped Bass. Many of the behavioral and physiological adaptations these species have evolved to survive in the bay environment—from migration timing to spawning strategies—are shared to some degree by myriad other organisms that call the estuary home (see p. 183, "Mini-Guide: Species in Peril").

Living Conditions

Environment in Flux

San Francisco Bay is a place of constant change. Conditions in bay habitats shift daily, seasonally, and annually, dictating which species are found where. Most of that change is driven by water conditions. The temperature of ocean waters, the strength of river flows, and whether the marine currents flow toward land or out to sea all affect how welcoming the bay may be for different species.

Species found in bay waters one month may turn up again next year, in 10 years, or not for half a century. "It's always interesting to see which organisms do well under a particular set of circumstances," says Randy Baxter, a senior fisheries biologist in charge of the California Department of Fish and Game's long-term monitoring program for fish and invertebrates. "The environment changes offshore and changes onshore, and you get this kaleidoscopic mix of different circumstances that favor one group of organisms over another group, over different years. It seems like it's never ending—there's always another combination that does something unexpected."

Salinity is a strong structuring component for all communities of bay organisms. How much salt a creature can handle dictates where it can live, feed, and reproduce. Seawater is typically 35 parts per thousand (ppt) of salt. But young Dungeness Crabs seek out areas with 15–25 ppt, making the bay an attractive haven. Species that prefer saltier water predominate in the Central and South Bay, whereas estuarine and freshwater species live in the upper bays and rivers. Two-thirds of the fish species swimming around the bay are marine.

The mix of salt and fresh water in the estuary can undergo dramatic shifts. In areas such as Suisun Bay, the water can turn from drinkable to tangy with salt within days. In deeper waters nearer the Golden Gate, conditions remain more constant. However, swings in salinity are not nearly as dramatic as they used to be in some areas; human management of the fresh water draining into the bay has smoothed out the extremes. The result is a more inviting delta for many nonnative freshwater species. Twelve of the 13 most commonly caught species in the bay are native; in the delta, less than 20 percent can claim local origins.

Beyond salinity, a number of other physical factors influence what lives

Scientists classify the species found in San Francisco Bay based on where they live.

- *Marine* organisms live in salty ocean water.
- *Estuarine* or *euryhaline* species prefer a salt water and fresh water mix.
- *Native* species are of local origin.
- *Non-native, exotic,* and *introduced* species hail from elsewhere but were brought to the bay by humans.
- *Pelagic* species such as Northern Anchovy inhabit open water.
- *Demersal* organisms are found on or near the bottom.
- *Structure-associated* organisms favor piers, rocks, and pilings.
- *Benthic* species live in the bottom mud or sand.
- *Resident* species live in the bay year-round.
- *Anadromous* fish live in the ocean as adults but return to the estuary and travel upstream through rivers and creeks to reproduce.

where: the material on the bay floor, currents, water temperature, and turbidity. Warmer waters, for example, put off sharks but please halibut. Turbidity—the murkiness of a given patch of water—affects the amount of light that can penetrate the water column. Turbidity from suspended sediments limits the types of plants and plankton that can grow and the amount of food available for fish; turbidity can also result from algal blooms.

The ocean exerts a powerful influence on local biodiversity. Positioned midway down the California coastline, the bay is a place where two distinct groups of coastal marine fauna overlap. One group is associated with warm, tropical waters that typically reach as far north as Point Conception, near Santa Barbara. The other is found in cooler waters, which generally extend from the Central Coast north to Canada. The mixing point of these zones can occur anywhere in between, including opposite the Golden Gate. When the ocean switches from cold to warm during one of its decadal regime changes, tropical species arrive in the bay within a few months.

Between 1998 and 1999, the Pacific Ocean underwent a regime change called the North Pacific Gyre Oscillation that sent cooler waters into the bay (see p. 45, "Weather and Ocean Cycles"). This shift also turned the bay's species communities upside down. At that time, biologists were shocked by a plankton bloom occurring in the bay as late as October. No one had seen such a phenomenon for decades. State Department of Fish and Game surveys showed the abundance of bottom-dwellers suddenly leap off the charts. Huge numbers of juvenile crab and English Sole migrated into the bay, while shrimp, Plainfin Midshipmen, and Sand Dab also prospered (see Figure 5). As larvae, all of these species rely on phyto-

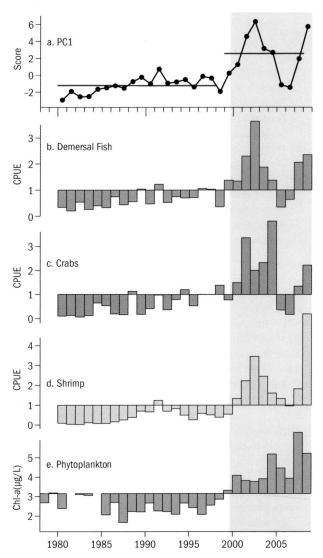

Figure 5. Changes at the interface between the ocean and bay—prompted by seasonal, annual, and decadal shifts—all affect which species thrive in the bay from year to year. Various common organisms such as fish, crabs, and shrimp (b, c, d,) appear on the left side of the figure, expressed in CPUE, an abundance index (catch per unit of effort), as well as a reference to their food supply in terms of phytoplankton (e). PC1 (a) is the index of community variability over time. On the right side of the figure, changing conditions are shown including the North Pacific Gyre Oscillation (f), Pacific Decadal Oscillation (g), El Niño and La Niña (h), sea surface temperatures (i), and coastal upwelling (j). (J. E. Cloern et al.)

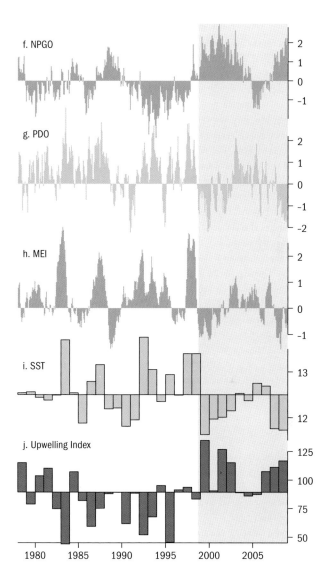

plankton. The dramatic switch in San Francisco Bay species was most pronounced in the area most closely connected to the ocean—the Central Bay.

Another boost to biological change and diversity comes from the fact that the bay is an outlet for so many rivers and creeks. These tributaries bring species that prefer fresh and brackish waters into the realm of the bay.

Geologic history, too, has helped shape the bay's present biodiversity. The 10,000-year-old bay is a recent feature on the Pacific Coast. The bay's geologic youthfulness means that relatively few clams, worms, and other species that live in the mud have had a chance to establish themselves in local waters. By the same token, the tides have had fewer seasons to carve out marshes, making bay wetlands less extensive than in older estuaries such as Chesapeake Bay on the East Coast. The relative rarity of local marshes further limits the amount of food available, because decaying plants and wetland ecosystems are important sources of estuary nutrients.

The last 200 years of human habitation have left a sizable mark on bay health and richness. During the Gold Rush, miners in the Sierra foothills unleashed tons of soil into the estuary's rivers, which eventually wound up on the bay floor as a thick layer of sediment. The sudden influx of mud smothered sedentary creatures such as the native Olympia Oyster, and bottom-dwelling crustaceans and worms, and changed the consistency of the bay floor. Because these species aren't very mobile, they had difficulty repopulating the new layers of mud. Eventually, foreign species filled the vacuum. To this day, scientists still characterize the bay floor as having low species diversity.

Bay Habitats

Habitats in and around the bay belong to one of three groups: open water, wetland, and upland. Open water areas are always submerged, and they range from the deepest depths of the bay to shallower patches near marshes that are never exposed to air. Beneath their watery surfaces lies the *substrate*, or bottom type, which can consist of soft sand, silt, rock, hard shells, and even peat in the delta. Shrimps and crabs, worms and clams live here. The water column itself is divided by depth into *deepwater*, *midwater*, and shallow or *subtidal* zones. Subtidal areas include most of the bay floor and shallows that are always submerged.

Wetland habitats ring the shores of the bay. These marshy areas are washed by tides or runoff that periodically leave them high and dry. *Seasonal wetlands* flood only during winter and spring rains. Many consist of flooded corn fields and other agricultural lands that provide important feeding and resting places for migrating waterfowl. The *tidal flats*, which include the broad mudflats that ring much of the bay, are only exposed at

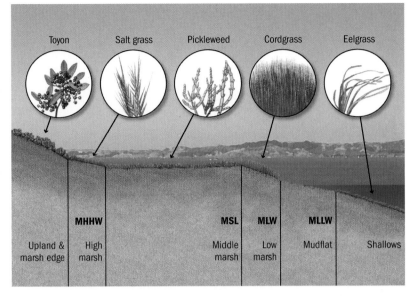

Figure 6. Intertidal distribution of representative plants and wildlife. MHHW, mean higher high water; MSL, mean sea level; MLW, mean low water; MLLW, mean lower low water. (Data from P. M. Faber and P. Baye, reference profile courtesy Brad Evans, drawn by Tim Gunther)

low tide. Farther inland, the tides sweep in and out of *tidal marshes* via twisting channels. *Brackish marshes* lie adjacent to freshwater outlets from the delta or near the mouths of rivers. *Managed marshes*, often owned by duck clubs, can be salty, brackish, or fresh, but are typically operated to optimize habitat for waterfowl.

The plants that grow in each type of marsh reflect both local salinity levels and the length of regular inundation by tidal waters. At their inland edges, tidal marshes are often sprinkled with less salt-tolerant, upland species, forming a particularly diverse transitional habitat. Species that use the bay for one purpose, and retreat to the uplands for another, rely on wetlands for cover and shelter during their commutes.

Upland areas are high enough in elevation to remain untouched by bay waters. Here, more than 20 feet above sea level, marine influences are muted at best. In the estuary's Mediterranean climate, grasslands and oak woodlands predominate. Creek drainages punctuate shorelines with riparian forest, willow groves, and riverbank habitats that inject splashes of species diversity to the shoreline.

During the past 140 years, many habitats in the estuary basin have been converted or degraded to accommodate humans (see p. 105, "His-

Low-tide habitats at the Palo Alto baylands. (Jude Stalker)

tory of Human Changes"). Development reduced open waters by 50 percent and wetlands by 80 percent, and urbanized 50 percent of the surrounding uplands.

The Marine Nursery

Like all good parents, aquatic organisms seek to give their young the most advantageous upbringing they can. The bay's many amenities make it an appealing site for marine species to rear their young. Gentle waves, a consistent supply of food, turbid waters that offer cover from predators, and warmer waters than the open ocean make the bay a nurturing environment for many kinds of helpless juveniles.

Some marine species, like herring, lay their eggs in the bay itself. But many others reproduce in the rich coastal waters just outside the Golden Gate. The majority breed in winter, when upwelling is at its weakest and less likely to carry young away from the shore. When spring arrives, upwelling produces plentiful food for their tiny offspring.

Species such as flatfish and Dungeness Crab travel into the bay during early life stages and remain to mature. Breeding out in the ocean, their parents strive to deposit eggs near enough to the coast for hatchlings to

Herring roe (eggs) on blades of eelgrass. Roe from San Francisco Bay are particularly prized by Japanese food buyers, who value their unusual golden hue.

crawl, swim, or ride the flood tides, or bottom current, through the Golden Gate. If parental timing and placement is off, these youngsters end up in other near-shore areas up and down the coast. Those larvae and juveniles that do maneuver themselves into San Francisco Bay find a sheltered, relatively warm, and food-filled place to grow up.

Entering the bay is one thing; managing to stay there is another. "There's no species that comes into San Francisco Bay to reproduce, or that is resident here, that hasn't got some mechanism or strategy to keep their young here, some way of reducing their chances of being carried out the Golden Gate or up and down the coast by tides or currents," says biologist Kathy Hieb of the California Department of Fish and Game. Hieb conducts a longstanding survey of bay life every month to monitor estuary health.

Some of these staying strategies include producing sticky eggs, building nests, bearing live young in safe shallows, and timing reproduction to coincide with currents or tides headed in the right direction. Such strategies are one reason species that live in and around estuaries are so special. "They sense which way is upstream. There's some gradient beyond just salinity, something in estuarine water like dissolved organics and plant materials, that they can detect using their olfactory senses," Hieb says.

Fundamental Food

The slate-grey waters of the bay can be considered a soup made up of nutrients, sediment, and microscopic organisms called plankton. The calories these minute creatures produce provide an essential foundation for all life in the bay and coastal ocean. Without plankton, the bay and ocean would offer little to eat.

A wide variety of bay creatures graze directly on plankton. These range from adult anchovies and herring to barnacles and larval fishes. Plankton not eaten while still alive sink to the bay floor and support filter-feeding clams, worms, and sponges. These bottom-dwelling species are, in turn, snapped up by organisms ranging from birds to fish, completing the link to the rest of the food web. Any plankton missed by these mouths decays into fertilizer.

Phytoplankton are the single most abundant source of food in the bay. Made up of simple plants, including single-celled, silica-walled algae called diatoms, as well as dinoflagellates and cyanobacteria, phytoplankton perform photosynthesis to transform mineral nutrients and sunshine into energy other creatures can eat. Phytoplankton range in size from roughly three-quarters of an inch to less than a millionth of an inch, and they include more than 5,000 marine species. Most live and die in the space of a few days.

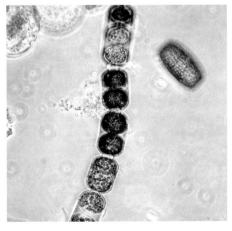

These *Melosira* sp. diatoms are among the phytoplankton responsible for algal blooms. Diatoms construct distinctive walls of silica that fit together like the halves of a pillbox. Using green chloroplasts such as those visible in this image, phytoplankton conduct roughly half of the photosynthesis that occurs on Earth. Conditions must be just right for plankton to bloom in murky San Francisco Bay. The winds that stir up water layers must weaken, so that freshwater runoff remains as a clear layer atop the bay's salty waters. Such water stratification encourages blooms in two ways: (1) sunlight penetrates deeper into the water column, reaching more phytoplankton, and (2) phytoplankton linger near the surface, far from the hungry mouths below. (Cary Burns Lopez)

Paddling about amid the phytoplankton and fish are the minute group of animals known as *zooplankton*. Unlike their photosynthetic neighbors, zooplankton cannot manufacture their own food from sunlight. Instead, they eat phytoplankton and one another in order to survive. This diverse group includes shrimplike copepods, microscopic rotifers, water fleas, and larval crabs up to half an inch in length. Over 200 species of zooplankton, many of which are non-native, can be found in the San Francisco estuary.

Larger zooplankton, such as Mysid Shrimp, migrate up and down the water column. They rise to the surface to feed at night, when they are less likely to be seen by predators, and return to the depths during the day.

Their movements dictate the behavior of many fish. From Pacific Herring to young Longfin Smelt, many fish travel to the surface in search of zooplankton, then sink back down into the water column to evade marauding seabirds.

Phytoplankton follow a cycle of bloom and bust. When conditions are right, they explode into algal blooms that may cover hundreds of square miles of ocean water. Any pond covered in green slime is the site of an algal bloom in action. Algal blooms form the base of the aquatic food web. But blooms that get out of hand can cause transient harm to estuary life. Most harmful blooms are triggered by too many nutrients, too much warmth, or relatively stagnant water. Filter feeders are unable to eat enough to keep up with the supply. The excess algae decays, depleting oxygen levels in the water and suffocating fish, crabs, and other species. Some living algae can produce harmful neurotoxins potent enough to kill fish and poison top predators such as pelicans and sea lions.

Not all blooms are harmful. Each year in the bay, phytoplankton blooms convert sunlight and dissolved inorganic carbon into about 120,000 tons of organic carbon, roughly equivalent to the number of calories required to sustain over a million adult humans. Despite these periodic blooms, San Francisco Bay is food-limited compared to other estuaries. Two main factors help ensure that bay blooms are rare. Turbid water blocks the sunlight required for photosynthesis, while the bacteria that recycle decaying organic matter back into the food web suffer from low abundance and growth rates.

Shifts in phytoplankton cycles are telltale signs of changes in bay conditions. The first shift came in 1987, when a species of clam introduced from Asia began invading the estuary's northern reaches. In Suisun Bay, where the mix of fresh and salt water brings good bloom conditions each spring, this exotic clam filtered phytoplankton out of the water column faster than the algae could reproduce. Levels of chlorophyll A (a measure of organic plant matter abundance) in the area, which once averaged about a hundredth of a gram per quart of water, dropped to roughly a fifth of that level after the clam's invasion. The virtual elimination of this bloom cut the heart out of the estuarine food web: the clams gobbled up all the plankton before the natives could get a mouthful.

The clam was not solely responsible for these abrupt shifts in bay plankton availability. Between 1977 and 1997, the most explosive blooms always occurred in spring, and remained relatively constant year after year. But this 20-year-old pattern came to an end in 1998. Phytoplankton abundance began exploding in one part of the bay and plummeting in another, and blooms occurred at times of the year never seen before. "We find ourselves in the midst of a big biological change, with biomass in the delta lower and in the bay higher, and both gradual and abrupt changes in the last two

THE POWER OF UPWELLING

The waters just outside the Golden Gate offer some of the most productive marine habitats in the world. Here, a phenomenon called upwelling introduces nutrients and oxygen to coastal waters, spurring a flurry of photosynthesis and plankton production (see Figure 7 below). Upwelling adds extra biological riches to San Francisco Bay, but the food exchange can go both ways. In spring, the bay's algal blooms may flow out to the ocean, whereas ocean blooms nourished by upwelling wash into the bay in summer. The ocean is a more important source of food for the bay during late spring and summer episodes of strong upwelling. Such influxes of nutrient-rich water, says UC Davis oceanographer John Largier, help explain why sea grass beds and phytoplankton blooms tend to be located in the Central Bay, nearer this water's source. San Francisco Bay's reliance on ocean productivity is unusual. In most estuaries, the majority of nutrients arrive via rivers and are exported out to the ocean.

Figure 7. Upwelling patterns off the central California coast. (Coastwatch, NASA)
Inset: The mechanics of upwelling. (Northwest Fisheries, NOAA)

decades," says the USGS's Jim Cloern. "On top of our regular seasonal variability we're getting larger regime shifts originating from the ocean."

The new blooms coincided with a cooling of the ocean off the Pacific coast and affected productivity in the saltier portions of the bay. These areas now experience blooms in fall and winter as well as spring. The cooler conditions also nurtured bumper crops of Dungeness Crab and English Sole. When these predators arrived in the bay, they found some tasty exotic clams to eat and the clam population declined—setting the stage for larger and more frequent bay phytoplankton blooms.

Plants

Beyond the microscopic phytoplankton sustaining the base of the bay's food web, bigger and more complex plants grow in the shallows and along bay margins. These plants not only provide shelter for other organisms to live but eventually decompose into the detritus eaten by filter feeders and into the organic matter that supports the entire bay ecosystem.

Growing at the edge of the bay is a challenge for plants. The pull of tides and waves churns soil, alternately uprooting young shoots and burying stems in the mud. Plant seeds also have difficulty sprouting in salty soil; seed coats must absorb enough water to break and sprout. This shrinks the germination window to a few months during the rainy season, even for species that tolerate high salinity when mature. Constant immersion in water can suffocate tissues. And constant exposure to salty or alkaline soils and seawater can desiccate even the hardiest plants. Plants adapted to marshes use several common strategies to overcome these problems. Hollow, air-filled roots and stems help deliver oxygen to submerged tissues. In addition to generating seeds, many marsh plants clone themselves via creeping rhizomes and runners. Such clones can make up a substantial portion of any pickleweed, salt grass, or tule patch. The resulting tangle of runners often forms a thick mattress that helps anchor the stems above.

Salinity, submergence, and competition all influence what species can grow where in a salt marsh. Of these, coping with the salt delivered by seawater requires the most specialized adaptations. Species found only in saltier soils—also known as *halophytes*—can tolerate levels of soil salinity that will inhibit or even kill potential freshwater marsh plants. The ability to withstand high salinities is costly, however. Adaptations for salt tolerance consume energy and nutrients that could otherwise be spent on growth and reproduction.

Marsh plants minimize such salt stresses in several ways, mostly by

In summer, the yellow flowers of gum-plant (*Grindelia hirsutula*, formerly *G. stricta* var. *angustifolia*) lend color to the green carpet of many bay tidal marshes. Its bushy shape, deep-green leaves, and daisylike flowers make this plant impossible to miss along the meandering edges of channels. Gumplant gets its name from the sticky white resin that accumulates within the flower heads and often varnishes the entire plant. (Kathleen M. Wong)

trying to equalize salt concentrations on either side of their root membranes. Some plants exclude salts when they absorb surrounding saline or brackish water, and some shed extra salt via special glands on their leaves—often evident as crystalline speckles or crusts—or when leaves die and drop. Because live, green leaves are a plant's source of energy and food production, dropping them can result in reduced growth. The most specialized halophytes deal with excess salt in their tissues with the help of creative chemistry. They remove salts from cell sap, store salts in membranous cell sacs called vacuoles, and balance the concentration of dissolved solutes in sap with organic salt substitutes.

Only a small number of plant species can tolerate the higher levels of salinity that occur in salt marshes, which range from the salinity of seawater (about 3.4 percent salt) to even higher concentrations due to evaporation. A much larger number of plant species in the estuary can tolerate diluted seawater, or less than about 2 percent of total dissolved salts. This is why only about 16 plant species are associated with bay salt marshes, versus about 100 species in brackish areas.

Another major challenge for tidal marsh vegetation is the wide fluctuation in salinity due to seasons, drought, and climate cycles that deliver extra rain. From the deluge of winter rain to the peak of summer drought, salinity levels around a plant can triple over the course of a calendar year. Stronger variations in climate can transform a cattail stand into a salt grass meadow within a few months. Many marshes fluctuate regularly between nearly fresh to seawater-salty over time, with extremes driving some plants to local extinction.

The plants of the bay and its wetlands segregate themselves within habitat zones. These include subtidal and intertidal zones in the bay, and low, middle, and high marsh zones onshore. The boundaries between marsh zones are seldom clear-cut. Tidal range, salinity, and drainage patterns vary throughout the estuary, affecting both zone positions and the distributions of marsh plant species (see Figure 6). Invasive non-native species, such as perennial pepperweed, grow across the middle and high marsh zones of brackish marshes, homogenizing the vegetation. The locations of creeks, freshwater seeps, and brackish areas at marsh margins jumble the picture further.

Eelgrass

Most bay waters are too turbid to support much photosynthesis, so most of the associated plant species grow in the shallows or tidal zones. One of the few that grows entirely underwater is eelgrass (*Zostera marina*). The long shoots of this emerald-green plant undulate over the muddy bottom like prairie grasses stirred by a breeze, but their brilliance is often dulled by a coating of algae. Each shoot is between 0.06 inches and 0.5 inches wide, but can grow up to 50 feet long. Growing in subtidal areas where the water falls less than 3 feet to 6.5 feet below mean-lower low water, eelgrass is easily viewed from the surface in a kayak or small boat. Eelgrass thrives in locations of lower turbidity.

Eelgrass grows in shallow underwater meadows covering 3,700 acres of the bay bottom. The biggest bed carpets a shoal between Point Pinole and Point San Pedro on the East Bay shore, north of Richmond. Two other large beds lie in Marin's Richardson Bay and off Alameda's Crown Beach.

In a world of mud where bottom cover is nearly nonexistent, the shelter of eelgrass is a magnet for many animals. Herring lay eggs on its strands, pipefish hide beneath its constantly moving canopy, Tubeworms burrow into the roots, and epiphytic organisms such as bryozoans and snails cling to its blades. The plants themselves form a baffle that slows the flow of water and traps sediments, improving water clarity. As eelgrass transforms nutrients into usable calories for the food web, its roots help filter pollution before it enters the ocean. The sheer number of species that shelter in eelgrass beds attracts predators such as Least Terns, which forage on the fishes hiding in this miniature forest. And at least one species of waterfowl, the Black Brant, relies on eelgrass blades for calories during its migration along the Pacific Flyway.

Though a valuable source of habitat, eelgrass is particularly scarce in San Francisco Bay. It covers less than 1 percent of the bay floor, compared to about 25 percent in other West Coast estuaries (see also p. 274, "Underwater Restoration," and p. 276, "Central Bay Eelgrass Beds").

Cordgrass

The first species to protrude above the surface of the water in the lower salt marsh zone is Pacific cordgrass (*Spartina foliosa*). It forms narrow bands or meadows at the edges of the bay and other areas subject to tidal inundation. Its pale, yellow-green stem sprouts narrow, green leaf blades and grows one to three feet tall, but it may be half submerged in salty water. Its leaves often appear grayish because of silt films left by high tides. Cordgrass manages its salt balance through leaf glands, cell sap, and sequestration, and its hollow stems deliver oxygen to its submerged roots. Cordgrass blooms from mid- to late summer, with the flowers appearing in clusters along the tip of the stalk. The seeds have a low germination rate, so the plant tends to reproduce by sprouting clones from underground rhizomes. Though few animals can stomach its salty foliage, cordgrass contributes to the estuary in other ways. These plants grow in wide meadows that absorb wave energy and slow the movement of water, protecting shorelines from erosion and encouraging sediments to drop out of the water column. Microbes, worms, and snails feed on cordgrass detritus, contributing to the food web, while the fine clays and muds help build marshland. Endangered California Clapper Rails rely heavily on cordgrass cover to hide from predators.

Unfortunately, smooth cordgrass (*Spartina alterniflora*), an invasive exotic cordgrass species from the Atlantic coast, has been hybridizing with the bay's native Pacific cordgrass since the 1990s. Left unchecked, the hybrids would threaten Pacific cordgrass populations with extinction in the San Francisco estuary (see p. 268, "Weeding by Satellite").

Spongy tissues help conduct air inside cordgrass stem. (Jude Stalker)

Native cordgrass, *Spartina foliosa*. Tidal marshes in the San Francisco Estuary differ from other central California coast marshes in several ways, among them the historic dominance of Pacific cordgrass (pictured here) and the presence of locally endemic species such as soft bird's beak (see p. 187) and Suisun thistle. Before Europeans settled around San Francisco Bay, this native grass lined hundreds of miles of local channels and shoreline, and also thrived in San Diego County and Baja, California. Today, Pacific cordgrass is competing for space at the water's edge with invaders from other coasts. (Jude Stalker)

Salt Grass

Salt grass sends out creeping runners both above and below ground to establish colonies of clones. These grow into thick mats of sod interwoven with fallen leaves and dead stems. Rhizomes may radiate out from the mother plant in a starlike pattern on bare ground. Stiff, coarse stems featuring sharply pointed leaves give salt grass (*Distichlis spicata*) a spiky appearance. Tightly overlapping leaf sheaths give the stem a scaly look that is echoed in the rhizomes. Salt grass tends to grow in dense, ankle-height stands that can dominate high and middle tidal marsh zones; it is often found with pickleweed. Salt grass contains spongy, air-filled tissues, which allow the plant to grow both underwater and in mud. Glands on the leaves exude salt. The flowers are bright, pinkish-purple, grow on spikelets, and mature into pale-green seed heads. Ducks seldom feed on the seed, but geese graze on the plant itself in the fall. Some fish and crustaceans may nibble on its roots, but primarily rely on the plant for cover.

Pickleweed

Dense stands of succulent pickleweed are found in the middle zones of many bay marshes but can also be found mixed among cordgrass. Perennial pickleweed (*Sarcocornia pacifica*) grows in thick clumps with semi-woody bases 8 inches to 25 inches tall. It can form prostrate turflike vegetation on marsh plains, or waist-high sub-shrubs in well-drained salt

Pickleweed and orange dodder. As its name suggests, pickleweed tastes salty, and humans have long made the most of this special quality. Early colonists pickled the plant, and local Native Americans used the stems to add zing to acorn mush, fish, and other dishes. Today, pickleweed can be found on fancy restaurant menus as "sea beans." (Jude Stalker)

marsh. The translucent stem segments have no leaves and resemble dark-green miniature gherkins. Succulent stems, a lack of leaves, and a waxy coating all reduce moisture loss. Like many plants, pickleweed changes colors with the seasons, appearing grey-brown in winter, green from spring through summer, and a drab reddish-green in fall (see cover inset photo). Perennial pickleweed has a higher tolerance to salinity than any other tidal marsh plant native to the estuary (save possibly its annual cousin), and it is capable of growing in soil salt concentrations many times higher than that of ocean water. Pickleweed tolerates soil hypersalinity by concentrating and storing salt in its tissues—"pickling" itself—and by balancing the saltiness of its cell sap and shedding its older segments.

Pickleweed shelters many estuary species. Secretive Black Rails and Salt Marsh Harvest Mice hide their nests amid its stems. Clapper Rails may build nests in dense, tall, shrubby pickleweed mixed with gumplant, and even Harbor Seals may use springy stands of pickleweed for a mattress. Song Sparrows hunt amid pickleweed's roots for snails.

In some areas, what looks like bright orange tangles of yarn drape over patches of pickleweed. These weird snarls are not silly string but a parasitic plant called dodder (*Cuscuta salina*). Dodder tendrils can grow several inches a day, and over time they may strangle entire plants in their day-glo grip and cover hundreds of acres of pickleweed marsh. Dodder relies on tiny suckers to penetrate the cuticle of marsh plants and feed off the nutritious sap. Dodder infestations can cause mass diebacks of pickleweed, creating vegetation gaps exploited by other plants.

Alkali Bulrush

In the midst of brackish tidal marshes, or in the fresher waters of the delta and intermittent lagoons, alkali bulrush (*Bolboschoenus maritimus*) grows in large stands up to 4.5 feet high. True to its name, it can tolerate alkaline conditions and survive prolonged flooding when dormant in winter. Its bright-green, robust stems have the triangular shape characteristic of all sedges. Large, hard "tubers" at its base and a spray of reddish-brown and hairy seeds, or awns, at the tips of its stems help distinguish these plants from other bulrushes. Geese, muskrats, and beaver consume the carbohydrate-rich tubers as well as the shoots, and use the plants for building material. Waterfowl eat the seeds and use the stems to build and conceal their nests. Alkali bulrush is one of the dominant species in poorly drained parts of brackish marsh plains or ponds, and on tidal channel banks in the North and South bays, and western Suisun Marsh.

Tule

"Tule" is an Aztec word meaning reedlike marsh plants including cattail and bulrush. In the estuary, tule refers to a plant also known as the Califor-

Tule marsh near Suisun Bay. (Jude Stalker)

Non-native Golden Star Tunicates (*Botryllus schlosseri*) come in many bright colors. Despite their primitive appearance, tunicates are most closely related to animals with backbones. Dozens of individuals live in flat colonies surrounded by a clear matrix, and they grow atop surfaces ranging from boat hulls to seaweed. These tunicates quickly colonized a plastic PVC plate hung from a bay dock as part of a 2006–2007 native oyster recruitment study (see p. 279, "Oysters Back in the Bay?"). (Jude Stalker)

nia bulrush (*Schoeneoplectus californicus*). Tule frequently dominates perennial brackish to freshwater marshes, often in the low tidal marsh zone. Among the tallest local marsh plants at 5 feet to 13 feet high, tule grows in large, dense stands. Its stems are dull olive-green and are three-sided like other sedges; however, the angles of tule stems are so obtuse as to make the stems seem nearly round. The inner pith consists of spongy, air-filled cells that allow the stems to float.

Many types of wildlife rely on tule for food and housing. Waterfowl feed on the seeds and nest within the extensive stands. Marsh Wrens attach their nests, made of a loosely woven ball of grass, to its tall stems.

Bottom-dwellers

Many species live in the zone of overlap between fresh and marine ecosystems along the coast. A surprising array of life—creatures with shells, claws, segments, suckers, and feelers—thrives in the ooze beneath many feet of water. The deep beds of mud coating the bay floor are riddled with cities of burrowing, filtering, siphoning, and sliding animals. These inhabitants of the benthos include the shrimps, worms, clams, and other creatures that filter the water or sift the mud for plankton and other microscopic meals. Today, 95 percent of these bottom-dwellers are species native to other estuaries. Only two native species—the Bay Mussel and a Polychaete Worm—are among the most commonly found species in the benthos. For this reason, scientists now consider the bay the most invaded estuary in the country (see p. 199, "Preventing Invasions," and p. 202, "A Few Bad Actors").

Clams

The bay's benthic communities were never as rich as those of East Coast estuaries, but local bivalves were more than plentiful enough to sustain the estuary's Native American residents. Scientists think the closest thing to a native clam from San Francisco Bay may be *Macoma balthica*. Reaching about an inch in diameter, this clam is a versatile feeder, able to dine both on bottom deposits and food suspended in the water. Its unusually long siphon sweeps across the mud like the hose of a vacuum cleaner. These long straws also enable the clam to survive extreme changes in salinity by burrowing deep into the sediments and finding pockets of salty water sequestered among rock, sand, and silt.

One not-so-native clam seems to surpass most of the bay's other benthic residents in sheer chutzpah and toughness: the Overbite Clam (*Corbula amurensis*). Though no bigger than a quarter, this bivalve has it all: speed, strength, and the ability to withstand extremes. It can siphon plankton from the water faster than any ordinary clam, spin anchoring byssal threads strong enough to secure its position in turbulent waters, and handle waters that are fresh one minute and salty the next. Other characteristics bolster its supercritter credentials: unusual stomach enzymes enabling it to digest bacteria; the ability to reproduce when just a few months old; and shells of unequal sizes (hence the overbite), buffered by a tough rubbery lip, that resist the prising of hungry crabs.

"The design of this clam is amazing," says the U.S. Geological Survey's Jan Thompson, an aquatic ecologist and engineer whose life work has been the study of bottom-dwellers and the physical processes that allow them to feed on the water column. "It's ecologically and biologically pretty plastic."

The Overbite Clam is a relative newcomer to San Francisco Bay. It most likely arrived in the mid-1980s by hitchhiking on an Asian container ship. The species occurs naturally in Korea, Japan, and China, but derives its scientific name from China's Amur River. The clam must have felt right at home upon arrival, because the Amur, like San Francisco Bay, is very turbid. Within two years, the clam dominated the bay's bottom community. Biologists like Thompson soon discovered that *Corbula amurensis* populations in Suisun Bay, for example, could filter the entire volume of water in the bay twice in one day. Like most clams, it feeds using two siphons: one to suck in water and mud to filter for food, and one to jettison the filtered water back out again.

The Overbite Clam's pumping rate is phenomenal. To study this, Thompson set up a bed of clams in a lab trough, then added water and phytoplankton and continued recirculating the water to simulate the moving waters of the bay. Then she measured how quickly the clams removed the phytoplankton from the water. In this case, a bed of 500 clams filtered all measurable phytoplankton out of 400 gallons of water within a day. In addition, scientists noted that clams on the leading edge of the bed remained burrowed in the sediment, whereas clams on the downstream end sat upright, leaving about half of their shell exposed to the flowing water. "By doing this the downstream clams are getting less of a shadow effect from what their brothers are eating upstream," says Thompson.

The Overbite Clam is now an established part of San Francisco Bay. At times, depending on estuarine conditions and predators, billions of them form a solid carpet across Suisun Bay. This intruder's sheer numbers have fundamentally changed the aquatic food web, and some even blame it for driving several species of delta fish to the brink of extinction.

The Overbite Clam is one of four clam species from Asia now found in San Francisco Bay and delta waters. One of the others, more commonly referred to as the "Asian Clam," arrived here in the 1930s and quickly colonized a different ecological niche: the fresher environs of the upper estuary and delta. But *Corbicula fluminea* can't match its overbite cousin, whose pumping rate per gram of tissue is considerably higher.

Shrimp

To glide over the bay floor is to observe the eyes and feelers of a thousand shrimp poking upward like blades of grass from the muddy surface. Most shrimp in the bay are tiny bundles no longer than a paper clip, bristling with delicate appendages and saturated in vivid hues. The Coon-striped or Dock Shrimp (*Pandalus danae*), common around Central Bay piers, may have translucent stripes and delicate red and yellow spots. Another, known as the Broken-back Shrimp (*Heptacarpus flexus*), has what appears to be a two-part body, whereas the Opossum Shrimp (*Neomysis mercedis*) is named for the females' habit of carrying eggs and young in a pouch by their last pairs of legs. Bay fishers trawl for the California Bay Shrimp (*Crangon franciscorum*).

Dungeness Crab

The native Dungeness Crab carries a distinctive V on its carapace, or shell, and has smaller claws but more edible flesh than the brilliant Red Rock Crab. Observers can tell a Dungeness (*Cancer magister*) from similar-looking species by examining the pincer-shaped claws. Rock Crabs have black-tipped claws; Dungeness have white ones. The sharp points of their remaining six legs are tipped with a biomaterial harder than acrylic glass. Because the material resists dulling, the animals can scuttle about for many weeks and still have feet sharp enough to cling to slimy surfaces.

Dungeness Crabs are present from the Aleutian Islands to Santa Barbara, but San Francisco Bay is at the southern edge of their range. The life cycle of the Dungeness Crab starts outside the Golden Gate, with hard-shelled males mating with soft-shelled females sometime between March and May each year. The following fall, each mated female produces up to two million eggs, carrying them as a spongelike mass under a belly flap until they hatch in December or January. The offspring first emerge as tiny plankton-eating larvae. They must grow through several life stages before they begin to resemble crabs around April to June. At this point, the young crabs swarm through the Golden Gate in large numbers, likely following chemical cues such as spring freshwater outflows.

Once they enter the Gate, young crabs seek out areas with lower salinities than the ocean, and they concentrate in the shallows. Juvenile Dungeness Crabs favor the shallow, soft, food-filled bottom of San Pablo Bay and nearby tidal marshes. After summering in San Pablo Bay, they follow that bay's deeper channels in their fall migration to the Central Bay and ocean. By that point, most will have grown to about four inches across.

To grow, Dungeness and other crabs must shed or molt their exoskeletons. These empty shells, called "ghosts," often wash up on beaches, where

Dungeness Crab on sale at Fisherman's Wharf, San Francisco. (Ariel Rubissow Okamoto)

they become treasures for beachcombers. Molting happens about 12 times as Dungeness Crabs grow from larvae to teenagers in the bay. Dungeness Crabs in San Francisco Bay molt more frequently than those reared in the near-shore coastal zone, thanks to both higher temperatures in the bay that allow them to grow faster and the availability of more food. They also mature and grow faster in rich bay waters than anywhere else along the Pacific Coast.

Dungeness are carnivores. While they're in the bay, the amount of habitat available determines how many will survive. Kathy Hieb describes it as follows: "If there's not enough food and not enough space, crabs will eat each other. If you're four weeks older than the next crab, you might be two inches across when the younger one is half an inch across—big enough to make a snack of the kid next door." One crab can only eat another if the latter has recently molted and therefore has a soft shell.

Although many of the crabs available in local restaurants and markets traveled into bay waters to mature, any Dungeness Crab caught in the bay must be thrown back. The law is among many designed to prevent the species from becoming overfished. So the animals waving their claws at seafood shoppers were actually trapped outside the Golden Gate.

Fish

San Francisco Bay is home to at least 120 species of fish, the majority of which are natives. Some live there year-round, whereas some linger only when young, using the bay as a nursery. Others use the estuary as a migration corridor to and from spawning and rearing grounds.

Most abundant among the bay's fish are the shimmering schools of anchovies, herring, and other small silver fish. Some may be fully grown, and others may be the young of larger fish. In certain seasons, the bay is full of fish not much longer than a human pinky finger.

The flatfish living on the bay bottom look as though they belong in a two-dimensional world. No thicker than a flapjack, flatfish see the world from a unique perspective, having eyes on only one side of their body. Among the bay's most common flatfish are California Halibut, English Sole, and Starry Flounder.

The strongest, fastest fish may be salmon—one of several anadromous fish that lead a two-part life, as adults in the ocean and as spawners and juveniles in the estuary's rivers. Salmon, Steelhead Trout, and Green and White Sturgeon are the primary native anadromous fish in the estuary system, but Striped Bass—a non-native—may be the most familiar as a favorite with anglers.

Chinook Salmon found in Battle Creek. (California Department of Fish and Game)

The bay fish with the most teeth and the fewest bones—with cartilage instead of a bony skeleton—are sharks. The presence of sharks in the bay at any given time is contingent on local water conditions. If the water gets too warm or fresh, sharks will depart for the ocean; if conditions remain cool, marine sharks will take up residence. Leopard Sharks and Bat Rays tolerate the lower-oxygen, warmer waters of the South Bay better than other marine species, and often hang out there. Sevengill, Leopard, and Dogfish Sharks all mate and birth their pups in estuary waters.

Though neither as big nor as glamorous as sharks or salmon, the most tenacious fish in the region may be the natives that live in bay creeks and small rivers. A surprising diversity of endemic freshwater fish survives in the streams that connect upland regions with the bay.

Pacific Herring

Pacific Herring (*Clupea pallasii*) have been known to enter the estuary by the millions. Imagine the main shipping channel between the Bay Bridge and the San Rafael Bridge as a 12-mile-long, 80-foot-thick river of silver. On a fish scanner, the biggest schools form what biologist Ken Oda dubs "giant sausage links" that stretch from one end of the bay to the other. Oda should know—he's studied herring runs around the bay for 20 years at the California Department of Fish and Game. On the surface, however, the only hints of the herring's arrival may be hovering gulls and bobbing sea lions, which come to gorge themselves on spawning fish.

Pacific Herring. Locals have been catching and eating Pacific Herring since the first humans settled around the bay. Native Americans stretched their herring nets between two tule balsas, and weighted the edge with stone sinkers. According to UC Berkeley's Kent Lightfoot, they also collected herring thrown up on the beach by storms.
(Ryan Bartling)

Pacific Herring collect in the bay starting in November and ending in March. The second and third waves of fish are typically the largest. After that, the Golden Gate becomes a revolving door as schools arrive, lay and fertilize their eggs, then return to the ocean. Herring may reprise this trip every year for their 11-year lifespan.

Herring will deposit their eggs on virtually any hard surface. In some months, San Francisco's entire waterfront, from Marina Green to Hunter's Point, may be covered with herring roe as ripe, full-bellied females unload a clutch of 4,000 to 134,000 eggs on any available rock, pier piling, sunken log, shipwreck, riprap block, and waterfront wall. Eelgrass blades and algae mats are also favored substrates. The fish have made a few modern adaptations too, spawning on the plastic mesh sacks used to package rice.

As female after female spawns on the same surfaces, some places acquire coatings of eggs up to nine layers deep. By late in the season, the pilings look like they're wrapped in tan rubber bands, says Oda.

The spawning of Pacific Herring is one of the easier wildlife events to witness. Anyone out on a lighted dock or breakwater in the evening, especially after a storm, might catch a swirl of activity in the waters below. "If you're in the right place at the right time, you can actually see it happening," says Oda's colleague Becky Ota, who managed the bay's commercial herring fishery for the California Department of Fish and Game for 10 years. "You'd see fish madly swimming around the piling—females getting really close to those pilings with their vents and depositing those eggs, and males zipping around and releasing milt. One morning I was headed over the Golden Gate Bridge very early and I knew right away there was a spawning event going on because the water at Fort Baker was just white with milt."

Once they've deposited their eggs, adult herring return almost immediately to the ocean. The egg masses left behind in the bay, meanwhile, attract gulls, Surf Scoters, and sturgeon. Within the 10 days or so it takes each batch of herring eggs to hatch, up to 95 percent are eaten. Eggs that aren't fodder for animals higher up the food chain develop from larvae to swimming fish within three months. By fall, these herring have left the bay, not to return until they are mature and ready to spawn at two to three years old.

In recent decades, juvenile herring in San Francisco Bay have suffered from loss of food, predation, and changing conditions. State fish managers estimated that the spawning biomass for the 2009–2010 season was 38,409 tons—down from an historical average of more than 49,000 tons but up from the 2008–2009 low of 4,833 tons. Though herring support one of the bay's handful of remaining commercial fisheries, the fishery's future remains uncertain (see p. 173, "Last of the Fishing").

Northern Anchovy

The Northern Anchovy (*Engraulis mordax*), the most abundant fish in the bay, is a small silver fish about the size of a french fry. As the foundation of a second commercial bay fishery, anchovies are used mostly as live bait for party boat fishing vessels and private anglers.

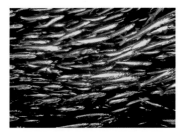

Northern Anchovies are easily distinguished from other small silver fish by their severe overbite—a characteristic scientists call "stupid mouth." (Aquarium of the Bay)

The life cycles of Northern Anchovy and herring are reversed. Whereas herring live offshore and come into the bay to spawn, most anchovies spawn offshore and move into the bay to grow up. Though this species can be found inside the bay for much of the year, their numbers peak from April to October. Scientists think that coastal upwelling and the subsequent plankton blooms trigger their spring arrival, and cooling bay waters spur their fall departure. Northern Anchovy can live for up to four years.

Longfin Smelt

At first glance, the Longfin Smelt is just one more of the half-dozen small silver fish species found in the bay. But the Longfin Smelt (*Spirinchus thaleichthys*) makes more complete use of the bay than any other small native fish. Its ability to tolerate a particularly wide range of salinities allows the Longfin Smelt to linger in the estuary's changeable water conditions. Within a month of hatching, their tiny larvae (roughly 0.4 inches in size), can tolerate some salt in the water. By the time they've doubled their length—to the size of a dime—they can handle full-strength sea water. Whatever their size, longfin do require a little time to acclimate as they move between fresh and salty conditions.

"Longfin Smelt have a broad-based strategy for life and multiple life history patterns," says Randy Baxter. "They spread their options out over a fairly extensive environmental gradient looking for conditions conducive to feeding and survival. If spawning conditions are good, they can reproduce as early as their first birthday. If not, they wait until the second or third. They take advantage of seasonal flows, positioning themselves up and down the estuary to exploit open niches. They also position themselves up and down the water column seeking the most advantageous conditions."

Like salmon, adult Longfin Smelt move upriver to spawn, but most only venture a short distance above the limit of saltwater intrusion. As larvae, they seek out brackish water. Outflows from rivers and tides disperse the hatchling fish downstream, increasing the likelihood they will find food. As Longfin Smelt age, they move farther downstream, eventually reaching the Central Bay or the ocean before the end of their first year.

In the San Francisco Bay estuary, Longfin Smelt have a short life span that averages around two years. That means small changes in conditions—shifts in freshwater flows, ocean currents, temperature, or food supplies, for example—can have a dramatic effect on their abundance. If one year-class doesn't make it, there isn't much wiggle room for recovery in the years before or after. Though their adaptable estuarine nature has made them survivors, Longfin Smelt are currently threatened by human changes to their habitat.

California Halibut

Many flatfish live in the bay, including California Halibut (*Paralichthys californicus*). But contrary to their name, halibut do not always stay flat. They may raise their heads off the bottom to snap up a goby or even swim into the water column to chase anchovies. Or they may get vertical to do one other important thing—reproduce. Halibut males and females release gametes in open water in close proximity to one another. "It's a surprising sight: adults swimming up off bottom into the water column and spawning like undulating stack of pancakes," says Randy Baxter. "Halibut are pretty big. Imagine a 40-pound fish about three feet long. So to see them swimming almost attached, and in tandem, head to head, tail to tail, undulating almost as one, is unexpected to say the least."

The undulations produce fertilized eggs, which drift, grow into larvae, and then undergo the transformation that leaves them peering at the world from only one side of their bodies. At this point juvenile halibut have the ability to swim under their own power. Like Dungeness Crabs, they hatch in the ocean and catch a ride on bottom currents into the bay to fatten and grow.

Larval flatfish drift at the whim of the currents for the first weeks—or sometimes months—of life. The longer the time spent adrift, the farther they are likely to travel from where their parents placed them as eggs. In one year, currents and El Niño conditions are known to have carried California Tongue Fish larvae all the way to Washington before they could settle near shore.

If and when larval flatfish do manage to find their way to the Golden Gate, research has shown that larger pulses of young flatfish enter the bay on flood tides during a new moon at night—a smart move. As Kathy Hieb says, "You don't want to be seen and eaten right away."

Once in the bay, halibut often head into the South Bay, looking for the warmest water they can find. But like most other flatfish species, as they grow halibut move into deeper, saltier main channels and Central Bay zones. Once they've reached one to four years old—it varies by species— flatfish start moving back out to the ocean. Whereas sole, Sand Dabs, and flounder rarely return to the bay, halibut may travel back and forth between the coast and bay following prey.

As adults, California Halibut will weigh about 40 pounds, only a third the size of their Pacific Halibut cousins. These ocean halibut are the ones that regularly end up in a steaklike filet covered in beer batter or a balsamic reduction.

California Halibut in San Francisco Bay do better in warm-water regimes. According to Baxter, you can look back over the decades and see how local halibut have fared just by studying ocean conditions. Halibut numbers dropped in the 1960s and early 1970s, when coastal waters were relatively cold. But warming periods in the early 1980s supported a decent local halibut fishery later in the decade. Warm-water periods ratcheted up the population another notch in following years, and a subsequent warm-water period in the mid-2000s helped maintain this higher population level.

Salmon

One of the signature species of the bay's watershed is the muscular, silvery pink, yard-long Chinook Salmon. Chinook (*Oncorhyncus tshawytscha*) migrate from the ocean, through the bay, and to the upper reaches of the Sacramento and San Joaquin rivers and their tributaries to spawn. Most of their historic spawning grounds are now blocked by dams. But salmon still work their way through the watershed to get as close as they can to the stream of their birth, and many now spawn in the main stem rivers below dams.

Once salmon arrive at a suitable spawning ground, they sweep their powerful tails across the bottom to dig a redd (rocky nest), deposit and fertilize their eggs, cover them up, guard them for a few weeks, and then die. For those who make it far up into tributary streams, the journey is arduous. They must swim against downstream flows, battle up natural rapids, climb fish ladders, and endure unhealthy warm-water reaches.

Adult Chinook travel inland through the bay to spawn in four different seasons. Scientists thus refer to them by the season of their spawning run—winter, spring, fall, or late fall—as they pass through the Golden Gate.

To reach distant spawning grounds, salmon likely rely on a medley of environmental cues. Biologists think day length, the sun's position, the earth's magnetic field, and water salinity and temperature gradients are among the signs salmon read to find their way from the open ocean to the coast. From there, these remarkable fish literally follow their noses, navigating upstream toward the distinctive scent of their natal waters. Salmon undertake their spawning journey at three to six years of age.

Scientists are tracking where juvenile salmon go and what they do in the upper reaches of the estuary. They saddle 3- to 5-inch-long juvenile salmon with one-gram radio transmitters and release them above river and canal junctions or pumping intakes. "The most dramatic result of our telemetry on smolts is the sheer magnitude of distances they move each day, twice a day, up and downstream with the tides," said Dave Vogel, a consulting scientist, in a 2004 publication. Vogel observed french fry–sized smolts traveling more than 9 miles with the tides in a single day. At delta channel junctions where flows split, the smolt didn't always go with the biggest flow or the straightest migration route. "What determines whether a fish turns left or right are site-specific conditions—velocity changes in the water over minutes and seconds related to tides and channel geometry and time of day."

Scientists outfitted this fingerling salmon with a transmitter in order to track its movements and habitat preferences within the estuary. (Dave Vogel)

Vogel's work has often been coordinated with research on flows from Jon Burau of the U.S. Geological Survey, so data on where the salmon went could be correlated with data on where the water was headed. In a more recent study, Burau and Columbia Basin biologists tagged and released 6,000 juvenile salmon smolts throughout the delta, each with its own identifying acoustic ping. Receivers placed at 70 delta channel junctions tracked the pings through the winter of 2008–2009. After running the data through a new statistical model, Burau thinks they will find out not only how many fish choose to take which routes but also how many survive that choice. "We'll know route selection and survival probability for each slough and channel within a few percentage points, which will help us make better restoration and water management choices for the fish," says Burau. (For more details on salmon, see p. 173, "Last of the Fishing"; p. 184, in "Mini Guide: Species in Peril"; p. 219, "Water Rights for the Ecosystem"; p. 223, "Production or Conservation Hatcheries?"; and p. 228, "Migrations: Two Salmon Travel Butte Creek.")

Sturgeon

Sturgeon resemble their dinosaur-age ancestors more closely than any other fish. Their most distinctive features include a long shovel nose, a skeleton consisting largely of cartilage, and five rows of armored plates called scutes that emerge from the skin on their backs. Drooping below a sturgeon's mouth are four fleshy feelers, or *barbels*. Each is covered with taste bud–like structures the fish uses to sense the presence of nearby food. Sturgeon are so large and powerful that they can easily inflict broken bones and bad cuts on fishermen and biologists who haul them on deck.

Sturgeon have been living in the Sacramento River system and traveling into the bay for between two million and five million years. Two spe-

Biologist Rob Fairey examines a White Sturgeon. Sturgeon have a storied life in the annals of California literature. In the crime novel *Dead Game*, author Kirk Russell describes poachers keeping an 8-foot-long, 50-year-old sturgeon tethered alive to a dock in a delta slough until she could be winched out of the water and sliced open for her ovaries. The roe must come from a freshly killed fish and be iced immediately to make the caviar grade. These ancient and magical fish can be seen at Pier 39's Aquarium by the Bay. (William Jakl)

cies of sturgeon—White (*Acipenser transmontanus*) and Green (*Acipenser medirostris*)—can be found in estuary waters.

White Sturgeon are both the largest and longest-lived freshwater fish in North America. They attain lengths of over 20 feet, grow up to 1,400 pounds—close to the mass of a small whale—and live up to 100 years. In California, however, the record is about 10 feet long and 495 pounds. They have a much stubbier snout than Green Sturgeon have. Green Sturgeon have slightly shorter life spans, and they are a third the size of White Sturgeon. Able to reach nine feet long and 385 pounds, they still outlive and outsize salmon.

Both species of sturgeon enter the bay and travel up the Sacramento River to spawn. Whites are found as far north as Colusa and Greens up to Red Bluff. Unlike salmon, they don't build nests and lay eggs in clear mountain streams where everyone can see them, so their spawning habits remain a mystery. Scientists do know that sturgeon frequent two kinds of habitat in bay watersheds: they favor 15-foot-deep holding pools, and they release their eggs and milt in turbulent waters near beds of cobbles and boulders. Their fertilized eggs settle on hard rock or in the crevices beneath rocks, where fast-moving water keeps them aerated and prevents smothering by silt. A single White Sturgeon female can carry up to five million eggs, and their mass can occupy up to a quarter of her body when she's fully ripe.

As befits their stately lives, adult Green Sturgeon don't start spawning until they're 11–18 years old—later than any other freshwater fish in North America. Once they enter the bay, these massive fish spend six to nine months breeding upriver before returning to the ocean. Juveniles live the first one to three years of their lives in the river and bay and then head out to the ocean, not to return for a decade or more. They may grow from an egg about the size of pearl barley to a fish a foot long in a single year.

Genetic and tagging studies show that the southern population of Green Sturgeon, which spawns in the Sacramento River, matures far from natal waters. After attaining a seaworthy size in estuary rivers and marshes, juveniles swim out the Golden Gate to wander as far north as the estuaries of Washington and Oregon. "One of the cool things about Green Sturgeon is that they go on these really long marine migrations," says sturgeon expert Josh Israel, now with the Bureau of Land Management. Israel's work on the species was instrumental in establishing that the Sacramento population is genetically distinct from all others along the Pacific Coast. "While young salmon will go out to the ocean for two to three years, Green Sturgeon will hang out in the ocean for 10, 15, 20 years. Then, over the course of their lives, they'll make multiple migrations in and out of estuaries, particularly in summer."

Israel chose to study Green Sturgeon because so little is known about these ancient survivors. "They've been around a long time, but they've managed to evolve to survive a lot of the variability because they produce a lot of eggs, can spawn multiple times, and are long-lived. So they can out-survive short-term variations that might be deleterious to other fish species," he says.

White Sturgeon don't stray as far as Green Sturgeon do. A good number will stay in and around the bay as long as there is something to eat. Adult sturgeon feed on the bottom, snuffling along in the sediments for invertebrates. Some have been found with large quantities of the invasive Overbite Clam in their bellies, not to mention lots of fish eggs. That sturgeon are major egg predators is ironic, because humans prey on sturgeon to obtain caviar. In California, strict fishing regulations have never completely deterred poachers. But UC Davis researchers have recently figured out how to raise sturgeon in captivity to produce sustainable and legal California caviar.

Striped Bass

"Stripers," as anglers call them, are not native to the bay's watershed. But soon after they were imported from New Jersey in 1879, these anadromous fish were spawning in the Sacramento River and the western delta, producing hundreds of thousands of eggs and young, and sustaining a regional commercial catch of over one million pounds of fish per year. *Morone saxatilis* is an unusually prolific fish: a nine-pound female can produce 900,000 eggs in one year; a 50-pounder, close to five million.

Not even the environmental degradation of the Gold Rush fazed the Striped Bass: their semibuoyant eggs, long lives, and wide-ranging nature helped them weather ups and downs in turbidity, salinity, and food supply. In their new environment, Striped Bass soon became top predators, chasing prey that had no evolutionary experience evading them, say scientists. The bass did well in wet years and not so well in dry, like native species. "An estuary that is good for Striped Bass by and large will also be good for remaining native species that require a fully functioning estuary," says UC Davis fish biologist Peter Moyle.

As adults, these silver fish with dark stripes can live more than 20 years and reach 50 to 100 pounds. No wonder these meaty prizes—whose high

Fishers both proud and nauseated by a Striped Bass catch. (Francis Parchaso)

metabolic rate enables them to put up a sustained fight—are favorites with sport fishermen. By the 1970s, Striped Bass had become such an integral part of the local sport fishing economy that the state developed an index of Striped Bass health to regulate water diversions. This well-adjusted transplant remained an indicator of estuarine health until the focus shifted to endangered fish.

Leopard Shark

The Leopard Shark (*Triakis semifasciata*) is easy to distinguish by its yellow eyes and the pattern of black spots and bars on its off-white skin. It is the most abundant shark in San Francisco Bay. It can grow five feet long over a life span of more than 20 years.

Researchers have found that Leopard Sharks in a given group never varied in size by more than 12 inches. No one knows why. (Aquarium of the Bay)

The Leopard Shark spends much of its time on the bay floor shoving its snout into the mud in search of bottom-dwellers such as shrimp, innkeeper worms, clams, fish eggs, and Plainfin Midshipman. It employs an ingenious method to nab shellfish: it will grasp the neck of a clam in its teeth and lever its long body against the bottom to yank the mollusk free from the mud. Another favorite food is the anchovy. Instead of chasing these tiny fish hither and yon, Leopard Sharks have been observed in San Francisco Bay swimming counterclockwise against a tight ball of anchovies schooling clockwise, so the little fish swim straight into their mouths.

In June and July, Leopard Sharks mate close to tidal marshes and then birth up to 36 pups later in the summer, often amid the shelter of eelgrass. For pups, it's a perilous existence—they are favored food for larger sharks, and they are also victims of poaching for aquariums. The Leopard Sharks that survive eventually move out from the sloughs and into open bay waters, where hungry Sevengills and sea lions await.

The Leopard Shark tends to correlate its movements with the tides,

The broad-nosed Sevengill Cowshark (*Notorynchus cepedianus*) is named for its great size and slow movements. The bay's top predator can grow up to 10 feet long and 250 pounds in weight. (Aquarium of the Bay)

swimming shoreward over the mudflats during inundation and retreating to deeper waters as the tide ebbs. In open waters, they swim about in groups made up of other Leopard and sometimes Smooth-hound Sharks.

Creek Fish

Local streams flowing into the bay are storehouses of aquatic diversity, no matter how urban their setting or how altered their condition. Fish biologist Robert Leidy of the U.S. Environmental Protection Agency has conducted several surveys in Bay Area streams over the past 25 years, and he finds that even dramatically altered urban streams still contain robust, diverse native fish assemblages. According to his latest survey, published in 2007, at least 24 of the 33 native fish species historically found within estuary streams still have reproducing populations. These range from Three-spine Stickleback to Sacramento Suckers and the California Roach. One reason for the persistence of native fish is that they may be better adapted to wide seasonal and annual variations in water temperature and flow than introduced exotics. Species such as Topsmelt and Pacific Staghorn Sculpin are accustomed to wide swings in salinity at the mouths of streams and in the delta.

"From the sky it can look like it's all concrete. But it's amazing how much native life there is in these little corridors weaving through neighborhoods and up into the hills. Creeks are surviving islands of biodiversity in our urbanized landscapes," says San Francisco Estuary Institute ecologist Robin Grossinger.

THE CREEK CONNECTION

Creeks connect the food webs of the uplands to the bay. Their waters carry nutrients—decaying vegetation, organisms, insects, and larvae—to the edges of the bay, where the mixing zone of salt water and fresh water provides a rich habitat. Creeks also connect regional ecosystems to those of the Pacific as a whole. Steelhead and salmon are the most obvious link, spawning and rearing in creek riffles, feeding in the brackish shallows of marshes, and maturing in the open ocean. But other species roam back and forth between the estuary and the wider world as well. For example, Yellow Warblers (*Dendroica petechia*) migrating between nesting grounds in North America and overwintering areas in Mexico often take a break from their grueling flight at San Jose's Coyote Creek. The creek is an oasis of available food within the urban sprawl of the South Bay. The majority of migrating warblers gain weight at this rest stop by feeding on insects that thrive in the creek's wet greenery. The creek and its food stores are even more critical to Pacific Flycatchers, which have exhausted their fat stores and are running on empty by the time they arrive.

FIELDWORK: NETTING UNDERWATER LIFE

The net comes up wriggling from a five-minute drag along the bay bottom. Flashes of white flap against the dark nylon mesh. While one crew member undoes the cinch rope, another places a plastic tray beneath the dancing sac to catch its contents. Out flop two halibut, three Bat Rays, a shark, and a pile of muck.

Scientists and crew aboard the state's *Longfin* research vessel count and sort juvenile crabs. (Kathy Hieb)

We are on the deck of the *Longfin*, a 42-foot research vessel the California Department of Fish and Game uses to sample what lives in the bay. The crew—scientists and technicians led by Kathy Hieb—quickly culls out the big creatures so they can be measured and thrown back before suffocating on thin air. After washing the mud through a sieve, they pour the remaining contents of this "otter" trawl, which had been dragged along the bottom, into another tray for further sorting.

A bell rings in the cabin and the crew winches in a second net. The captain shouts "mid." This net samples the open midwater zone where the bay's schooling fish reside. Minutes later, the crew heaves in their second catch; drops instruments into the water to measure temperature, salinity, and turbidity; and records our location on the GPS unit.

As the *Longfin* sets off at high speed for the next sampling site, the crew unloads the midwater trawl. "Chovs," announces one girl, as several hundred bait fish bright as polished chrome fill the tray. Their number likely includes Northern Anchovy, herring, and half a dozen kinds of smelt. But all of these slim silver fish look pretty much the same to my untrained eye—a bit like the sardines from the super-market canned goods aisle.

The crew knows better. Dumping these three- to six-inch-long fish on a white sorting table, they tell me that herring have a fatter gut and bluer back than "chovs," which have a "stupid mouth," or overbite. Telling one smelt from another is trickier—you have to count the number of scales between two of the fins on its back. In this case, the trawl's silver fish bonanza resolves into 1,400 anchovies, 27 Jacksmelt, 6 Pacific Pompano, and 2 Pacific Herring. At completion, the tray is awash in clear slime dotted with rubbed-off scales. The slime protects fish skin from bacterial and fungal infections but rubs off easily when fish are handled.

Next, the muck from the otter trawl goes on the table. Dragging our bare fingers through the heavy clump of mud and algae, we pull out the largest things first: a baby Dungeness Crab with a distinctive V on its back; a number of Pear Crabs with long, spidery legs; a pregnant goby fish; and a Plainfin Midshipman fish. Upside down in a bucket of water, the Midshipman shows off a row of luminescent photophores, which resemble the gleaming brass buttons of its sailor's uniform namesake.

Next we push shrimp of all sizes into a corner pile, ignore a bunch of yellow-and-grey many-legged isopods (the aquatic version of roly-polys), and tease out several dozen translucent rubbery blobs about the size of a quarter that the crew dubs "Philine" (pronounced like the name of the movie director Fellini) after their

Measuring a ray. Bat Rays are most closely related to sharks, skates, and other fish with cartilaginous skeletons. They feed by flapping their winglike fins while hovering just above the bottom. This creates a vacuum that removes sand from the surface, exposing bivalves, worms, shrimps, and crabs. Their short, flat teeth, which are replaced throughout the Bat Ray's life, grind easily through shells. (Kathy Hieb)

scientific names. These are snails with a rosy internal shell that cruise the sediment on a muscular foot.

As the *Longfin* crew repeats the otter and mid-water trawls at eight stations during the course of that August day, I see other forms of bay life. A midsized fish called a White Croaker shines with a white-gold purity in the sunlight, belying the poisonous mercury that tends to build up in its tissues (see the California Department of Health Services illustration on p. 177). Most difficult for the crew to handle are the Bat Rays, whose tails include barbed spines that can make a good nick in a forearm. The crew breaks off spines entangled in the net to avoid unintended jabs. A smaller version of the ray, a skate, looks up at me with half dollar–sized dark circles that I soon notice aren't its actual eyes, just a diversion for would-be predators.

Onboard the *Longfin*, followed by cawing gulls and inquisitive cormorants, the bay seems implacably grey. I am thankful that the crew has brought so much of what lies obscured under the surface up to the deck for me to see. It is from these trawls that we know what lives in the bay, and how species change from season to season, and year to year. Whatever they draw from the bay, the crew knows it's more likely to be slippery and slimy than monstrous. As Kathy Hieb remarks, "most of the things that come up in the net don't bite us." ARO

Mammals

Amid the finny, feathered, and many-footed residents of the bay are more than a few mammals. As the most sensitive to human disturbance, these species have gone into a sharp decline since the years when Sea Otters, River Otters, Steller's Sea Lions, and beaver were seen in abundance around the bay. Those that remain are versatile survivors, their populations having held through recent decades of industrial exploitation. As environmental conditions improve, mammals such as beaver and mink appear to be returning to estuary watersheds.

California Sea Lion

The California Sea Lion (*Zalophus californianus*) is familiar to most people as the trained seal of circus and marine park shows. A sable brown coat, streamlined body, large front flippers, and visible ear flaps distinguish the California Sea Lion from other bay pinnipeds such as the Harbor Seal. Though two other species of sea lions frequent the Central Bay, the wet, dark heads visible along San Francisco's waterfront are most often California Sea Lions.

Sea lions can be easily seen at San Francisco's Pier 39. In the waters of Aquatic Park nearby, sea lions have been known to butt or harass bay swimmers. Because these marine mammals use subtle currents in the often murky water to find fish, they may be drawn to the wake left behind by paddling hands and feet.
(Anna Davison)

California Sea Lions can grow to an intimidating size, with males—distinguishable by the sagittal crest or bump on their heads—reaching 800 pounds and just shy of 10 feet long. Females are considerably smaller at 250 pounds and less than eight feet long.

The bay's sea lion population is small (1,000–2,000) relative to the state's population of 200,000. Sea lions stay in the bay through fall and winter, then move to southern California and Mexico to breed. Their presence in San Francisco Bay coincides with herring spawning season. The masses of fish make easy pickings for sea lions, pelicans, gulls, and other predators. Around the estuary, sea lions are generalists that will eat anchovies, rockfish, salmon, and even Smooth-hound Sharks. Sea lions have been known to toy with their smooth-hound prey, tossing them out of the water several times before ingesting the victims whole and headfirst.

Most visitors to San Francisco's Pier 39 have visited the docks crammed with California Sea Lions. No one knows why these marine mammals abandoned Seal Rock off Ocean Beach in the late 1990s, though some suspect it was due to the dwindling numbers of salmon traveling through the Golden Gate. These opportunistic predators certainly may have been drawn to the pier's newly constructed docks by the waste fish and crabs discarded off Fisherman's Wharf.

Harbor Seal

The Harbor Seal (*Phoca vitulina richardsi*) has shiny, nickel-grey fur with an all-over peppering of darker spots. At roughly 300 pounds and six feet long, males are the size of a big man, females slightly smaller. This plump, relatively stubby seal finds the bay so comfortable that it lives here year-round. Scientists say about 600 Harbor Seals can be counted among the permanent residents of the estuary.

Harbor Seals dive and forage throughout the open waters of the bay, especially around islands and isolated rocks where they haul out. Harbor Seals must get out of the water almost daily to digest their food and rest. Being relatively small, they are not as well insulated as other marine mammals and must spend a fair amount of time basking in the sun to maintain their body temperature.

For safety, Harbor Seals seek areas that offer long-distance views in every direction and allow them to slip quickly into deep waters at the first sign of danger. That's an uncommon combination in the noisy, developed modern bay, but these seals use at least 20 shoreline spots on a regular basis to rest in the estuary.

The bay's seal population has remained stable for decades. "They're unusually urbanized seals," says National Park Service biologist Sarah Allen, author of *Field Guide to Marine Mammals of the Pacific Coast*. "They're more tolerant of people than colonies along the coast. The seals on Castro Rocks, for example, have the Richmond Bridge, with all sorts of vehicle noise, over their heads and big oil tankers constantly going by. They've learned these kinds of disturbances aren't really going to hurt them. If the same tanker went by the seals on the Farallon Islands or Devil's Point, it would flush the whole herd into the water."

Harbor Seals may not be as imposing as sharks, but they certainly rank among the bay's top predators. They rely on their sensitive and luxuriant whiskers to find fish. By spreading their whiskers out they can detect minute disturbances in the water: a fish swimming by or flapping its tail changes the currents around it, creating what scientists call a hydrodynamic trail (or "hydro-trail"). Even blindfolded, seals easily trail fish around.

Harbor Seals can dive to depths of nearly 350 feet and can reach speeds of up to 12 miles per hour while pursuing fish. (Max Eissler)

Whether after large or small prey, these seals' talent for following hydro-trails is particularly useful in local waters, where visibility often drops to a few feet or less. Studies of their gut contents suggest these seals eat goby, sculpin, and croaker in the extreme South Bay but focus on the Plainfin Midshipmen of the Central Bay. This single fish makes up over 90 percent of local Harbor Seals' diets. Perhaps the unique luminescence of these fish gives them away in the murky water.

Like their human neighbors, bay seals thrive on the variety of the local cuisine. Allen once saw seals eating a halibut that was about the size of a pizza. They were out of the water on Castro Rocks, holding the halibut in their flippers and rotating the fish, "eating it around the edges like a chocolate chip cookie," she says.

Birds

Of the many types of bay life, perhaps the most visible to humans are waterbirds. These aquatic avians include the ducks, sandpipers, gulls, egrets, and other birds that can be seen year-round seeking food, rest, and shelter on bay waters and shores.

Waterbirds fall into different categories based on their habitat usage. Shorebirds include the skittish, flighty birds that sprint across the sand and probe at water's edge for insects and crustaceans. Seabirds such as pigeon guillemots, gulls, and cormorants frequent the open bay or ocean, diving for their fishy dinners and often nesting on rocky offshore islands. Another common category of waterbirds, waterfowl, encompasses ducks, geese, and other aquatic game birds. Some waterfowl live on the open ocean, but more of them frequent estuaries such as San Francisco Bay, as well as brackish and freshwater lakes.

Waterbirds flock to the California coast for much the same reason people do: the mild winters. Species winging in from the arctic arrive by the millions every year to rest in the shallows and wetlands of San Francisco Bay. The bay provides critical refueling and foraging habitat for vast numbers of shorebirds that breed on arctic lakes, as well as for waterfowl that have raised their young on North American prairies and in northern woods. As soon as the air cools around their nesting sites, these travelers take flight for the long journey to estuaries and wetlands of the temperate coast. As the biggest estuary along the Pacific and the one with the widest variety of habitats, San Francisco Bay is the destination of many. During peak migration periods, up to a million shorebirds may pass through the bay in a single day.

"San Francisco Bay is not discrete," says Jules Evens, an avian ecologist with an abiding interest in wetland birds, and the author of *California Bird Life*. "It's part of a network that's built into the life history of these critters. Their wintering grounds are just as important as their breeding grounds. These birds tie the continent together."

Waterbirds begin arriving in the bay in August. More than 50 percent of the diving ducks traveling the Pacific Flyway winter here, as well as one of the largest populations of Canvasbacks in North America. Biologists and volunteers counting birds from shorelines, boats, and airplanes have tallied up more than 700,000 waterfowl in the bay and delta in recent winter surveys. And more than a million shorebirds—the sandpipers, plovers, phalaropes, and dowitchers that wade in the water and probe the mud for food—are estimated to take up winter quarters in the bay each year. Most won't leave the estuary until April.

The 30 species of waterfowl commonly found in the bay can be divided into several distinct groups. Swans and geese feed on plants by grubbing in the sediments of wetlands and fields. Dabbling ducks feed by filtering small invertebrates and plants from surface waters or by tipping tail-end-up to yank plants from the shallows. Today the most abundant dabblers in estuary waters are Mallards and Cinnamon Teal, but historically Northern Pintail dominated the scene.

Another group is the diving ducks. These species use legs set far back on their bodies to propel themselves underwater after fish or to pick mollusks and other food off the bottom. These ducks may dive to depths of 40 feet. The abundance of fish and relative scarcity of plants in the bay's open waters mean that diving ducks here outnumber dabblers two to one.

Many other types of birds use the bay's shores and creeks as critical rest and refueling sites. Still other species breed to the south, rather than the north, and live in the bay the rest of the year. These include the prehistoric-looking Brown Pelicans that fly in bomber formation around the bridges and shores. Many seagulls and cormorants—marine birds—also frequent the bay.

Bufflehead

The most diminutive of the bay's native ducks is the Bufflehead (*Bucephala albeola*), also nicknamed the "butterball" or the "bumblebee dipper." The male, or drake, of this black-and-white duck has a disproportionately large domed head that inspired the species' original name: the buffalo head.

Buffleheads make a strenuous autumn flight from the midwest or from northern boreal forests to the California coast. Upon arrival, these diving ducks must first rest and recover, and then they must eat enough clams, shrimp, snails, and seeds to build up fat reserves for the return flight. Over the next several months, some will indulge enough to amass a quarter of

In the water, Bufflehead Ducks raft together in groups to rest. In flight, Buffleheads can be recognized by their small size, black-and-white feathers, and rapid wing beats. (Norris R. Dyer)

their body weight in fat. Toward the end of this overwintering period, Buffleheads begin to select mates, often staying with the same individual for several years. To keep pair bonds strong, Buffleheads engage in year-round courting behaviors involving flyovers and head shakes, wing lifts, and head bobs, as well as a variety of squeaks, chatters, growls, and guttural rolls.

In San Francisco Bay, Buffleheads frequent marshes and salt ponds, and they forage in waters less than ten feet deep during dives averaging over 12 seconds in length. On the ground they look awkward, with feet set seemingly too far back on their bodies. But in the air they fly faster than most other waterfowl.

Great Blue Heron

The Great Blue Heron (*Ardea herodias*) is an elegant and powerful bird. Like sharks and seals, Great Blue Herons are among the region's top predators. They have plenty of tools to accomplish their hunting tasks—tall, slender legs for wading and long, sharp beaks for snapping up all manner of prey. Anyone driving around the bay has seen the Great Egrets—smaller, white-plumed relations of the Great Blue Heron—fishing on wet highway verges. The heron is equally common around the bay, just less visible against the brown-and-green backdrop of marshes, ponds, and streams.

Great Blue Herons stand up to five feet tall. At least half of that height consists of leg. In flight, their six-foot wingspan seems to flap in slow motion. But standing in the shallow tidal waters of the bay is where this bird is in its element. Herons remain absolutely still to stalk prey—unlike egrets, which tend to mince slowly along. A couple of uniquely flexible vertebrae in a heron's long neck enable it to perform a slingshot maneuver as it thrusts its bill out for unsuspecting fish, gophers, snakes, or frogs.

"The whole heron family is phenomenal in their ability to find good places to stand," says Audubon Canyon Ranch's John Kelly, author of an atlas of egret and heron rookeries throughout the Bay Area. "They're really adapted to foraging in places where water levels are receding, or in places

Great Blue Heron. (Richard Bohnet)

where their prey tend to concentrate, or anywhere fish might be swimming by. Once they get there, they're pretty patient. You watch them and they'll stand for long periods of time and nothing will happen, and all of a sudden they'll pull up something really big. I opened up a dead Great Blue Heron once that had a 14-inch Sacramento Sucker occupying most of its insides. They're generalist feeders. Whatever they can cram into their beak, they will."

Kelly says herons are also primarily solitary feeders, and they can be quite territorial about their feeding grounds. He's seen herons chasing each other away on the ground, and even engaging in full-body blows to protect their foraging turf. Kelly estimates that, on average, the San Francisco Bay area supports at least 500 pairs of Great Blue Herons, nesting in at least 62 colony sites.

Though not nearly as tall and slim as great blues, Black-crowned Night Herons are also fearsome fishing birds and predators (see cover inset photo). These black, white, and grey herons live and nest around the bay, especially on Alcatraz Island. They come out to hunt at dusk, dawn, and through the night, preying on fish, insects, crabs, and amphibians. They have even been known to eat other birds. A South Bay birdwatcher once watched a couple of Night Herons make a meal of six Gadwall Ducklings in the South Bay. A copycat Western Gull made 17 similar attempts, with no success.

Peeps

The most diminutive of the bay's shorebirds are the "peeps," small sandpipers that can be difficult to tell apart. The peeps of San Francisco Bay include Dunlin, Western, and Least Sandpipers. In winter, all have mottled brown backs and snow-white bellies. These tiny birds use their relatively long beaks to probe mud and sand for invertebrates. Peeps comprise approximately 75 percent of all shorebirds in the bay during spring migration season.

The bills of peeps and other shorebirds are cylindrical and vary in length and curvature. Shorter beaks are best for picking prey off the surface; long beaks are best for probing deep mud. The longer a bird's bill, the deeper it can forage, with the effect that shorebirds often sort themselves into bands along the tide line by bill length. Peeps stab the moist ground like mad in search of small invertebrates. Sanderlings, in particular, often scuttle in small groups before the waves, and startle into a swooping, synchronized flight that alights moments later a few feet farther along the shore.

At less than 0.7 ounces and the size of a sparrow, the Least Sandpiper (*Calidris minutila*) is the world's smallest shorebird. It frequents smaller wetlands as well as the margins of larger wetlands, and it is typically found in groups of dozens or hundreds rather than the gatherings of thousands preferred by other peeps.

Its relative, the Western Sandpiper (*Calidris mauri*), weighs in at just shy of one ounce. The Western Sandpiper is the most abundant shorebird in California during fall and spring migration seasons, and it is the second most abundant one during winter. Roughly 100,000 Western Sandpipers overwinter in San Francisco Bay out of a total population of four million. In winter months, nearly 60 percent of all of the bay's shorebirds may be found in the mudflats and salt ponds south of the San Mateo Bridge.

Western Sandpipers make the most of a variety of bay habitats, ranging from mudflats and salt pond levees to tidal sloughs, drained ponds, and seasonal wetlands. How and when they use these habitats depends on whether it is low or high tide, and if they are in search of food or refuge. (Max Eissler)

Dunlin (*Calidris alpina*) breed in the subarctic and arctic and migrate down the Pacific Flyway to wintering grounds up and down the coast. At two ounces, it is the largest of the estuary's peeps. A long, drooping bill and spring and summer breeding plumage of rusty-red back feathers set off by a black belly patch distinguish it from other peeps.

Whatever their size, most peeps split their time between the food-rich waters of the estuary, breeding grounds in the subarctic and arctic, and winter in Mexico and Central America. Peeps spend more time resting and recuperating in San Francisco Bay than anyplace else they pass

It is early August, and the male Western Sandpiper is nearly starving. He has flown over 400 hundred miles since his last stop in Coos Bay, Oregon, many hours ago. He began his trip south a week earlier in the Kuskokwim Delta of Alaska, more than 1,800 miles to the north. At this moment he is flying into the southerly breeze alongside thousands of his fellows on the avian highway known as the Pacific Flyway. Below, the glint of the sun off San Francisco Bay is blinding, but his journey is nearly done.

He soars above the roar of Dumbarton Bridge, alighting on a mudflat on its eastern edge amid a handful of other shorebirds. Barely settled, he plunges his beak rapid-fire into the mud to fill his empty belly. He has escaped the clutches of raptors and made safe harbor here to spend another winter.

This male sandpiper is hardly the first of his kind to arrive this year. He has been preceded by other birds whose nests failed, their eggs or chicks snapped up by foxes and jaegers, as well as by the females, who left in late July right after their eggs hatched. His mate was among them, using San Francisco Bay as a brief stopping point on her way to a balmy winter in Panama. After the females departed, he and the other males remained behind for several weeks to finish raising their chicks. The youngsters will follow their parents south several weeks later. Male sandpipers typically spend their winters at higher latitudes, where they will have a head start in their spring quest to secure a good nesting site.

For the next few months, the male's life is dictated by the tides. Day or night, he probes the muck with his sensor-laden beak to sniff out the clams, worms, amphipods, and other morsels hiding below. At other times, he uses the pointy, brush-coated tongue only males have to mop up the nutritious slime known as biofilm that coats the muddy surface. Biologists call this behavior "snot feeding," after the gooey texture of this mixture of single-celled organisms. Calories from biofilm may constitute half of a sandpiper's diet.

At high tide, the male sandpiper retreats from the mudflats to the drier territory of the salt ponds to roost, or drops in on nearby salt ponds for a meal. The surrounding levees can be black with swarms of tasty Brine Flies and fatty fly larvae. When the waters in the ponds are shallow enough, he may also indulge in "twinkling"—hovering above the surface to stab at wriggling balls of Brine-Fly larvae and the occasional Brine Shrimp without getting wet. When the ponds are nothing but mud, he joins thousands of others like him to forage on the oozes.

Though accustomed to long-distance travel, sandpipers are homebodies once they reach their destinations. Over the 10 months the male sandpiper lingers in the bay, he hardly budges from the same four square miles he visited last year and the year before that.

When it's time to roost, he picks his way along the wrack-littered edge of one of his chosen levees, raising a cloud of Brine Flies with each step, until he settles amid other birds in a place where he can easily spot the approach of predators.

But no wild creature can afford to sleep too deeply. As the white face of the moon begins to appear in the pond's shallow waters, other shore residents pad toward the dozing flocks in search of a meal. Coyotes, non-native Red Foxes, and feral cats all take advantage of the cover afforded by brush and salt grass.

This year, the male is lucky. Nearby birds catch a whiff of predators before they can pounce and all the birds take flight, the male sandpiper with them. He survives to see another spring. In February, his appetite grows. He begins to eat more frequently, increasing his featherweight grams by a third or more. His guts shrink, his fat stores swell, and his behavior grows more flighty. By April 21, he departs his winter home for the multiday trip that will bring him to Alaska by early May. The females follow days later to renew the cycle of life amid the tundra and low-lying marshes of Alaska's coastal regions. KMW

Peeps in flight. (Max Eissler)

through in their travels. In spring, more than a million Western Sandpipers will pause to refuel along bayshores on their way north to Alaska; more than 500,000 may be present in a single day by late April.

Double-crested Cormorant

Drive east across the San Mateo–Hayward Bridge, and it's impossible to miss the chunky black bodies and snaky necks of Double-crested Cormorants (*Phalocrocorax auritus*) roosting on the cement footings of the power pylons. The species is named for its summer breeding plumage: twin head tufts of white feathers reminiscent of Alfred Einstein's eyebrows. As the only cormorant in North America associated with fresh, brackish, and sa-

Double-crested Cormorants roost, fish, and congregate in the Central Bay, but a great place to see them up close is Oakland's Lake Merritt. Look for them drying their wings on the buoy lines that separate the wildlife sanctuary from the navigable part of the lake, or swimming and diving together in groups while fishing. (Max Eissler)

line water, it is far more common in the estuary waters than Brandt's Cormorant (*Phalacrocorax penicillatus*), which also fishes in the bay. An orange throat pouch further distinguishes the species from the blue or grey throat of Brandt's.

Agile swimmers, cormorants may hunt in groups of up to 600. They eat small invertebrates and fish such as sardines, smelt, the Plainfin Midshipman, and Yellowfin Goby. They can remain underwater for about 30 seconds, diving from 5 to 60 feet deep.

Unlike many waterbirds, cormorants lack oil glands to waterproof their feathers. To prevent their plumage from getting waterlogged, the birds repair to roosts whenever they are not fishing. On rocks and bridge platforms, they prop themselves up on stubby tail feathers, often perching with wings akimbo to dry their feathers in the sun.

These cormorants are monogamous and breed from April to August. Unlike most other birds, Double-crested Cormorant parents wrap their webbed feet around their three to four eggs during incubation. Young are ready to begin fishing on their own within 10 weeks.

In recent decades, double-crested cormorants have been enjoying a major population rebound after nearly a century of human persecution. First fishermen tried to eradicate them because the birds competed for their catch; then pesticides took their toll. Laws protecting seabirds and banning DDT helped the cormorant population to recover. Then the construction of bridges, power lines, and other structures on bay waters gave the birds new nesting sites. Today, all 12 Double-crested Cormorant colonies in the bay are located on human-built or altered environments. More than 10,000 Double-crested Cormorants may be counted in the estuary during midwinter.

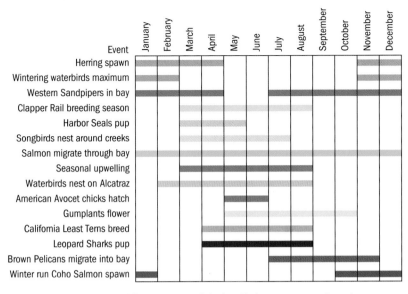

Figure 8. Seasonal wildlife events around the bay. Each season presents a showcase of biological marvels—migrating ducks, spawning salmon, pupping Harbor Seals, blooming gum plant—against the shimmering backdrop of the bay. (Kathleen M. Wong)

Conclusion

The array of plants and animals in today's San Francisco Bay is very different from what lived there before Europeans arrived 300 years ago. The modern mix of estuary inhabitants bears the distinctive stamp of human history. These newer residents range from stowaways on Gold Rush–era ships, to discarded aquarium pets, to species planted here by immigrants who missed familiar species from home. Hundreds of such alien species have taken root within the bay's welcoming waters and established thriving populations. The estuary, like the cities around it, has become a melting pot from around the globe.

The majority of these species have settled seamlessly into existing biological communities. But others are shouldering aside the natives at an alarming rate. These include invasive clams that now carpet Suisun Bay, cordgrasses that sprout with eerie vigor, and a bass that seems more at home here than the estuary's native fishes.

Whether native or introduced, the organisms found here must contend with both the estuary's natural environmental variability and sweeping human manipulations of their environment.

"Though urbanized, the bay still has high biodiversity, mostly because of conservation efforts that have retained some historic habitats and restored others," says John Takekawa, a wildlife biologist with the U.S. Geological Survey. "The wildlife populations have protection, but their presence is not assured. Increased population pressures will continue to affect their habitats. We must reduce disturbance and create undisturbed reserve areas for wildlife. And we must value and teach an ethic of conservation and pride in the natural resources of the estuary."

HISTORY OF HUMAN CHANGES

1800s–1960s

[Up the Sacramento River] steamed our little craft, scaring myriads of ducks and other water fowl by the newness of its form and voice, scaring deer that hid in the tangled woods, and even the grizzly bear, so abundant in the river bends. . . . [At the site of Colusa] . . . the wild oats that surrounded me were much higher [than six feet] . . . [and] beyond was as beautiful a scene as ever met the vision of man. There was one endless sea of white and blue, purple and gold. It seemed a sea, as the gentle breeze made those myriads of wild flowers wave and glisten. . . . I seemed to be reveling in the very Garden of Eden. . . . [At the same site, after the flood of 1867] Colusa and its environs is now an island: above, below, to the right and left is one vast sheet of water. Between the water and the Coast Range the water presents the appearance of an inland sea.

WILL GREEN, COFOUNDER OF THE TOWN OF COLUSA, 1850 AND 1867

Among [the] curious phenomena connected with the last floods, was the fact of considerable breadths of tule floating in the bay, on the surface of which there was generally found a number of land snakes, some of which floated into the Pacific, others landed under the wharves, and for a long time after the floods had in a great measure subsided, numerous snakes were to be found about the wharves of San Francisco. . . . Most singular of all, however, was the fact that bay fisherman frequently caught freshwater fish in the bay for from two to three months, [and] the surface portion of entire waters of the Bay of San Francisco consisted of fresh water, to the depth of eighteen to twenty-four inches. [Also curious was that] the oysters placed on oyster-beds fattened and died; mussels became fresh and flavorless. . . . For nearly a fortnight, the water was brackish at the Farallone [sic] Islands.

THOMAS ROWLANDSON, NOTABILIA ON THE FLOODS OF 1861–62

SQUINTING AT THE BAY in the playful light at dawn, on a day when fog hides the tall buildings and cell towers and muffles the first sirens and car alarms, it's possible to visualize a scene from 200 years past. Historic accounts describe a place where there were as many ducks and salmon as there are people today, and where it was not unusual to encounter grizzlies or mountain lions, or to see otters playing offshore.

In the dawn haze, a historic visitor might have seen a woman with a basket dig with a pointed stick in the shoreline mud for clams, or four men rowing a wide canoe woven from tule rushes on their way to collect Murre eggs from the Farallon Islands. The visitor's eye might be caught by the white spray of a whale spouting, or their ear startled by the howl of a coyote or rush of a thousand pintails beating their wings. With very good hearing, a visitor might have even heard the ring of a ship's bell passing outside the Golden Gate on Pacific explorations.

Fog could not hide San Francisco Bay forever. Eventually, a party of Spanish explorers climbed a hilltop and gasped at the sight before them: an expanse of quiet blue water encircled by golden hills, spreading oaks, and lofty redwoods. Ever since, the bay's inviting geography, sheltered waters, and natural riches have made it a magnet for people from all over the world.

At the time of Spanish discovery, more Native Americans lived in California than in any region north of Mexico. They gathered food, hunted game, cultivated plants, and even dammed streams—the first in a long line

Painting of the Golden Gate circa 1890 by Colter. (GGNRA Park Archives, Martin Behrman Negative Collection)

of human inhabitants to tinker with the region's ecosystem in an effort to better serve their own needs. Soon after the Spanish arrived, the bay region became an important destination along the Pacific coast for ships. Even as these early Europeans explored and settled, the bay environment remained relatively undisturbed until one event: the 1848 discovery of gold. At that moment, the world made a beeline for California.

So many people in such a rush to make their fortunes made their presence felt on the land and water. Between 1849 and 1920, thousands put their backs into extracting gold, cutting timber, catching fish, and hunting furry animals, as well as into building farms, businesses, and towns in California. Soon they were constructing levees to protect these investments from floods, and to develop swamps into real estate. In a land of space and plenty, early entrepreneurs worried little about the disruption to natural ecosystems they left in their wake.

But the biggest changes made to the flow of water through northern California and San Francisco Bay occurred between the 1920s and 1960s. During this period, Californians constructed hundreds of dams, dug miles of aqueducts, and raised levee upon levee—all in an attempt to control and exploit the annual winter flood of water from the mountains to the sea.

Though Californians gained in a more stable water supply, flood protection, and agricultural and mineral riches, each activity also damaged the ecosystem. These impacts in turn inspired early attempts to protect natural resources and water quality. Thus commenced the tug of war between exploitation and preservation that endures today. Whatever the outcome, one thing is clear: humans changed so much in this ecosystem, so fast, that San Francisco Bay remains one of the most altered estuaries in the world today.

Earliest Inhabitants

Those who lived around the bay a thousand years ago had a very different relationship with it than people do today. The lives of California's coastal Native Americans were so linked to the bay and ocean that nineteenth-century ethnologist Stephen Powers described them as "almost amphibious." They used the bay region's fish, birds, and acorns for food, and its marsh plants and trees to build homes and weave baskets. Historians say that for perhaps as many as 10,000 years, about 10,000 Native Americans, living in 30 to 40 communities, were the Bay Area's only human residents.

Though early perspectives suggest a "primordial paradise" where humans lived in harmony with the natural world in a region of plenty, more recent research suggests that Native Americans around the bay didn't always have it easy. The droughts and deluges of California's climate meant food supplies could be inconsistent. To cope with this, some moved between winter and summer settlements; some used strategies such as burning fields, clearing wood, and spreading seeds to enhance certain types of plant growth; and some smoked and dried food for storage.

Though individual families might claim specific oak trees, clam beds, or fishing grounds as their own, the Native Americans hunted and gathered food as communities, and they shared their harvests. "They handcrafted small-scale economies that were tailor-made to the specific environmental parameters of local places in order to weather El Niño events, droughts, and periods of global warming and cooling," write Kent Lightfoot and Otis Parrish in their book *California Indians and Their Environment*. "This emphasis on local, small-scale enterprises that are ecologically sensitive may be prudent for us to consider in . . . California today."

Around the bay proper lay communities that spoke mostly what have come to be known as the Coastoan or Ohlone languages; up in the river valleys people spoke Yokuts, Patwin, and Nisenan; and in the lower delta and in modern-day Marin and Sonoma counties people communicated in Miwok and Pomo languages.

The bay region's Native Americans built both permanent villages and temporary camps where they lived while harvesting a particular kind of food. Almost everywhere they lived around the bay, however, they left behind evidence of their long residence. Shell mounds, some in piles almost 30 feet deep and a quarter-mile wide are testimony to "thousands of years of feasting on shellfish," according to Malcolm Margolin, author of *The Ohlone Way*.

The bay provided the Ohlone with the two staples of their lives: shellfish to eat and tule reeds with which to build both homes and canoes, and weave mats and baskets. They dug for mussels, oysters, and clams in the mudflats at low tide using a special stick, sharpened and hardened at one end with a flame. They also collected willow branches from creeksides—another connection to the water—to create the structures of their dome-shaped huts, weaving the tule reeds in between. To craft canoes, they made three 10-foot-long bundles of tules and lashed them together with willow branches. Each boat could carry four people out to gather bird eggs from nearby islands, to hunt seals and sea lions, or to trade with other tribes across the bay. "The extreme lightness of the tule gave it a fine buoyancy," according to Margolin.

Of course the bay offered the Ohlone much more than shellfish to eat. The tribe waded with dip nets for smelt, lured ducks into traps with tule-stuffed decoys, wooed whales to their beaches with songs sung by shamans, and used whale blubber as a kind of butter. They poked at crabs and

Lake Pomo woman gathering tule reeds. Bay Area Indians used tules to construct everything from homes to canoes. (Edward Curtis, Courtesy of the National Anthropological Archives, Smithsonian Institution)

octopus in tide pools with a stick, provoking them to grab hold with claw or tentacle. Each tribe had a different way of hunting salmon. Some built weirs to trap the fish, some made fires at night on creek banks to attract salmon within reach of harpoons, some fished with seine nets stretched between two poles, and some threw poisonous soap root into stream pools to stun the fish just long enough to pluck them out of the water.

According to Robert Kelley, author of a book about California's early water history called *Battling the Inland Sea*, "drying salmon strung up in the Indians' tule reed houses gave their villages a reddish aspect" throughout most of the year.

Color was not the only by-product of the Native American's harvest of aquatic riches. They worked clam shells into dime-sized beads for wearing and trading, crafted mussel shells into spoons and tweezers, made coats from Brown Pelican skins, and stuffed blankets and robes with duck and goose down.

Native Americans shared the bay's terrestrial environs with large herds of antelope, elk, and deer, as well as with foxes, beavers, bobcats, and grizzly bears. "The ecological diversity of the Bay Area was enormous. In some parts of the Ohlone region over 50 inches of rain fell a year; in other parts, less than 15. Tribes only a few miles apart hunted different animals, gathered different plants, and developed different customs and food preferences," according to Margolin.

COMMON YARROW

Native Americans favored the native plant common yarrow for making certain kinds of baskets. Many local tribes in the watershed still weave today. To help them maintain their basketmaking materials, those planning riverbank restoration work for the Merced and San Joaquin river projects have been including common yarrow in their planting palettes.

Even though Native Americans living around San Francisco Bay enjoyed unusual access to aquatic foods and did little to alter the salt marshes, dunes, and beaches, they did harvest and manage plants. According to Kat Anderson in her book *Tending the Wild*, "Through coppicing, pruning, harrowing, sowing, weeding, burning, digging, thinning, and selective harvesting, [California Indians] encouraged desired characteristics of individual plants, increased populations of useful plants, and altered the structures and compositions of plant communities. Regular burning of many types of vegetation . . . created better habitat for game, eliminated brush, minimized the potential for catastrophic fires, and encouraged a diversity of food crops."

By the time Europeans arrived, the Native Americans around the bay had been living in a sustainable, balanced relationship with the fish, trees, and wildlife around them for thousands of years. "The white man sure ruined this country," said James Rust, a Southern Sierra Miwok elder quoted in Kat Anderson's book. "It's turned back to wilderness."

Explorers, Missionaries, and Hunters

Spanish explorers discovered San Francisco Bay in 1769, finding it by climbing a ridge rather than sailing into the Golden Gate. Sir Francis Drake and others exploring the coast had already passed the bay's narrow opening, often masked by fog, several times. But when Gaspar de Portola climbed up onto what is now Sweeney Ridge on the coastal mountains near Daly City, he saw what he described as "an arm of the sea" immense enough "for all the navies of Europe" to shelter in. From the very beginning, the Spanish saw in this "arm" what other explorers, settlers, entrepreneurs, and immigrants were to see who came after them: an extraordinary natural harbor.

At first, the Spanish merely set up a small fort at the Presidio to defend their find, allowing their Franciscan padres to build missions to convert and conscript the Indians. During the Mission Period (1770–1834), thousands of Native Americans were converted to the Christian faith, kept within adobe mission walls, and forced to tend crops rather than hunt and gather. Many died from European diseases or lost their culture to this alien way of life.

In addition to building missions, the Spanish set up vast ranchos for cattle grazing and farming and reworked the landscape to suit their needs. Creek straightening may have been among their activities. For example, the earliest topographic map of Sausal Creek, located near what is now the Fruitvale BART station, depicts this segment of the stream as unnaturally arrow-straight and ending prior to entering the estuary. Aquatic biologist Christopher Richard of the Oakland Museum of California speculates that the creek was ditched and drained through a connection with the bay to reduce habitat for marauding bears and swarming mosquitoes.

The Spanish weren't the only foreigners on the scene. Other Europeans soon arrived to hunt, fish, and make the most of the region's natural riches—beginning a century-long era in which the bay served as an important collection, processing, and distribution port for the fish, furs, and other natural products harvested from the watershed and Pacific coast. Hunters from England, France, Russia, Spain, and America pursued natural riches ranging from bear skins to skunk tails in the bay region as early as 1800. But it was those mammals with a special relationship with the water that hunters coveted the most: otter, mink, seal, muskrat, and beaver. These furs—dense and luxurious enough to help a warm-blooded mammal survive in frigid waters—brought top dollar on the world market.

Sea Otters were once plentiful in San Francisco Bay, but hunters attracted by their valuable pelts decimated the species between 1800 and 1830. They sent many of the pelts to be sold in China, stowed out of reach of moths and damp in empty rum casks. (Max Eissler)

Sea Otters were among the first casualties of this new California commerce. According to one account, Russian hunters took up to 800 pelts from the bay in one week in 1812, and 50,000 skins within their first five years of hunting these waters. Another account says that in the early 1900s, 16 American and British ships were making regular trips around Cape Horn, stopping at several ports including San Francisco, and collecting thousands of otter skins for export to China. Still another report depicts Sea Otters as so abundant in some coastal waters that paddling through any kelp bed might deal fatal blows to the animals.

Though otters inspired the most greed, the pelts of many other aquatic mammals also filled the wagons and ship holds of early hunters. These men hunted Pribilof and Guadalupe Fur Seals on the Farallon Islands just outside the Golden Gate, as well as Harbor Seals in the South Bay; trapped beavers on what one observer later called the "rush-covered" islands in delta rivers; and slayed sea lions for blubber rendered into oil for reading lamps.

During this early era of hunting and gathering, the overlap among bay, coastal, and riverine ecosystems in the San Francisco region provided abundant resources to each new wave of entrepreneurs and adventurers.

The Allure of Gold

When John Sutter's foreman discovered gold in the channel below California's first sawmill on January 4, 1848, few could have guessed how immense a change it would bring to the wild frontier state on the nation's westernmost shore. The mill, built on the south fork of the American River upstream from San Francisco Bay, was powered by the flow and tumble of the river. John Sutter was among the earliest European settlers to begin farming in the Central Valley, and his mill processed some of the timber that built California's first homes and towns. Sutter's activities exemplify the many ways in which settlers and gold diggers changed San Francisco Bay's watershed in the next half century.

The immediate effects on the bay were obvious. In one year, 100,000 people arrived in California, most of them via ship into San Francisco Bay. More than 10,000 vessels entered the gate between 1849 and 1850. On some vessels, the entire crew caught the gold fever from their passengers. Sailors abandoned hundreds of ships in the coves around the tiny city of San Francisco. These rotting hulks eventually collapsed and merged into the city's first bay fill.

As the would-be miners traveled up toward the gold fields of the Sierra Nevada, they began visiting creeks for drinking water, chopping and collecting wood from banks, and fishing and hunting for food. Employment for a whole second wave of Californians involved supplying the miners with tools, food, hotel rooms, and transport. Small settlements around the bay grew larger, and new towns sprang up along Central Valley rivers as farmers discovered the rich soils on the floodplains.

In the beginning, the miners simply swarmed around every creek and river bank looking for glints of gold. Their early methods involved collecting and sifting through streambed deposits, or "placers." They used picks and shovels to loosen the sediments, and rinsed water through the ore in grooved sluice boxes designed to separate the silt, sand, and gravel from their precious quarry. But the streambeds soon gave up the flakes they had collected in their running waters over millennia, and the miners expanded their search to the nearby hillsides. To dislodge these more ancient deposits, they experimented with ways to wet the soils. They also took to adding mercury to their sluices because it attaches to gold.

Even in this first mining wave, hundreds of small streams at the highest levels of the bay watershed were disturbed, and their environs eroded.

In 1853, a miner from New England named Edward Matteson had the bright idea to reroute his water supply so that it poured down from above the mine onto the excavation site with more force. With the addition of a nozzle, this new pressure hose blew the ground into a muddy slurry that could be run directly into a sluice box. The water was made to do the work of many miners. These hydraulic mining methods—with their distinctive hiss and roar—were soon brought to mines in the ancient gravel beds of four of the rivers upstream of San Francisco Bay: the Feather, Yuba, Bear, and American.

Gathering the water from far up the mountains and delivering it to hydraulic hoses ignited some of California's first large-scale engineering projects. By 1867, miners had built 300 water systems, operating 6,000 miles of mining flumes and pipelines, and storing nearly 15,000 acre feet of water. In the 1870s, the Bloomfield mine in Nevada County consumed a hundred million gallons of water a day.

"Turning their powerful jets on the hillsides, the hydraulic miners soon excavated great pits in the flanks of the Sierra Nevada, their red-dirt interiors gleaming through the dark green forest. Out of these broad cavities stretched long lines of sluice boxes, three feet wide, through which rushed torrents of brownish-red muddy waters. The nearby air echoed to the steady deep rumbling of gravel and rocks rolling along the bottoms of the sluices. Out of their mouths shot spraying catapults of debris-laden waters that tumbled on down the hillsides into adjacent creeks. Much of the debris lodged there, where it permanently remains, wide glaring white deposits of sand and gravel. Great volumes of tailings, however, also

Hydraulic mining blasted water across the landscape to expose gold-bearing deposits. According to a *Butte Record* newspaper article in 1871, at the Hendricks mine up the Feather River from Oroville, "the earth melts away, and even the bedrock is torn up and thrown high in the air, shivered to atoms and whirled away down the flume by the rapid current." (UC Davis, Eastmans Originals)

washed on down these upland creeks to flow into the deep river canyons," writes historian Robert Kelley.

Mining debris soon choked the deep canyons of the American, Bear, and Yuba rivers with deposits up to 100 feet deep. The upper reach of the

Yuba alone received 10 million cubic yards of debris, and the 15-mile-long lower reach between the canyon and its confluence with the Feather River held six times that amount.

As early as 1856, just three years after miners turned the hoses on the hillsides, a steamboat on its regular route between Sacramento and San Francisco ran aground on the Hog's Back shoal in the Sacramento River. The vessel had to wait hours for high tide before it could proceed. Steamboat Slough, where the shoal was rising, had collected more mining debris than shallower waterways due to its deeper, more rapid conditions.

More grounded steamers, plus plumes of brown water and debris downstream, brought about a ban on hydraulic mining in 1884. But this was not before the industry had gone through a second boom with more powerful equipment—and not before the first dams had been built to check the debris flow. Indeed, the mining did not cease until after enough mercury had been added to sluices to contaminate estuary fish more than a century later. Between 1850 and 1884, miners worked more than 1.5 billion tons of placer gravels in the Sierra Nevada, releasing an estimated 3 million to 8 million pounds of mercury into the environment in the process, according to the U.S. Geological Survey.

All that mining waste worried those downstream in the growing farming towns at river confluences: Marysville, Colusa, Yuba City. After a few short years of living in the valley, residents had become attuned to watching the rivers. Valley farmers had every reason for such vigilance. In winter and spring, the rivers often rose up to flood both homes and fields. Any fool could see that the mining debris reduced the amount of water that rivers and streams could carry, and pushed floods to higher levels. In some years, so much debris came with the floods that it blanketed entire fields in a new layer of sediment. In one instance, according to Kelley, debris covered 39,000 acres of farmland, burying orchards, gardens, and crops from sight.

In most years, however, the creep of Sierra soil down into the valley and bay was more insidious. "The debris produced by the mines was gradual in its impact, and it arrived on the flatlands anonymously, as a kind of natural fact. No one could tell from which mine the mud was originating. . . . Litigation was difficult to conceive of. . . . Who could be sued and for what?" writes Kelley.

Blaming the miners didn't sit well with many Californians, who viewed them as heroes and the source of the state's wealth. Like most Americans at the time, Californians also believed that the environment and its resources were "limitless and resilient," according to Kelley, and that it was the inalienable right of individuals and businesses to do whatever they pleased on their private property. In the same vein, people had few qualms about relying on rivers and the bay to carry away whatever unwanted liquids and solids humanity might produce.

Fighting Floods

Though the mining debris worried the town and farm folk in the valley, the floods that seemed to arrive year after year worried them more. As they planted crops and trees with diligence, and laid out homes, schools, and city halls, floods kept soaking or sweeping away their investments. The Native Americans had told the region's first visitors that the valley regularly filled with wall-to-wall water. As Kelley describes it: "During the annual winter cycle of torrential storms . . . or in the season of the spring snow melt . . . the Sacramento River and its tributaries rose like a vast taking in of breath to flow out over their banks onto the wide Valley floor, there to produce terrifying floods. On that remarkably level expanse the spreading waters then stilled and ponded to form an immense, quiet inland sea a hundred miles long, with its dense flocks of birds rising abruptly to wheel in the sky and its still masses of tule rushes stretching from the delta to the Sutter Buttes and beyond. Not until the late spring and summer months would it drain away downstream."

Historic floods on the Sacramento River outdid those of even the great Mississippi in magnitude. The Mississippi takes days to rise, gathering water slowly from a vast area encompassing half the continent. But snowmelt and storm water swell the Sacramento with great speed, coming from

Flooding on 4th Street, between L and M Streets, Sacramento, during 1862. (Department of Water Resources)

nearby mountain ranges and quickly overtopping riverbanks to spread across the Central Valley.

The settlers that came to the valley were full of the vim and vigor of conquering the West. Taming nature was just part of a day's work, and the fertile river plains of the Central Valley were worth the risk. They didn't really believe the size of the floods described by the Native Americans or in the speed with which such waters could arrive on their doorsteps. But flow gauges set up by the U.S. Geological Survey in the early 1900s confirmed that the Sacramento River could rise from its normal flow of 5,000 cubic feet per second (cfs) to 600,000 cfs in less than a week—an amount that could never be contained within its natural banks.

On January 7, 1850, the small riverfront town of Sacramento experienced its first flood. The river rushed and swirled through the entire town, rising to the first floor of most houses and stores, and soaking others. The flood brought citizens together for a meeting, where they decided to build an earthen flood wall around the entire town. This first California levee would kick off decades of individual communities or property owners building small levees or dams willy-nilly, and of floods every few years that wiped out what crops, goods, and livestock the people had managed to amass.

Localism ruled, and the rights of individual property owners remained sacred. The response of most landowners threatened or engulfed by water was to redirect the water to a neighbor's doorstep. If you built a levee on your side of the river, the owner on the opposite bank had to build a higher one. Accounts from the late 1800s describe midnight moments when masked men stole up on dams, disarmed guards, and dug trenches—breaking open the barrier so that the water might flood one part of the valley and spare another.

Reclaiming Swamps

Within the natural river system, the first lands to absorb winter floods from storms and snowmelt were the delta's freshwater tule marshes. The state soon labeled these "overflowed" lands. Farther down in the bay watershed, this designation encompassed shoreline mudflats and salt marshes. Early Californians viewed marshes as wasted land that could be put to better use once drained. They called this activity "reclamation." Little did the empire builders know the critical function these marginal lands served in the estuarine ecosystem—and how much it would cost their descendants to restore them.

From the very beginning, those with an eye for the future began buying up these "swamps" for a song and imagining corn, rice, wheat, and orchards standing in place of the sea of bulrushes. The state had been granted ownership of two million acres of California wetlands by the federal government under the Swampland Act of 1850. Eager to raise revenue, California began selling off overflowed lands with incentives to drain and reclaim.

Californians got so busy building levees for both flood control and reclamation that they invented a special piece of equipment—the long-boomed clamshell dredge—to get the job done. "The dredges moved along rivers and tidal channels, scooping up bucketfuls of mud, swinging them to the island side, and dropping a row of loads," writes historian John Hart in *San Francisco Bay, Portrait of an Estuary*. "A dike would be built in two or more passes, with pauses in-between while the sediments drained and consolidated. Once the barrier was complete, remaining water within the walls would be pumped out, and farming could begin."

Central Valley settlers began building levees and dams in the 1800s to protect their homes and fields from floods. (U.S. Army Corps of Engineers Transcripts Collection, Courtesy of the Department of Water Resources)

Entrepreneurs organized holding and construction operations to reclaim delta marshes, leading to the farming of hundreds of thousands of acres. A few of these small reclamation districts—usually organized and run by a board of local landowners—formed in the 1860s. The first large-scale district, RD 108 in the Colusa Basin, came into existence in 1870 and is still functional today. Between 1860 and 1930, Californians diked and drained 97 percent of the delta's freshwater marshes, isolating them from tidal influence. By 1918, 700,000 acres of the valley had been "reclaimed." Large acreages of wetlands around San Francisco Bay were similarly withdrawn from the reach of the tides and developed. Early Californians had converted over 80 percent of San Francisco Bay's original tidal marsh to farms and pastures by 1920.

Reclamation and flood-control efforts occurred on many different scales throughout the lowlands of the watershed. People built levees, weirs, dams, and other structures wherever they felt like it. At times, some enterprising individual might propose a more coordinated approach to controlling the flow of water through the landscape, organized by river or basin or county. But politics was not to overcome the individualistic free-enterprise tendencies of those times until the 1940s, when the Sacramento River Flood Control Project finally put the needs of many before those of the individual.

Farms and Towns Expand

As nineteenth-century Californians planted more crops and built more homes, towns, and cities, their impacts on the waters of rivers and bays intensified. Upstream, people began diverting water to irrigate their farms and orchards. Downstream, they set to work developing the shores of the world's greatest natural harbor and using the bay for business, fishing, transportation, naval activities, waste disposal, and coastal commerce.

On the agricultural front, enterprising farmers built the first two "big ditches" in the 1850s, importing water from the Merced River to the San Joaquin flatlands, and from Cache Creek to the Capay Valley near the town of Woodland. In the decades that followed, an irrigation boom brought water to several hundred thousand acres of land. By 1890, one million acres of semiarid land were wetted by ditches, pipes, sprinklers, and hoses. The large-scale diversion of water for agriculture, and subtraction of natural flows to the bay, had begun in earnest. Later, it would transform the Central Valley into the breadbasket of the world.

On the urban waterfront, the town of Sacramento grew up at the heart of the Central Valley. Downstream, the first three Central Bay cities to incorporate—San Francisco, Oakland, and Alameda—rapidly added fishing piers, breakwaters, ferry docks, and waterfront warehouses. Shipbuilding and naval support, soon to fire the engines of the Bay Area economy, got an early start in the North Bay at Mare Island Naval Yard with

Remnants of the North Bay's agricultural history still linger along the shoreline. (Francis Parchaso)

the creation and launching of a wooden paddlewheel steamer called the *U.S.S. Saginaw* in 1859.

Not content with shorelines and hinterlands, residents began to fill the open water of the bay itself, creating new lands off Alameda in 1902, ridding San Francisco of earthquake rubble by dumping it in Aquatic Cove in 1906, and claiming open waters once under today's Marina District to host the 1915 Panama Pacific exhibition.

While new cities and military communities expanded around and into

Roberts Landing in San Lorenzo, one of numerous landings along the bayshore where small vessels fetched and delivered produce, fish, and other goods via local waterways in the late 1800s. (David Rumsey Historical Map Collection)

the Central Bay, numerous small towns popped up near shoreline coves and promontories to form Benicia, Antioch, Redwood City, Hayward, Port Chicago, and Port Costa. Ferries geared up to carry passengers and daily cargo between these population centers. Other vessels carried fruits and vegetables produced around the edges of the South Bay in Santa Clara, Ardenwood, Hayward, and Fremont—and even wine grown in the vineyards around Mountain View—from agricultural landings to the urban markets of the Central Bay.

Just as the Sacramento River provided good boat transportation for the agricultural production of the valley, the bay afforded quick transportation for those seeking to ship products to an even broader market. By the turn of the century, businesses began to crowd out farmers around some bay landings. At Point San Pablo, on today's Richmond waterfront, the arrival of the railroad at the landing in the early 1900s attracted a whale processing plant, an oil can factory, a brickyard, and the world's largest winery.

Fishing for a Living

Nobody had to go far, or risk a stomach-heaving trip out through the Golden Gate, to catch something to eat or sell in the Bay Area in the decades after the California Gold Rush. Many locals came to know the life in the water—and the seasons and habits of different fish species—intimately. Indeed, the heart of the regional economy lay in harvesting the species swimming around and dug into the mud of this rich coastal estuary. Word on the dock back then was that the best fishing for smelt was in the South Bay, for flatfish in San Pablo Bay, for salmon in the Sacramento River and northern bays, for sturgeon in Suisun Bay, and for carp and catfish in the San Joaquin River. And if fishermen preferred smaller or more stationary prey, shrimp teemed in the shallows, and oysters and clams burrowed through acres and acres of mudflats.

It wasn't long after the Gold Rush that Bay Area fishermen began landing every available species in record quantities. They could drop their fresh catch off on a town dock lined with restaurants, or sell it to canneries to be sent to the miners or overseas via the growing fleet of transoceanic ships. San Francisco Bay soon evolved into an important collection and distribution point for fish products, and for a short time it even bragged of being the whaling capital of the world. At that time, there were more than 80 fishing ports ringing the bay, according to John E. Skinner. Skinner's 1962 historical review of the San Francisco Bay's fish and wildlife resources offers a unique glimpse into the region's fishing and hunting past, some details of which follow.

Though Italian immigrants organized the bay's first commercial fishery, other new arrivals soon took up their own lines and nets. Chinese fishers sailed out for sturgeon in their junks, staked out shrimp nets in bay coves, and hooked sharks to send the fins back to the land of their forebears. Fishers of Portuguese descent also swelled the local fleets. For a long time salmon remained the primary fishery.

Wharves sprang up on San Francisco's shores to support all of this fishing, and canneries opened to preserve the catch. Hapgood and Hume established the Pacific Coast's first salmon cannery in 1863 across the river from the town of Sacramento. Here, the cannery packed salmon in salted water, added a pickle, boiled the can, and then dipped the tin in a combination of red lead, turpentine, and linseed oil. This way, even if the label fell off, the buyer always knew the contents of the red can. By 1882, 20 salmon canneries producing 200,000 cases per year lined the Sacramento River. Canneries also set up shop on San Francisco Bay's shores to package both local sardines and fish from out of town. Vessels delivered Alaskan codfish to Union Fish of Belvedere to be dried, brined, filleted, and repacked in tins.

By 1875, 85 boats worked the bay's fishing grounds. Five years later, San Francisco was processing more fish than any Pacific coast port between Mexico and the Puget Sound. Locals also went after crab, dropping and reeling in pots and traps over the sides of 50 different vessels. To support the burgeoning fishing and crabbing trade, the state built the first fishermen's wharf at the corner of San Francisco's Union and Green streets. The wharf was soon handling 10 million to 11 million pounds of fish each year.

Chinese immigrants, meanwhile, set up shrimping camps in coves all around the bay. According to local legend, they weren't particularly enchanted with Bay Shrimp until a pivotal day in 1870. As Harold Gilliam recounts the legend in his 1950s book *San Francisco Bay*: "An unemployed Chinese cook begged a handful of shrimp from an Italian fisherman near Hunters Point. He cooked his meal over a driftwood fire, took one bite, and was so startled by the delicious taste that he raced to San Francisco's Chinatown and showed the delicacy to the head of his tong (association). The tong chief knew a good thing when he saw it. He thought of the thousands of unemployed Chinese who had been imported for the building of the Central Pacific Railroad across the Sierra, had spent some time in the diggings of the Mother Lode, and had drifted down to the city when the gold ran out. He immediately sent to China for a supply of nets and a few experienced fishermen. . . . Within five years, fifteen hundred Chinese

The *Ming Lee*, an early Chinese fishing boat, at San Francisco's Fisherman's Wharf in 1899. (S.F. History Center, S.F. Public Library)

A shrimping camp (note drying grounds) at Point San Pedro in San Francisco Bay. (Gulf of Maine Cod Project, NOAA Marine Sanctuaries, Courtesy of the National Archives)

China Camp State Park in Marin preserves remnants of the bay's last active shrimping camp. The nets, baskets, drying ovens, and other elements of the shrimping life are on view, and the *Grace Quan*, a replica of a historic shrimping junk, can occasionally be found tied up at the dock. (Kathleen M. Wong)

were engaged in the shrimp industry around the bay. . . . Dried shrimps were exported and fresh ones sold in San Francisco," where it was the custom in restaurants at the time to place a plate of fresh shrimp before patrons perusing their menus.

The shrimpers fished just offshore using time-honored techniques they had practiced in China. They staked poles in the bay's extensive mudflats, strung hand-woven nets between the poles, caught the shrimp in a kind of bag in the middle of the net, and took up the nets at each slack water of the flood and ebb tide. According to an early fisheries surveyor, Captain Edgar Wakeman, 12–15 boats, with three men each, worked the nets and brought in the shrimp. The catch was then "boiled in large vats of salt water, . . . spread out on the cleanly swept ground and dried in the sun, being raked over frequently during the day. The scales or skin become separated from the meat and looks like a fine sawdust. The meat and refuse is then sewn up in [the] best quality of bags . . . [and] shipped to China."

The Chinese shrimpers were so successful that they put their predecessors, the Italians, out of business. But the Italians had other fish to fry. They set out in small Mediterranean-style lateen sail boats from which they fished by hand and nets not only for salmon upriver but also for smelt, sardines, anchovies, sole, and flounder in Richardson Bay and the South Bay. Surveyor Wakeman observed that they built picturesque fires on the beaches at night, which could be seen twinkling from other shores, and sometimes slept next to these fires, between daylight fishing trips, face-down in the sand. In 1876, when the Italians introduced the paranzella net (also called a "drag net"), it pulled so many fish up out of the bay and into the market that prices went down. Drag nets were among the first types of fishing gear to be restricted.

Even back then, people such as Wakeman were taking note of how all this fishing affected the bay itself. The surveyor lamented the loss of so many young and unwanted fish, fish that might have survived if thrown back into the bay but had instead perished from compression in the nets. On April 2, 1870, in response to "serious inroads in all segments of fish and wildlife resources," the state set out to preserve and restore its fish by creating Wakeman's employer, a body now known as the California State Fish and Game Commission. The first things this new regulatory body did were to pass legislation to help salmon navigate all the new obstructions in their migratory path upstream, to import new species to the bay, and to curb the hunting of waterfowl and shorebirds.

San Francisco remained the hub of fishing in the region. At the Vallejo Wharf, home of the Italian fishing community, up to 400 men relied chiefly on fishing for a living, and their families and friends built up the complex of restaurants, fish markets, and shops that now extends into and around Fisherman's Wharf today. Beyond San Francisco, every town of any size on the bay shoreline or along the Sacramento River had its fishers and vessels. By the late 1800s, there were nearly 5,000 men in more than 1,000 vessels out fishing every year in the San Francisco Bay region, and producing $2.8 million worth of product.

This was also a time when Californians got the bright idea of making fish populations bigger and better. In 1872, a man named Livingston Stone set up the nation's first hatchery for the artificial culture of salmon eggs and fry on the McCloud River. His initial purpose was to supply fertilized salmon eggs to the East Coast, but he was soon working with the state of California to augment local supplies. Gold miners had sent enough rubble and dirt into state rivers to smother much of the habitat the fish used to spawn. Fish biologists found, however, that fertilizing and rearing young salmon was quite straightforward. All they had to do was slice open a female, spill out her plump red roe, and mix the eggs with the milky milt of a hook-nosed male. Releasing fry only after they were larger kept the fish safe from predators during their most vulnerable life stages.

The Baird hatchery on the McCloud River helped augment depleted Pacific and Atlantic Salmon stocks, while nearby Campbell Hatchery set about rearing native Steelhead and Mountain Trout to stock lakes and rivers (see also p. 223, "Production or Conservation Hatcheries?").

In addition to trying to pump up existing native populations, the early fish commissioners decided to bring in some favorite species from other parts of the country. The most successful introduction was likely the Striped Bass. In 1879, after California's fish commissioners decided Striped Bass would enhance the region's fisheries, their envoys pulled 132 stripers out of a New Jersey river, put them on a train, and released them in the Carquinez Strait. Soon afterward, they relocated another 300 live fish from Jersey to a new West Coast home in Suisun Bay near Benicia.

The Striped Bass certainly took to West Coast living. Just 20 years later, commercial fishers caught over one million pounds of this species. Striped Bass soon became not only a valued food item and commercial fishery but also a prized angling catch, which it remains to this day.

Culturing Oysters

Though the beaches south of San Mateo glistened white from the native oyster shells, early nineteenth century diners preferred the larger, plumper, whiter oysters familiar from Boston and New York dinner tables over the smaller, leaner, browner California native. The bay's sheltered temperate

Workers cull oysters grown In San Francisco Bay by Morgan Oyster Company in 1889. As a teen, Oakland writer Jack London pirated oysters from cultivated beds like these, then joined the fledgling California fish patrol in 1892 to enforce early fishing laws. He recounts these adventures in *Tales of the Fish Patrol*. (Gulf of Maine Cod Project, NOAA Marine Sanctuaries, Courtesy of the National Archives)

waters and mudflats seemed ideal for the cultivation of oysters, and locals were quick to introduce the region's second major non-native species.

In 1868, a Mexican company shipped in the first foreign oysters, but the business didn't take off in the bay until a decade later, when East Coast oysters were able to travel coast-to-coast on ice by railroad. Three carloads arrived. Entrepreneurs planted them in beds around the Marin, Oakland, and Alameda shores. As other oyster ventures sprang up, they abandoned these beds and moved to different areas. After 1875, most of the oyster production shifted to the South Bay. The industry began importing seed oysters, rather than adult oysters, to save on shipping costs. At the time, the bay was considered too cold for oysters to spawn.

Though shipping oyster seed could be costly, land for growing the oysters was cheap. Bay tidelands could be had for as little as $1.25 per acre. The state was as eager to sell the tidelands as the tule marshes of the valley.

The new oyster industry thrived, especially on the mudflats off the town of Dumbarton. By the 1890s, it had become the most valuable fishery in the state. At its peak, it imported over 3.2 million pounds of seed oysters from the East Coast to plant in bay beds and harvested up to 15 million pounds of eastern oysters per year.

Fish and Wildlife Protection

The rapid development and exploitation of San Francisco Bay and its watershed soon took a visible toll. Salmon runs diminished sharply as this delicious red fish became the staple food of the region, and its habitats remained under assault from mining, logging, and farming.

In the bay itself, pollution and human activity overtook the fish. In an 1878–1879 report to fish commissioners, Mr. W. N. Lockington noted: "The constant hurrying to and fro of the numerous ferry-boats and other steamers, indispensable to our comfort, tends to drive away the timid finny tribes, whilst the ashes and cinders let fall injure the character of the bottom. But the injury from this source is small compared with that inflicted by the constant fouling of the waters and consequent destruction of life by the foetid inpourings of our sewers . . . , [harming] creatures on which human beings are largely dependent for a means of life."

The pollution, which included both sewage and oily bilge water from the hundreds of vessels plying bay waters, soon affected the oyster industry. By 1908, production had sharply declined to one million pounds per year, and low output continued through 1936. In mudflats now laced with sewage, oysters took too long to grow, and often ended up thin, watery, and flaccid—not to mention unsafe for diners to consume, even with a liberal squeeze of antibacterial lemon juice. The industry moved most of its beds to cleaner outlying waters in the 1930s in Bodega and Tomales bays, and in Drakes Estero near Point Reyes, where they remain to this day.

Californians did not turn a blind eye to the pillage and pollution, and they began expanding on the state's first salmon protection measures. In the 1897, the state prohibited using certain nets and building weirs, required all commercial fishing vessels to carry a license, and banned the harvesting of female Dungeness Crab. During the same decade, when sturgeon populations suddenly took a dive, the state prohibited set lines (dozens of hooks set on one line strung across a river), and by 1901 it was outside the law even to possess a sturgeon. The state also beefed up licensing requirements and established a closed crab season with a catch size limit of six inches or more. In 1911, California restricted shrimp fishing, and by 1915 both fishers and wholesalers had to keep systematic records of the species, weight, and catch date of their haul. These detailed records of early landings paint a stark picture of the bay's falling biological productivity.

"Duck-a-Minute" hunting club in Schellville near Sonoma shows off a day's take in 1927. (S.F. Call-Bulletin Collection, S.F. History Center, S.F. Public Library)

Other creatures reliant on the bay also received protection. State legislators passed laws to protect shorebirds, waterfowl, and other game birds whose numbers had been cut in half by 1918 by hunting and habitat loss. Californians hunted duck both for food—over 250,000 were sold in San Francisco markets annually in the early 1900s—and for finery. Between 1900 and 1920, during the "plume boom," every color and shape of feather, even whole birds and wings, topped the most fashionable of ladies hats.

These early environmental protections did little to slow the momen-

Officials declared Oakland's Lake Merritt a National Wildlife Refuge in 1869, making it the first wildlife refuge in North America. Five bird islands were constructed in the lake starting in 1925. Today, waterfowl by the thousands feed, rest, and nest in the refuge. (Kathleen M. Wong)

tum of a period in California history characterized by fast growth and quick consumption. In the decades between the two world wars, people came up with dozens of new ways to enhance their lives and livelihoods around the estuary, and to mediate the impacts of flood and drought. By the 1930s, when gasoline-powered engines became commonplace, it seemed there was no dirt that couldn't be moved, no fishing ground too deep or too far, and no chasm or bay that couldn't be crossed by a highway or bridge. Industry and infrastructure began to take on shapes recognizable today. Despite the arrival of the Great Depression, the region continued building, even filling in 400 acres of open water to create Treasure Island and celebrate the 1939 World's Fair.

All of this fast growth and development had an ugly side. Those attending the World's Fair teased the locals about the "cesspool" smell wafting in from the water. The needling goaded the legislature to require the first sewage treatment plants to be built, and stricter fishing laws were passed. Nature, it seemed, was not quite as resilient and absorbent as the empire builders of the West had first imagined.

Industrialized Fishing

When industrialization brought gasoline power and improved gear to the local fishing fleet, San Francisco boat builders upgraded the old Italian feluccas moored at the Union Street Wharf into something called the

"Monterey clipper." The clipper could go after more species and spend multiple days at sea outside the Golden Gate. Venturing as far as Monterey to the south, the fleet brought more catch back to the canneries and packing plants all around the bay, and trucks, railroads, and ships carried more of these products to other parts of the country and abroad.

The seafood processing and distribution system boomed around the bay. Fish deliveries to San Francisco averaged about 43 million pounds per year between 1920 and 1950, but they fluctuated wildly from year to year with the ups and downs of natural ocean cycles and the size of the fishing fleet. This was a time when a turn-of-the-century lag in the local fishing industry revived, when most of the activity moved outside the Golden Gate, and when limits on catch and recognition of the bay's importance as a nursery ground for future catch grew.

The local crabbing boats, equipped with pots to trap San Francisco's signature Dungeness Crab, numbered 200–250 vessels during this period, and often pulled 90 percent of the total statewide catch from coastal waters offshore of San Francisco Bay. Meanwhile, the Chinese shrimping camps around the bay flourished. Sport fishing for Striped Bass gathered popularity in the delta, and charter boats for day fishing trips both to the ocean and upstream were moored side-by-side with the commercial fleet in San Francisco.

But the biggest boom in the region's fishing history came in the 1930s, when San Francisco Bay suddenly became one of the three major sardine

Fishing boats at San Francisco's Fisherman's Wharf in the 1940s. (S.F. History Center, S.F. Public Library)

TABLE 2. San Francisco Bay Area Commercial Fish Landings: Lowest and highest annual catch between 1920 and 1950 in pounds

Product	Catch
Bay Shrimp	235,000–3.4 million
Dungeness Crab	715,000–5.98 million
Oysters	86,328–1.8 million
Salmon	648,000–8.5 million
Sardines	154,000–492 million

Source: California Department of Fish and Game, J. E. Skinner report, 1962.

ports in the state. As Harold Gilliam writes, "[Those were the] great days on the Wharf, when sardines ran in schools of countless millions along the coast, when there were some 40 sardine canneries and reduction plants going full blast around the Bay, when the big 16 man purse seiners were moored so thick between piers that you could walk from one pier to the other by climbing across their decks. . . . They used to go out the Gate at night in the dark of the moon, and suddenly, a few miles offshore, the water below the surface would turn white, ablaze with the phosphorescence stirred up by millions of sardines." Unfortunately, the sardine boom eventually collapsed.

Bay and Riverfront Enterprise

Fish were not the only thing locals were pulling out of the bay for profit in the first half of the twentieth century. Various industries grew up to har-

Sardine can label from San Francisco canneries. (James Bridges, www.Sardineking.com)

vest its by-products and access its raw materials. Down in the South Bay, the Leslie Salt Company brought together a dozen small operations to create a 40-square-mile ring of salt ponds between Redwood City and Fremont. This important bay industry, which had converted about 40 percent of the bay's tidal marsh to salt production by the 1930s, took bay water through nine stages of ever increasing salt concentration, from evaporation to crystallization, then harvest. The entire process took a little over a year, and it evaporated more than 90 percent of the bay water—producing one pound of crude salt at the pond bottom for every five gallons of bay water.

According to Gilliam, nowhere else on earth did the elements combine in such perfect proportions to make salt as in San Francisco Bay, with its long rainless season, warm sun, moving air to evaporate water rapidly, and acres of sea-level marshland sealed by hard clay, creating a watertight floor. "Unlike most places where man extracts wealth from nature, here he has made little change in the ancient landscape. He has put his levees around it and his power lines across it, but he has not tamed it. A sense of the primeval remains, owing perhaps to the fact that man's job here is not to conquer nature but to facilitate its work," writes Gilliam.

The proportions were just as harmonious for another type of industry in the South Bay: the manufacture of cement. In the 1920s, dredgers with snouts inhaled a mix of mud, water, and old oyster shells from the bay

A South Bay salt pond at Eden Landing. (Jude Stalker)

floor. These materials made a near-perfect blend of raw materials for the Ideal Cement Company of Redwood City. Another company ground up the shells from the oyster beds to make a calcium supplement for chickens to eat on the poultry farms in the North Bay. Writes Gilliam: "Bay Area residents who find their breakfast eggs do not crack in boiling water may owe their thanks to an oyster who lived on the bay bottom five hundred centuries ago."

Local entrepreneurs tapped the bay for many other raw materials. At Marine Magnesium workers developed an early process for extracting magnesium from seawater. Three other companies mined sand from shoals where high river or tidal water velocities swept away silt and mud, leaving behind only the heavier particles. At first, this building material was shipped by sand scow from Central Valley rivers to the bay for the construction of bridges, roads, and buildings. In the 1930s, however, sand miners adapted the hydraulic suction hoses once used by gold miners to supply local construction projects. Sand sucked out of the bay in one place was often redeposited in another to create new land out of open water. Treasure Island, for example, is built on sand mined from the east side of Alcatraz Island, and the Alameda Naval Air Station stands on sand from the Presidio Shoals near the Golden Gate. Sand mining trucks can still be seen today rolling on and off Alameda Island in the East Bay.

The sucking, scooping, and digging was not only focused on resource extraction. In the Sacramento River bed between Collinsville and Rio Vista, two massive dredgers were in the midst of a 25-year project to dig out a giant plug of mining debris so that flood waters could flow more freely out to sea, rather than backing up into the valley. Once complete, the cut removed more soil than was excavated to create the Panama Canal, according to Kelley.

Transportation Facilities

As the Bay Area developed, the use of its shores for transportation intensified. Roads, rail tracks, docks, bridges, warehouses, military shipyards, ferry terminals, and industry soon created a zone of traffic and commerce all around the bay, and this growth separated neighborhoods and downtowns from the waterfront.

The intercontinental railroad stopped short of San Francisco proper in Oakland, unable to cross the bay. Thus the shores of the East Bay became the region's overland transportation hub. East Bay ports and waterfronts served as important transfer points between steamers from Central Valley rivers and Pacific coastal trade, oceangoing ships, and the railroads and

Steamers and ferries moved passengers and goods across the bay and upriver into the delta for more than a century. *Top:* Wharf at the foot of San Francisco's Broadway Street in 1865. *Bottom:* The *San Joaquin #3* steamboat upriver in Corning, California. Such vessels were often called "floating stores." (GGNRA Park Archives, Martin Behrman Negative Collection)

trucks that served the continent. All around the bay, the "harbor to beat all harbors" flourished.

Within the bay and delta itself, fleets of small steamers, ferries, and other vessels carried goods and people from shore to shore. Taking the ferry to work was a regular part of the day for the thousands commuting to and from San Francisco.

"To the ferry commuters the Bay was more than a fragmentary glimpse of blue water in the distance; it was a direct experience, a working part of their lives," writes Gilliam. "Every morning and every evening they smelled the salt spray from the deck, heard the sound of its waves, breathed its cool winds off the water, sensed its changes as the boat moved in response to tides and currents. . . . Quite possibly San Francisco's reputation as a city of serenity and of vision is due to some degree to the effect on three generations of that twice daily journey across the waters."

Ferries shared the bay waters with ever larger oceangoing vessels lumbering in and out of the Golden Gate. To accommodate these vessels, San Francisco razed old wooden piers and built new concrete piers with wider slips, and it expanded its port facilities south of Market Street down into Hunter's Point. Oakland, meanwhile, saw the need for larger berths and established the Port of Oakland in 1927. Richmond developed a long wharf to receive oil tankers.

With such good connections both to the continent by rail and to the world by sea, heavy industry clustered along the eastern shores of San Pablo and Suisun bays. Indeed, so many oil refineries, explosives factories, and steel and chemical plants located along the Contra Costa County shore between Richmond and the Carquinez Strait that it became known as the "Chemical Coast."

The navy and the air force added to the region's harbor-oriented activities. In the 1930s and 1940s, the military developed new bases and air stations on all shores of the bay—from Sunnyvale's dirigible-friendly Moffett Field and Marin's Hamilton Field, to the weapons depot at Port Chicago, and to what was to become the nation's busiest military airfield, Travis Air Force Base in the delta. In 1941, looking for a place to repair its Pacific fleets, the navy also took over one of the world's largest dry docks, at the Union Iron Works, for the Hunter's Point Naval Shipyard in San Francisco. These facilities bolstered a long-established network of defenses for the great coastal assets of the bay.

Amid all this maritime and military activity on the bayshore, another kind of waterborne commerce was thriving: the delivery of the fruits, vegetables, grains, and animal products of California's interior to urban and international markets via the bay.

By the 1920s, farmers upstream were expanding into new crops—fruit and rice—aided by the introduction of irrigation water to 1.2 million acres

THE BRIDGE & TUNNEL CROWD

Concrete island supporting western span of Bay Bridge. (Max Eissler)

The challenge of building in the bay has kept engineers tossing and turning at night since the 1930s. Those building the Golden Gate Bridge encountered particularly treacherous, deepwater conditions. Early construction trestles, for example, were swept away by storms and rammed by freighters. Bay Bridge engineers struggled with soft footings in bay mud, murky waters that kept divers in the dark, and long expanses of open water to cover. Both bridges rose with the help of unimaginable amounts of concrete. One engineer built a football field–sized underwater room and drained it, in order to create a safe, dry spot where his workers could build a particularly deep pier; the other built a brand new bay island out of concrete to hold up a very long suspension span. Concrete also figured prominently in the transbay BART tube. Rather than dig an expensive 3.8-mile tunnel beneath the mud, the tube consists of 57 hollow concrete segments joined underwater. Each was constructed on land, towed by barge into the bay, and sunk into an underwater trench.

of the Central Valley. "Fruit culture encouraged a level of rural civility in the care of homes, the founding of schools, churches and libraries, the nurturing of social and recreational amenities which stood in complete contrast to the Wild West attitudes of wheat," writes state historian Kevin Starr. A vast fruit belt 800 miles long and 200 miles wide soon extended down the valley. This investment in a fruit belt and rice farms moved the valley another step toward its current dependence on estuary waters for irrigation and transportation.

The opening of the Panama Canal gave California agriculture a speedier route to world markets. The trivial cost of local water transit in the bay–delta region helped as well. Back then, every piece of fruit, can of fish, wooden plank, and workaday commuter needing to get from one shore to another traveled across the water. At the time, four navigation companies ran 26 steamboats and numerous barges out of Sacramento. Vessels carried both freight and passengers between Sacramento and San Francisco. "If a farmer had freight, he would put up a little flag . . . boats would stop for even one bag of potatoes," writes Robert Kelley. "Carrying the equivalent of twenty-two carloads of freight, boats from the Valley could tie up directly beside ocean-going vessels in San Francisco harbor, short-circuiting all the switching and handling of railroads."

That intimate connection with the bay and rivers that locals got from their ferry rides, fishing trips, and goods deliveries via water changed forever with the advent of the automobile and bridges to convey the four-wheeled wonders from shore to shore.

Controlling Water Supply and Floods

The region's growth soon increased demand in the valley and around the bay for a more stable water supply system. California suffered several devastating floods in the early 1900s and equally challenging multiyear droughts in 1917–1920 and 1923–1924, not to mention a six-year dry spell starting in 1929. The droughts and diversions generated water and power shortages in rural and urban areas, and spawned lawsuits and battles over water rights. California's perpetual water wars had begun. The competition for this precious liquid kicked off an era when the natural watershed would be re-engineered on a grand scale to serve human needs. These alterations, and those that followed, changed the entire flow of water around the state, and set in motion the virtual collapse of the estuarine ecosystem 75 years later.

Engineers built dams, laid pipe, dug aqueducts, and greased pumps to bring water from the Tuolumne and the Mokelumne rivers to the fast-growing urban centers in the Bay Area, and eventually to take water from the Sacramento and San Joaquin rivers to the deserts of the Central Valley—to irrigate lands never before farmed—and to Los Angeles. These water-development projects grew in tandem with completion of Sacramento River flood-control projects begun in the prior century. Many projects had multiuse aims, designed to generate hydropower, store and deliver water supplies, regulate floods and flows, and improve vessel access to inland waterways. In the three decades between 1920 and 1950, humans made the largest physical alterations to the estuary in its history.

At first, these alterations just involved dams. By 1920, myriad small dams blocked creeks and rivers flowing into the estuary, as local landowners worked to store water or fill irrigation hoses and kitchen faucets. Not long afterward, much bigger dams were in the works, among them Hetch Hetchy and Shasta.

Hetch Hetchy's O'Shaugnessy Dam submerged a glacial canyon as dramatic in its topography as neighboring Yosemite under 360,000 acre feet of Tuolumne River water. The battle over whether to flood this beautiful canyon galvanized the nation's young conservation movement, including one of its early visionaries, John Muir. Dam advocates in the early 1900s argued, "the 400,000 people of San Francisco are suffering from bad water and ask Mr. Muir to cease his aesthetic quibbling." The people prevailed, and the City of San Francisco completed the Hetch Hetchy Dam in 1923, as well as the water connections to the city miles away a decade later. The inundation of the valley devastated Muir, and ignited a battle to remove the dam that continues today.

Shasta Dam, completed in 1945, dwarfed anything built before or since in the estuary watershed. Its reservoir covers 29,500 acres and stores up to 4.5 million acre feet of water. The dam itself backs up the mighty Sacramento River into the Sierra foothills just above Redding, stopping a huge river from spilling down into the Central Valley plains.

Shasta Dam under construction in 1942. (Lee Russell, Library of Congress)

FIELDWORK: FISHING FOR MERCURY IN THE BAY

Walking in the bay is a test of your patience, the strength of your quads, and the quality of your waders. The water is too murky to see your feet. If you lean over too far or move too fast, a gush of cold water may lap over the tops of your waders and wet your belly. If you fall, you're soaked. The bottom, meanwhile, seems to suck and grip your rubber-encased foot as if it were a pacifier and the bay a teething baby. Your toes grope along, feeling for solid spots, snarls of wires, snags of roots. With each step, your heart follows your foot—the farther it sinks, the harder it will be to pull out.

I walked into the bay with scientists from the San Francisco Estuary Institute to fish for mercury. The institute regularly tests the bay for contaminants to measure whether water quality goals are being met. On this day, however, our team, led by environmental scientist Ben Greenfield, is on a special mission: we must catch 100 Topsmelt, gobies, and silversides, all of roughly the same size and weight, to be tested for methyl mercury. Where each individual fish hangs out, what it eats, how far it travels: all of these factors affect the body burden of mercury in their tissues. These species neither live long nor stray far, so their bodies reflect immediate, localized conditions and can serve as what scientists call "biosentinels" of ecological health.

Though the bottom of the bay may not be the black mayonnaise of spilled fuel and industrial effluents found in Boston or New York harbors, it contains its fair share of contaminants, including mercury washed down from gold mining in the Sierra foothills more than 150 years ago.

As we unload our gear on the bay shore on this sunny fall day, we are surrounded by signs of human changes to the bay. There are the levees we've driven over to reach the shore, built in the 1890s to drain and reclaim these marshes for farming; the wooded cove sheltering the rundown shacks and docks of a circa-1800s shrimping camp; and a pickleweed field furrowed with unnaturally straight tidal channels created by the rapid deposition of mining debris on mudflats. Of the 200 million cubic yards of mine spoils that ended up in San Pablo Bay, the majority arrived over a period of only 21 years (1856–1887). Some of those spoils ended up here, on the shallow shores of San Pablo Bay at Hamilton Air Force base in Marin County.

On this fishing trip, we use a net not dissimilar to the one the Chinese used to catch shrimp long ago: a sack with a drawstring connected to two poles staked in the water. Ours too has a sack, with two net wings, each attached to a pole. It has floats on the top and weights on the bottom. The guy who knows where the fish are, Andy Jahn, takes one pole and I take the other, and we lumber across some salt grass into the water.

It's an odd feeling, for the uninitiated, to walk up to your waist in water and not feel wet. Coolness but not wetness tickles your skin. Andy coaches me as I totter, struggling to keep my footing. He says to go slow, to place the pole bottom in the mud ahead of me for support and then catch up to it. My leg muscles are screaming after only a few minutes. When Andy gives the nod, we both walk back the way

Seining for small fish in Arrowhead Marsh. (S.F. Estuary Institute)

we came, the net stretched between us, trying to catch the inch-or-so-long fish that dart through the shallows. The net grows heavy. We move toward each other slowly until Andy takes hold of both sides of the sack, rinses out some of the mud, and then drags the whole shebang onto shore.

Upon a bed of salt grass, we sort our catch. We use one bucket to wash the fish and another to keep them. Hands sift through the brown mud feeling for tiny fish, striving to tell the smelt from the gobies and silversides. On our first haul, we are lucky to trap quite a few Topsmelt. But the rest of the hauls only yield one more. Andy says these slivers of marine life prefer higher salinity waters, and with the tide going out now we start seeing more lower salinity species like silversides.

As the tide retreats over the course of the afternoon, it reveals our two sets of muddy footprints. Expedition leader Greenfield has the truck tailgate down and a suitcase full of instruments open. He takes each fish out of the bucket and sorts them into plastic baggies by type and size, pausing now and then to confirm with Andy that the sliver of scales, fins, eyeballs, and a tail on his finger is one species or another.

At the end of the day, we have 25 Mississippi Silversides, 25 Topsmelt, and 51 Arrow Gobies. Later they will be frozen, sent to a lab in Wisconsin, dissolved in acid, and run through a machine called a cold vapor atomic absorption spectrometer that spits out a reading on the amount of methyl mercury in each fish. So they don't have to kill so many fish in the name of science in the future, scientists are busy creating a new plastic substitute: a dish containing a gel that can monitor pollutant diffusion.

The tide has left our shore as we pack up to leave Hamilton. Sunlight bounces off the smear of water on the mudflat, creating a blinding mirror for the heavens above, illuminating a flock of white shorebirds picking worms and shrimp from the exposed mud. Bigger birds dabble and dive in the shallows, scooping up the small fish we have been chasing all day, and carrying the mercury farther up the food chain—a reminder of the reverberating impact of human activities around the bay.

ARO

Between 1920 and 1950, these dams and other water storage systems increased the reservoir storage capacity within the Sacramento and San Joaquin river basins from one million to nine million acre feet.

The biggest leap in water storage came in the late 1940s, when Shasta Dam, Folsom Dam on the American River, and Friant Dam on the San Joaquin River were constructed as part of the multipurpose Central Valley Water Project, or CVP. This project grew out of the state's first attempts at a water plan in response to the droughts, floods, and shortages of the early 1900s. The federal government took over development of the CVP in 1937. The project included dams and storage facilities on five rivers feeding into the estuary, as well as eight canals and various pumping facilities. Together they moved water within an area 400 miles long and 45 miles wide. Water deliveries from the first CVP facilities began in 1940; eventually, they would carry Shasta Dam water all the way to Bakersfield.

As part of the CVP, four major canals— the Contra Costa, Friant-Kern, Delta Mendota, and Madera—moved water from one basin to another. In addition, two local municipalities built aqueducts to bring water from new headwater dams to their bay-front cities. One connected the Tuolumne River and Hetch Hetchy reservoir to San Francisco, and the other hooked the Mokelumne River to the faucets of the East Bay. Together these six new aqueducts totaled 594 miles in length. They could convey 11,000 cubic feet of fresh water per second away from its natural course and across places where water had never flowed before.

All of these new facilities—aided by big pumps and water turbines— helped California's engineers control and move flows to new areas thirsty for water. But they also provided another level of flexibility for keeping water out of areas it wasn't wanted. While others were off building dams and aqueducts, Central Valley towns and reclamation districts had been working with the state on ways to free themselves from fear of floods and manage the spread of the "inland sea." Their approach, which embraced the accumulated wisdom of 50 years of flood fighting and political turf wars, involved a combination of stronger, longer levees, designated overflow zones, and continued mining debris removal at the clogged mouth of the Sacramento River to speed the flow of water out of the valley and into San Francisco Bay.

By the 1940s, the major elements of what came to be known as the Sacramento River Flood Control Project had finally been put in place. In addition to walling off nearly every important riverbank in a line of continuous unbroken levees across the valley floor, the project created seven bypasses—large tracts at key pressure points, where floodwaters could be let loose across fields and wetlands without doing permanent damage. By 1944, local and state sources had contributed $66 million to the flood con-

One of many agricultural drains on the Sacramento River. (Department of Water Resources)

trol project, and the feds had allocated $23 million. According to Kelley, "Its authorized works included 980 miles of levees; 7 weirs or control structures; 3 drainage pumping plants; 438 miles of channels and canals; 7 bypasses . . . encompassing an area of 101,000 acres; 5 low water check dams; 31 bridges; 50 miles of collecting canals and seepage ditches; 91 gauging stations; and 8 automatic shortwave radio water-stage transmitters." Californians had achieved their goal of replumbing the bay–delta watershed.

Shasta Dam also helped to put a big dent in the 600,000 cubic feet per second of water that the valley's first settlers so dreaded sweeping through their towns and orchards. Behind the dam, runoff could be trapped and released more slowly over time; other, smaller headwater dams promised to bolster flood-flow regulation capacity further.

As these measures were being taken to control flows, people living on the valley floor acquired a new sense of security. In the rural counties of Colusa, Yuba, Yolo, and Sutter, the population grew by 170 percent between 1910 and 1950, and in more urban Sacramento County it increased by 309 percent, according to Kelley. During this time period, the system finally seemed to weather flood years with only minor, not major, levee breaks. But the lull would not last forever. And the flood-control project—originally designed to protect agricultural lands—now found itself charged with protecting many urban communities with much higher property values.

The people of California now had a more stable water supply, stronger flood protections, and regular dredging programs to speed inland navigation. But as these activities started to curb the flow of fresh water into the bay and divert it outside the system, and as droughts further depleted these outflows, the tides crept upstream. This phenomenon marked the beginning of a saltwater intrusion problem—in which salt water reaches fresh drinking water intakes—that continues to plague water managers and engineers to this day.

At the time, federal engineers proposed building a giant dam across Suisun Bay to solve the problem. The thought was that the dam would keep the salty ocean on one side and the fresh river water on the other, and remake the lower delta into a giant reservoir to boot. Dickering over how and where such a salinity barrier could be built lasted 30 years, but resulted in nothing concrete except the creation of the extraordinary Bay Model in Sausalito. (This three-dimensional, 1.5-acre model, open to visitors today, simulates tides and currents in the estuary.) Later, engineers turned their attention upstream and sought to solve the intrusion problem with a peripheral canal (see p. 190, "Warring over Water").

Growing through War

World War II fueled another growth spurt around the bay, and the region's second major population boom in a century followed. The first boom attracted people with the promise of "gold in them thar hills," and the second with permanent jobs in the aftermath of the war. Thousands had come to work the military and civilian production lines of the wartime period. After the war, many of these workers decided to stay on—attracted not only by the growth in industry and jobs but also by the region's unique coastal beauty and mild climate.

The Bay Area population tripled during and after the war, swelling to over three million by 1960. Houses, shops, businesses, and industries grew up all around the bay, taking over space once occupied by small farms and pastures. Many acres of the surrounding watershed disappeared under buildings and pavement with the swell of urbanization; many acres of open water also disappeared as developers filled them in to create cheap new real estate. More roads, and more railroads, laid their lanes and lines along the bay's accommodatingly flat shoreline.

Though many of the region's residents moved toward land-based work,

The navy's mothball fleet has been a fixture of Suisun Bay for generations, but it is in the process of being dismantled. Many of these vessels were built in Bay Area shipyards or had served as part of the Pacific fleet. (Max Eissler)

some still eked out a living from the bay itself. Fishing occupied the lives of a dwindling number of people, and focused on fewer species. Every commercial catch required a permit and couldn't exceed a state-set limit. Dredgers still mined sand from the bay floor and deepened the berths of the region's six major ports to accommodate the new container ships coming into Oakland and the new supertankers coming into Richmond, and to clear the Gold Rush sediments still creeping downstream 100 years later. Workers still scraped salt crystals off the bayshores to fill cardboard cylinders in kitchen cupboards.

Upstream in the delta, agriculture continued to thrive, but years of cultivating delicate wetland soils spurred the sinking of diked islands farther below sea level. Farmers had to shore up dikes and expand drainage systems. Farther afield in the drier valleys, growing crops required more inputs of water and chemicals, as well as tile drains to remove salty irrigation water. Demand for water grew neck and neck with the state's population, resulting in another network of pipes, canals, ditches, dams, and pumps being laid down over the already extensive water infrastructure built in the first half of twentieth century.

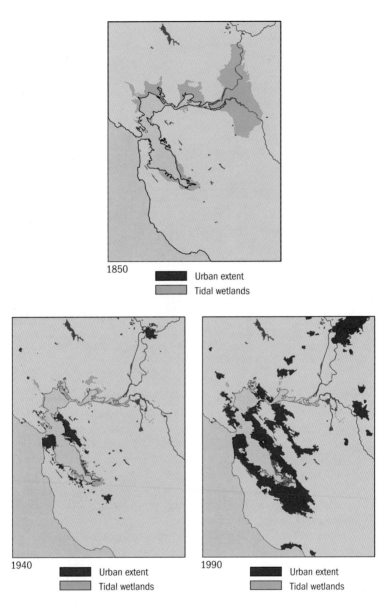

1850
Urban extent
Tidal wetlands

1940
Urban extent
Tidal wetlands

1990
Urban extent
Tidal wetlands

Maps 3, 4, and 5. San Francisco Bay–Delta urbanization and wetland loss. (Data from U.S. Geological Survey, redrawn from Carle 2004)

Conclusion

The bay and its environs accommodated all of this development—but not without consequences to the ecosystem. By the 1950s, the results could be seen and felt in the form of oily beaches, salty drinking water, trashy shores, and the stench of sewage near the bay.

The impacts of water development were less obvious but equally important. The extensive replumbing of the rivers flowing into the bay blocked salmon migrations with dams and trapped sediment in upstream reservoirs. It changed the seasonal pattern of flows out to sea. It diverted millions of acre feet of water to irrigation pipes and city taps, and more millions of acre feet to arid spots of California that had never seen Sacramento or San Joaquin river water before.

This replumbing assuaged the fear of anything but the "100-year flood" and the five-year drought. Though Californians benefited from this stabilization in the flow of water across their land, their actions eventually destroyed what the system's smallest fish and biggest birds had long adapted

The neon sign of the C&H sugar refinery is a landmark for those traveling between Sacramento and the Bay Area. Ships have unloaded raw cane sugar from Hawaii here since 1906. But not everything produced along this shore is sweet. Since the 1920s, it's been known as the "Chemical Coast" for its cluster of oil refineries, smelters, and munitions plants. (Max Eissler)

to rely on: the instability and diversity of a habitat mixing river floods and ocean tides, in a climate subject to both drought and downpour.

By this time, however, the promise of California had changed. A life based on the natural riches of the golden state was passing. A life more dependent on chemicals, petroleum, pumps, cars, and technology lay ahead.

THE ENVIRONMENTAL BACKLASH
1960s–Present

PORT OF OAKLAND

When I was a kid in the 1970s, we used to go out on the Emeryville mudflats, where they had all the tire and driftwood sculptures. Enough of them were always falling down, or in various states of disrepair, that we could gather up a bunch of driftwood and make something. Then we'd have to wash off before getting in the car, because we would be completely covered in mud, just black all over. These days it's all clean; it looks beautiful; it even has an intact marsh. But I miss the old sculptures on the bay.

MICHELLE ORR, WETLAND ENGINEER, PHILIP WILLIAMS & ASSOCIATES

TAKE A LOOK and a sniff of the bay and most days you'll find it relatively refreshing. Four decades ago, however, San Francisco Bay smelled like old sneakers. Locals heading down to the bay for a Sunday stroll were more likely to find a garbage dump than a shoreline path edged with wild strawberries and purple sage. No one took their toddlers to wade in the gentle chop or donned a wetsuit to windsurf back then—bay water was too unappealing. In those days, residents of the East Bay hills could actually see the bay shrinking as cities filled their shallows with sand and rock to build out beyond their natural shores.

The bold strokes of environmental protection that saved the bay and nurtured today's upwelling of conservation and restoration work had their seeds in the 1960s. It was in this decade that the bay arrived at a visible breaking point. In just 250 years—a much shorter time span than most civilizations—the region had grown from a wilderness at the edge of an ocean into an urban metropolis. In the process, millions of people, thousands of vessels, hundreds of industries, and acres of development had arrived on the bayshore, along with all the unpleasant by-products of their activities.

Storm drains spilling into San Francisquito Creek in East Palo Alto. (Jude Stalker)

Former *San Francisco Chronicle* journalist Harold Gilliam wrote of the first citizens to stand up for the bay against big business and "progress" in the 1960s and 1970s: "It would be absurd to compare saving the bay to saving the earth, which will require revolutionary changes in the way all of us on this planet live and work, but it should give us courage and perspective to remember the first environmental activists, who didn't realize that what they were trying to do was impossible."

Since then, many initiatives have succeeded in tackling the "impossible"—saving birds, redwoods, wetlands, and creeks from urban pressures, and creating a body of federal and state legislation to protect the quality of the environment. As a result, by the late 1980s, the bay was much cleaner and healthier than it was after World War II. It was also surrounded by communities with a special commitment to its welfare.

Stopping Fill

Moving the bay's best interests to the front burner of the regional agenda took decades. It wasn't so long ago that city fathers saw a fortune in real estate glimmering under the bay's blue surface. In the 1960s, every city lucky enough to have shorelines had a plan to grow its borders by filling the bay. Dumping sand and rock in the shallows would enable the construction of new houses and commercial buildings, thereby increasing both municipal acreage and tax revenue. The natural topography made landfill relatively easy to accomplish—most of the bay was, and still is, less than 12 feet deep and easy to "reclaim." Developers drew maps of the bay showing more streets and subdivisions than underwater topography.

"The Bay was seen chiefly as a thing to get rid of, and the solemn superstructure of western property titles rose upon a quicksand of epic fraud and theft from the public domain," UC Berkeley historian Gray Brechin observed in a speech about early views of the bay.

The grand schemes for new in-bay subdivisions were a far cry from the reality of the shoreline in the 1960s. At that time, the edge of the bay was a forbidding zone of barbed wire, railroads, industry, firing ranges, shipyards, and salt ponds. Decades of trash and sewage dumping had turned the gravel beaches and sandbars into reeking wastelands. Living by the water was not for the rich but for the poor.

"The pattern of development was for communities to be walled off from the bay. So cities that once had a landing or a small port didn't, when I was growing up in the '60s, even think of themselves as bayside cities anymore. You couldn't get to the shore of the bay as a member of the public," says David Lewis of Save the Bay, an organization founded to protect the region's watery heart.

Though unable to reach the water's edge, local residents could see and smell the rot in their midst. Mounds of garbage grew taller by the day along the shorelines of communities such as Berkeley, Albany, Hayward,

Mountain View, and Palo Alto, and choked baylands in San Francisco's Candlestick Cove and San Jose's Alviso. At that time, 20 major landfills pushed into the bay "like deltas from rivers of consumption and waste," writes John Hart in his book *Portrait of an Estuary*.

These and other landfills took a noticeable toll on the remaining open water. At the time of the Gold Rush, experts estimate, the open water area of the bay was around 787 square miles. By 1960, so many extensions had been added to islands, shores, and seawalls that only 548 square miles of bay remained.

But up in the hills, someone was watching the bay's disappearance. In 1961, three women accustomed to beautiful bay views from their front windows began noticing the changes to the shoreline. "We could all see it being filled in," says Sylvia McLaughlin, wife of a mining magnate and University of California regent. "Then I saw the headlines in the *Berkeley Gazette*, how the city was going to double its size in the name of 'progress.' And every time I went downtown, I'd see these huge trucks rumbling down to the bay, filled with dirt and refuse from university building projects."

Others could see the travesty on the shores, too. The *Chronicle*'s Gilliam remembers fires burning out in the bay at night. Where Berkeley's Eastshore Freeway is today, he recalls dikes crisscrossing the shallows, trucks dumping garbage inside the dikes, and the burning of the garbage. By that time, most of the bay bottom had been sold off to railroad and real estate companies for development. Everyone saw this as progress, not pillage. "The word *environment*, as we now use it in relation to total ecology, was not even in anyone's vocabulary yet," Gilliam says.

Concerned, Sylvia McLaughlin met with her friend Kay Kerr, at Berkeley's Town and Gown Club, and soon afterward with another friend, Esther Gulick. They discussed, with some horror, their hometown's plans to pave several thousand acres of the bay—an area that might have stretched streets out to the end of Berkeley's long wharf (three miles). They vowed to try to halt the filling.

The three women had a lot going for them. Not only were they fired up about the plight of their bay but they had the means and connections to do something about it. In addition to the business and university ties of McLaughlin's husband, Kerr was the wife of the president of the University of California, and Gulick was married to a professor.

As a first step, they invited the leaders of 13 conservation groups to Esther's living room. "Kay gave a pitch about the bay being filled in and they all agreed something must be done, but said they were too busy saving birds and redwoods and wilderness," recalls McLaughlin. "So they all wished us luck and filed out the door, and we sat down and started our own organization, Save the Bay."

Aided by the gift of mailing lists from the Sierra Club, the Audubon

Three women who saved the bay in the 1960s: Esther Gulick, Sylvia McGlaughlin, and Kay Kerr. The full story of how they did it, and the fascinating story of how San Francisco Bay came into being and then was settled, developed, polluted, and finally restored by its human populace, is beautifully presented in the 2009 documentary film *Saving the Bay* by Ron Blatman. (Save the Bay)

Society, and other groups, the fledgling Save San Francisco Bay Association sent out hundreds of letters calling attention to wanton development in the bay. Most of the people who received the mailing sent back $1 to join, giving the organization a base. Their reach soon extended beyond Berkeley, with membership swelling to 18,000 by 1970, and into the halls and offices of the state capitol. Locals heard the call to save the bay on the radio, read about it in newspapers and on bumper stickers, and talked about it around family dinner tables and in grocery store parking lots.

"With surprising rapidity, the movement to save the bay became a mass political uprising . . . a wildly popular cause, and hundreds of people (including me), were converted to environmentalism in the process," writes Richard Walker in his history of the greening of the region called *The Country in the City*. "Nothing was more essential to the Bay Area's green culture. It all goes through Save the Bay."

The intense lobbying gave Save the Bay two immensely powerful allies. Seeing the popularity of the cause, state Senator Eugene McAteer and Richmond Assemblyman Nicolas Petris agreed to propose legislation creating a single regional agency to regulate bay fill and environmental quality. Some supporters sent baggies of sand to their state legislators to make the point. Others crowded into buses to throng hearings in the state capitol. Their presence turned the tide in many battles. For example, when developers seeking to fill an area off Alameda Island claimed it had no important avian species, Professor Junea Kelly of UC Berkeley responded by pulling one stuffed bird after another out of a dress box. McLaughlin in a Bancroft Library oral history recalls the incident as a "sensation." McLaughlin also remembers dressing up in a blue linen suit, a straw hat, and red high heels to impress a key finance committee. She was thankful that she'd done her homework when they asked her to explain the nature of an anadromous fish.

The McAteer–Petris Act passed in 1965, creating the San Francisco Bay Conservation and Development Commission (BCDC) to take charge of the bay's future. The commission got to work immediately—putting a stop to fills, dams, and other developments threatening the bay. McLaughlin, Kerr, and Gulick attended nearly every commission meeting in those days, sitting "where we could always be seen," she says. Gulick regularly got on the phone to bend the director's ear on policy issues.

One early triumph occurred when the fledgling bay commission saved a mountain from ending up underwater. Real estate moguls David Rockefeller and Charles Crocker had hatched a plan to shave the top off Mount San Bruno south of San Francisco and use it to create new land off Redwood Shores. An area of old oyster beds the size of Manhattan was to be filled. But BCDC and Save the Bay soon put the brakes on the mammoth development project.

Whereas Save the Bay's early leaders were feisty women, the commission's early leaders were strong men, among them *Sunset* publisher Mel Lane and director Joe Bodovitz. These men set a new tone for bay-related business, and it was not "as usual."

Today, BCDC is a commission of 29 members drawn from diverse public agencies and transportation interests, and headquartered in downtown San Francisco. These days, a BCDC permit is a prerequisite to do almost anything in the open water, from repairing a dock or mooring a vessel, to dredging a marina or placing any kind of solid in the liquidity of the bay.

Since its creation more than four decades ago, BCDC has guarded the interests of the bay in many ways. The organization has protected wetlands and championed their restoration, negotiated with ports and airports seeking to dredge or fill for new projects, and overseen mitigation for oil spills and habitat losses. It has weighed in on military base reuse planning, facilitated public access to the bayshore, fined lawbreakers, brokered environmental agreements among diverse interests, and reviewed every imaginable proposal to fix a bridge stanchion or build a deck on a waterfront cafe.

"Passage of the McAteer–Petris Act brought overnight changes to San Francisco Bay," says Phyllis Faber, a wetland biologist who once served on California's Coastal Commission. "The creation of BCDC with its Bay

Chevron oil refinery along the East Bay's "Chemical Coast." (Jude Stalker)

Plan signaled a monumental shift in public consciousness, and provided the positive attitude toward good planning for the bay that prevails to this day." BCDC has since won international recognition as a model citizen's initiative.

At its inception, BCDC was the first coastal zone management agency in the world. Both the commission and Save the Bay have been strong voices for the bay ever since. According to Gilliam, who was in Gulick's living room in 1961, the save the bay movement marked the origin of an *environmental* movement, one with goals distinct from the *conservation* movement to save wild things and places that preceded it. "It was the first major revolt against the dominant postwar mindset of unrestricted development, the mandate of 'progress,' the tyranny of bulldozers . . . demonstrating the power of grassroots action," Gilliam writes in a 2007 retrospective article.

In the decades immediately after Save the Bay galvanized ordinary people into action, many other groups materialized to keep watch over other aspects of the bay's business. On the peninsula, two women succeeded in saving Palo Alto's baylands in 1965, and two couples endeavored to champion tidal marsh restoration and wildlife-friendly salt ponds. Noting that the bay could not be cut off from the rivers and runoff that feed into it, Bill Davoren launched The Bay Institute in 1981, and Friends of the River stepped in to help with upstream issues. Ducks Unlimited, United Anglers, and the Pacific Coast Fishermen's Federation soon got involved protecting the habitats and quality of the bay, where they so enjoyed hunting and fishing. Many other initiatives followed—making the region one of the most environmentally mobilized in the world (see p. 319, "Learning More, Helping Out: A Few Places to Start").

"I remember one dinner party at our house, when the president of Ideal Cement, a friend of my husband's, winked and said, 'Well, Sylvia, you're just too naïve to understand,'" says McLaughlin, guessing he was trying to put her in her place concerning a huge bay fill project. "Years later, I met his partner in the project, David Rockefeller, at a party. He held out his hand, looked me in the eye, and said, 'Well, you won.'"

Clean Water

The environment, scientists often remind us, is a closed system. Things don't go away; they just change forms or shift from place to place. Yet for centuries, humans have trusted creeks, rivers, currents, and tides to carry their sewage, refuse, and waste away. Out of sight, perhaps, but not out of mind for long.

Waste is not borne away quickly in the bay. Though the tides sweep beaches and mudflats smooth twice a day, only a small fraction of the bay's water exits the Golden Gate. In the decades preceding the 1970s, this recirculation made the bay particularly rife. Raw sewage traveled directly from toilets into the bay via more than 80 points of discharge. Industries and refineries also discharged untreated wastewater. Farms upstream watered their crops and let the excess—laced with fertilizers, pesticides, and minerals—run off into rivers feeding the bay. Meanwhile, every refueling or repair of a vessel spilled a little oil.

Back then, fish bloated and turned belly up in the bay every few weeks, particularly in the South Bay, where waste from Santa Clara Valley fruit canneries often overwhelmed local sloughs. At this end of the estuary, tides and freshwater inflows weren't strong enough to flush and clean the shallows. Nutrients from sewage and cannery effluent triggered algae blooms. When these blooms died, the decomposition process stole so much oxygen from the water that none was left for the fish (a phenomenon scientists call anoxia).

"The shore stank and the bay reeked of sulfides, peeling the paint off the houses in Milpitas," says Sam Luoma of the U.S. Geological Survey, a hydrologist who arrived in the Bay Area in the early 1970s to research contamination, and went on to lead several large estuary restoration initiatives. "That's why they called Milpitas the armpit of the bay, because it smelled like one from July through September." Similar anoxic conditions plagued the cannery-lined Sacramento River around Stockton and areas of the delta receiving sewage inputs. When the smell of decomposing algae reached the nostrils of nearby residents, the public complained.

The bay was not the only convenient place to get rid of waste. Early studies documented the pollution in San Pablo Bay's Castro Creek, and later San Francisco's Islais Creek, around which clustered a variety of heavy industries. Land along the bayshore also accumulated every kind of refuse. The great shipyards at Richmond, Oakland, and Hunter's Point piled up scrap metal, old fuel drums, and oily engine parts on their waterfronts. They scraped chips of lead paint onto the ground and poured paint thinner onto the tarmac. Military bases and munitions plants used the convenient coves and corners of their shorelines as landfills and sewage outfalls. Aerial photos of the era show a bright yellow-and-orange plume oozing out into the bay from the slag heap of the Mountain Copper Company at the south end of the Benicia Bridge. According to John Hart, the shoreline was a place for "anything that stank or was dangerous."

By the early 1970s, the bay was absorbing 786 million gallons of wastewater from municipalities and industries every day. A 1972 study noted 14 out of 16 shellfish beds exceeded bacterial standards. It was not safe to swim or surf in the bay.

Down on the bottom of the bay, meanwhile, traces of all this human activity were accumulating in the sediments. To read this record of contamination, Sam Luoma sank steel pipes into the floors of San Pablo and Richardson bays. The pipes captured five-foot-long cores of sediment layers laid down by erosion and deposition over the years. Within the older layers, Luoma found signs of terrestrial soils from agricultural runoff and erosion. Above these layers sat hydraulic mining debris with its signature mercury content. In the more recent layers contaminant levels gradually increased, because humans used more and more mechanical and chemical tools between the 1930s and 1970s.

According to the cores, the bay suffered its most extreme contamination between 1950 and 1970. In this period, the additives of choice were both persistent and toxic. People sprayed DDT (dichlorodiphenyltrichloroethane) on their pest problems, cooled their electrical transformers with PCBs (polychlorinated biphenyls), and smoothed various industrial processes with heavy hitters like copper, lead, zinc, and chromium. These additives were rarely removed from any effluent or by-products of human activities. Though each of these contaminants may have only ended up in the bay and its sediments in traces, scientists soon discovered that some

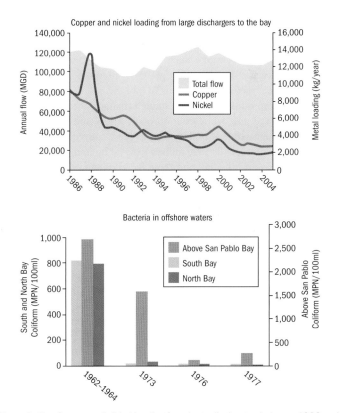

Figure 9. *Top:* Copper and nickel loading from large discharges between 1986 and 2004. The bay's biggest discharger, the San Jose/Santa Clara wastewater plant, reduced its copper loading by more than 90 percent with the help of a tertiary treatment facility operational as of 1979. *Bottom:* Bacteria in offshore waters between 1962 and 1977, showing the dramatic reduction of contaminants due to the initiation of wastewater treatment. Coliform bacteria are typically used as indicators of disease-causing organisms. (S.F. Estuary Institute)

had a nasty way of becoming more concentrated as they passed up the food chain.

In the bay region, efforts to curb pollution began in earnest with the construction of nine publicly owned sewage plants in the 1950s. The plants used screens and sedimentation tanks to remove materials likely to float on the water or settle on the bottom. By the 1960s, some plants also used disinfectants and biological processes to consume organic materials in the waste.

Pollution control efforts gained political muscle and money in 1969 after passage of the state's Porter Cologne Act, which established water quality controls, and again in 1972 from the federal Clean Water Act. These laws produced rapid improvements and huge investments in treating waste and reducing contamination. Both nationwide and in California, the feds offered to cover up to 75 percent of the costs of building sewage treatment plants. Despite such sweet financial incentives, many communities dragged their feet. To get their attention, the state water board banned new sewer connections in half the cities in the Bay Area, leading many communities to have a sudden change of heart.

Putting sewage and wastewater through filters and settling ponds worked. Treatment reduced pollution from these sources by 80 percent. The region currently spends $500 million per year operating sewage treatment facilities around the bay, and these facilities and other dischargers flush 900 million gallons of treated wastewater into the bay every day. That's equivalent to the contents of more than 1,360 Olympic-size swimming pools daily. Despite this copious discharge, the bay is clean enough to swim in. Says Luoma, "We made the really egregious contamination go away. The fact that the bay is so much cleaner today is a central part of our regional environmental history."

The proof is in the organisms. In the 1970s, when Luoma first visited the mudflats of Palo Alto to test the pollution levels, he measured copper and silver levels off the charts compared to anywhere else in the world. In looking at what was left of the estuarine food web in the sediments, Luoma discovered that entire groups of animals were missing. The clams he did find, after digging around, had absorbed so many heavy metals they could no longer reproduce.

His sampling location lay within a kilometer of a suburban sewage treatment plant in Palo Alto. The metals in its discharges came from photography and copper plating industries in the watershed. These pollutants adhere to sediments. Looking for those benthic animals that lay their eggs on the sediments, or that feed directly on the sediments, Luoma counted fewer benthic animals than those that feed from the water column. Since pollution controls were implemented, he's found both types of feeders, as well as predators, in the same Palo Alto mudflats, signs of a healthier food

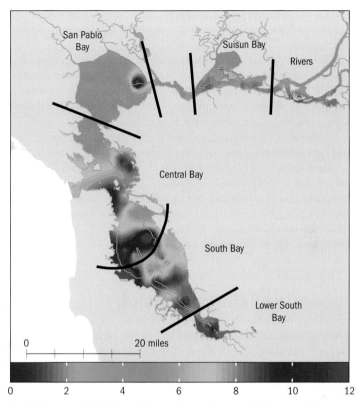

Map 6. The sum of PCBs found in bay sediment (parts per billion, or ppb) between 2004 and 2008, based on 235 data points in the Regional Monitoring Program. Maximum concentrations (30 ppb) occurred in the South Bay in 2008, with a bay-wide average in the same year of 9.4 ppb. (S.F. Estuary Institute)

web. In other words, organisms that couldn't live in the bay 30 years ago have been making a comeback.

Clean Water Act investments delivered immediate reductions in organic and bacterial pollutants, as well as in some heavy metals. Yet other metals, and chemicals such as DDT and PCBs, persisted in sediment and water samples. Though banned in 1972, DDT drove several bird species to the brink of extinction, weakening the eggshells of the California Brown Pelican and Peregrine Falcon until they broke during incubation. California's Brown Pelicans proved especially sensitive due to a combination of their reliance on ocean foods such as sardines and heavy DDT dumping on the ocean floor near their nesting areas. Their California numbers plummeted from about 5,000 pairs in the 1950s to just a few hundred pairs by 1969. Though bans reduced terrestrial sources of these persistent pollutants, old ocean dumps were harder to tackle. Impacts on fish-eating birds remain.

No one, of course, intended to hurt either pelicans or marine ecosystems when they sank barrels of DDT or radioactive waste in the ocean off California's coast, or allowed farm runoff and wastewater to enter local waterways. In all cases, the convenience to humans trumped any thought of the repercussions for the health of the region as a whole.

"We've yet to learn two lessons," says Rainer Hoenicke, who once managed regional programs testing water quality and who now runs the San Francisco Estuary Institute. "It's a bad idea to release manmade substances into the environment before their persistence and unintended side effects are known; and it's a good idea to turn off the tap to the overflowing sink before mopping the floor. To this day, thousands of substances are being released about which we know nothing—the tap is still flowing—while we are still cleaning up old messes."

Preventing Spills and Runoff

Spills and pollutants are much easier to contain on land than in the bay. The bay is particularly vulnerable to oil spills because of its high volume of marine traffic, its semi-enclosed nature, and its myriad bridges, rocks, and other navigational hazards. Since 1984, a handful of notable spills have sullied the bay and nearby Pacific coastline. That year, the tanker *Puerto Rican* leaked 1.5 million gallons of oil when it broke up outside the Golden Gate. The feather-fouling petroleum stayed mostly in the ocean but killed an estimated 5,000 birds. In 1988, a Shell Oil storage tank spilled 420,000 gallons into sensitive wetlands near Martinez. In 1996, a ship being repaired at the San Francisco dry docks leaked 80,000 gallons of fuel. About a tenth of the fuel reached the bay, spreading a sheen along shorelines from Treasure Island to Tiburon, and oiling at least 100 birds. In November 2007, a 900-foot-long container ship—the *Cosco Busan*—ran into the Bay Bridge. The collision ripped a gash in its side, and over 53,000 gallons of bunker oil poured into the bay. In October 2009, a refueling accident of the *Dubai Star* spilled hundreds more gallons of petroleum products. In such a busy port, the spill list is bound to go on.

"The trouble with oil spills in San Francisco Bay is that you have the bathtub effect," says California League of Conservation Voters CEO Warner Chabot, formerly of the Ocean Conservancy. "The oil sloshes back and forth from shoreline to shoreline. Once oil gets into the marshlands and wetlands, it stays for many years, and it's impossible to clean up." Chabot says great risk to the bay from commercial shipping remains, because the deadline for ships to be fitted with double hulls that provide on-board containment is still years away. Another problem is that San Francisco bar pilots—who guide foreign ships through the bay—must rely on navigational screens displayed in other languages.

Birds are generally the most visible victims of oil spills. During the *Cosco Busan* incident, about 3,000 birds perished, though some estimates put the number much higher. When people saw that the scale of the disaster was much greater than officials could handle, they rushed to clean oil off beaches and riprap, and rescue oiled birds. Birder Lisa Owens Viani remembers her sense of shock at the scene: "The morning after, the shoreline felt desolate, like a war zone. Huge gobs of tar were washing up at the water's edge; it took four or five of us to haul these gobs out of the water with sticks and bag them. Most of the birds we rescued in Richmond were already exhausted, hunkered down in the riprap or high marsh, and pretty easy to catch." The volunteers enlisted the help of bicyclists and joggers on the shoreline, some of whom ended up driving the suffering avians to the International Bird Rescue Research Center north of Vallejo.

After such spills, staff at the center work to keep the oiled birds hydrated and warm. Once stabilized, the birds get a series of washes (with Dawn dish soap), rinses, and blow dries. Those that survive this stressful process are then transferred to outdoor ponds and aviaries, and when deemed healthy, the birds are released back to a nonoily part of the bay.

For two weeks following the *Cosco Busan* spill, volunteers returned to the shoreline to try to save as many lives as they could. Recalls Owens Viani, "We worked quietly in teams of two in the hot sun, the smell of bunker fuel permeating the air. One of us would capture a bird in his or her net; the other would gently untangle it and place it in a cardboard transport box, trying to avoid inflicting yet more stress. Holding these small victims in my purple-gloved hands, I was awed at their beauty and dignity, and sick about what we humans had done."

Two years after the *Cosco Busan* debacle, the *Dubai Star* spilled hundreds of gallons of bunker fuel while refilling one of its tanks. Although the ship was carrying an absorbent boom, the crew did not notice the spill until a one-mile-long sheen was headed for beaches in the East Bay. The spill prompted environmentalists to call for mandatory placement of booms around vessels before fueling. This mandate is now enforced in the Puget Sound and Alaska's Prince William Sound, where oil from the 1989 *Exxon Valdez* disaster is still trapped in the beach sands 20 years later.

In the wake of these spills, California has taken several steps to improve response. In 2008, Governor Arnold Schwarzenegger signed seven bills that together require faster notification of local emergency responders during the next spill, more funding to train bar pilots and new volun-

Booms deployed during fuel transfers in Puget Sound, Washington, to help prevent any spilled oil from contaminating the ecosystem. (Washington State Department of Ecology)

teers in oiled wildlife care, and more stringent spill reporting. But California is still not doing a good enough job of coordinating with responding agencies and mobilizing volunteers, according to BayKeeper, a water quality watchdog group.

Most critical for the bay in the future is whether clean-up crews can speed up their response time. Says Chabot, "What you do in the first two hours after a spill is more important than what you do in the next two weeks. If you can't contain the oil in San Francisco's tides and currents, you've lost the war and are suddenly faced with having to use thousands of volunteers to clean up the coast."

Though in-the-water spills continue to defy the logistical skills of state planners, management of polluted runoff across the land has progressed in the last two decades. Unfortunately, runoff from farm fields, city streets, and other contaminated surfaces into the bay doesn't come conveniently out of the end of a pipe, where it can be captured and cleaned up before discharge.

Tackling such diffuse sources of contamination has required both federal and local actions. In 1987, the nation's leaders passed an amendment to the Clean Water Act requiring local municipalities to come up with storm-water management plans. Suddenly cities and counties everywhere were scrambling for ways to stem the flow of pesticides, gasoline, fertilizers, flame retardants, and other chemicals off the landscape and into waterways and estuaries.

"What people forget is that the bay is at the bottom of all of it; it's the terminus of all the activity going on in the Sacramento–San Joaquin watershed," says Hoenicke. "All these interconnected waterways and landscapes drain into the bay."

Most of the runoff management momentum came from cities. In the latter half of the twentieth century, the volume of runoff pollutants had risen at an alarming rate due to new home construction, urban expansion, and the paving of more roads and driveways. Curbing these inputs is a matter of public education more than anything else. Most Bay Area residents have since seen or heard a message via billboard or radio urging them to use biodegradable products to wash cars or spray weeds, or to take old paints and motor oil to collection sites rather than pouring them down a nearby storm drain.

Getting farmers to keep fertilizers and pesticides out of irrigation drainage proved more difficult. Agricultural runoff not only conveys chemicals sprayed and sprinkled on the farm into the estuary but can also have unexpected impacts on soils and surrounding ecosystems. In the San Joaquin Valley, where the soils are naturally laden with salts and selenium, the long-standing practice of sending runoff through evaporation ponds concentrated the salts and poisoned the food chain. This practice contrib-

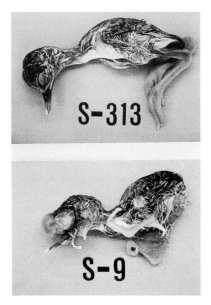

Selenium occurs naturally in California soils but is toxic at high concentrations. Selenium from farm drains accumulated in Kesterson Reservoir in the 1980s, poisoning fish, waterfowl, and other wildlife. A normal Black-necked Stilt embryo is shown above; the one below, hatched at Kesterson Reservoir, has serious deformities. Because the invasive Overbite Clam (*Corbula amurensis*) also accumulates selenium, it causes similar problems among North Bay Diving Ducks and White Sturgeon, posing a health risk to human duck and fish eaters. (Courtesy of the U.S. Fish and Wildlife Service)

uted to the ecological catastrophe at Kesterson National Wildlife Refuge in 1983, where many ducks turned up dead or deformed by selenium poisoning. Scientists warn that if the San Luis Drain—the channel that delivered the contaminated agricultural drainage—is ever connected to the North Bay as originally planned, it will increase bay selenium concentrations to levels that endanger ducks, fish, and other species. Many environmental groups and agencies now say that retiring large tracts of land with problem soils is the only sustainable solution.

Down in the urban region around San Francisco Bay, cities and counties are now pushing storm-water initiatives far beyond the public service messages and waste motor oil collection of a decade ago. At Brisbane City Hall, rainwater from the roof and parking lot that used to race into the bay now flows into a green depression—a "rain garden"—planted with sedges and rushes (see p. 197). In San Bruno, street runoff flows into a bulb-out planted with trees and native grasses. In Oakland, a bioswale treats polluted storm water that would ordinarily flow into Lake Merritt. Around the bay, municipalities are working on ways to slow, spread, and sink the storm water that used to speed into the bay. These "green infrastructure projects" mimic how a forested landscape would handle runoff. Regional regulators now require all new or redevelopment projects over 10,000 square feet to treat their storm-water runoff on-site.

Emerging Contaminants

In the twenty-first century, the brew of pollutants turning up in everything from tiny fish to human infants is a reminder that the battle to keep our bay and environment clean is far from over. Not only do some "legacy" pollutants never seem to go away—such as mercury from mining days, selenium from irrigated San Joaquin Valley soils, and PCBs from old dump sites—but moves to ban certain chemicals like flame retardants or pesticides simply lead to their replacement with something equally problematic for the environment. And industry isn't solely to blame. Scientists have been disturbed to see personal care products, medicines, and birth control hormones turning up in organisms, water, and sediments. They think such contaminants may be the reason some fish and frogs have been found with indistinct genders and incomplete reproductive equipment.

"The real issue is the relative costs and benefits of all these chemicals we're putting in our diapers, plastic bottles, make-up, deodorant, drugs, furniture, cars—all these different things we use to keep things from catching fire, to make them smell nice, to stop them from getting moldy, or to prevent pregnancy," says scientist Ben Greenfield of the San Francisco Estuary Institute. "The bay, and every waterway in the world, is becoming this petri dish that all these things are leaching into at very low concentrations, and we're starting to see some stresses on the fish and wildlife."

Sadly, nature doesn't always cooperate with humanity's best intentions. The processes at work in such a large water system complicate cleanup. In the past, for example, rivers were constantly adding new layers of sediment eroded from upstream to the bottom of the bay. As a result, a lot of contaminants—which naturally attach themselves to sediment particles—got buried and immobilized, or "sequestered," semipermanently within bay mud. However, since dams have trapped the supply of sediments from upstream, the bay floor has started to erode. When long-buried contami-

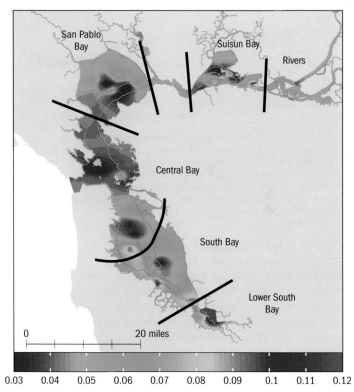

Map 7. Distribution of total methyl mercury, the most bioavailable and toxic form of this heavy metal, in water in San Francisco Bay, measured in nanograms per liter (ng/L). Plots based on 75 data points collected from 2006 to 2008 as part of the Regional Monitoring Program conducted by the S.F. Estuary Institute. (S.F. Estuary Institute)

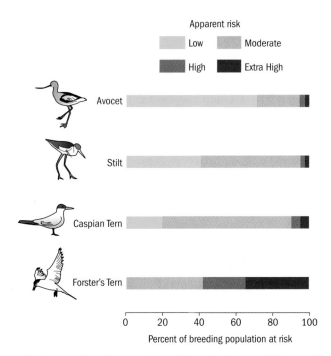

Figure 10. Percent of breeding population of fish-eating birds at risk from methyl mercury. Recent U.S. Geological Survey research suggests that nearly 60 percent of the Forster's Tern population breeding in San Francisco Bay are at high risk due to current methyl-mercury concentrations in their blood. Scientists think there may be particular risk to those species of birds that forage on invertebrates in pickleweed marshes, such as stilts, or on small fish along the margins of the bay, such as terns. (Collin Eagles-Smith, S.F. Estuary Institute)

nants are exposed to water, or disturbed and mobilized, they can be quick to change chemical forms and enter the food chain.

"In our estuary we're generating pollutants from a wide range of activities, and each pollutant has different chemical characteristics, timescales of storage, and transformation processes," says Jim Kuwabara, a U.S. Geological Survey hydrologist. Kuwabara has the unflagging attention necessary to track the journey of a contaminant molecule from source to water to sediment to water, over and over again. "As good as treatment processes have become, it's wise for the public to understand that because so much of the contamination is happening around an estuary, these contaminants will continue to mobilize, flux in and out of the water column, become biologically available, and transfer up the food web," Kuwabara says.

While scientists uncover the behaviors of different contaminants, other

POISONS IN LOCAL PINNIPEDS

The Harbor Seal is an apex predator in the estuary. These 200-pound-plus pinnipeds fear only big sharks and dine on fish large and small during life spans of 30 years or more. But lately, the top tier of the food web has become a perilous place to be. Recent studies have shown that environmental pollutants called polybrominated diphenyl ethers, or PBDEs, have been accumulating at an alarming rate in local Harbor Seals.

PBDEs were first used intensively in the 1970s as flame retardants in upholstery foam, rigid plastics, textiles, and electronics. They also resist degradation and have been accumulating in the bay food web, so much so that the Bay Area ap-

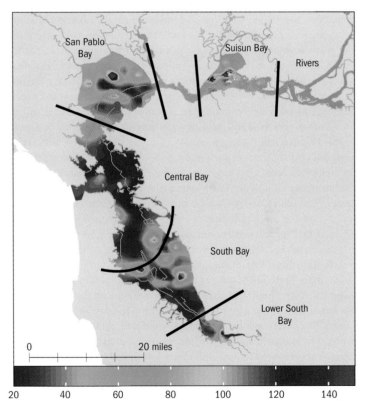

Map 8. BDE47 in water (in picograms per liter, or parts per quadrillian) based on 203 data points measured between 2002 and 2008 by the Regional Monitoring Program. BDE47 is one of the most abundant PBDEs (ingredients in flame retardants) detected in the bay. (S.F. Estuary Institute)

pears to be a hotspot of PBDE contamination. Concentrations of this contaminant in bay fish are 10-100 times higher than found in Japan and Europe; likewise, levels in local bivalves are among the highest reported worldwide. A recent study found that PBDE concentrations in bay Harbor Seals have doubled every 1.8 years throughout the 1990s. The same study found elevated PBDE concentrations in the breast milk of Bay Area women.

In the laboratory, high doses of PBDEs cause reduced learning and memory capacities for young animals, disrupted endocrine functions, and decreased muscle control, and they led to abnormal responses to fearful situations. Though PBDEs were banned in 2003, new flame retardants designed to replace them may be equally troublesome.

---

concerned parties are ensuring that environmental protection laws are being implemented. Today, the bay and its watershed come largely under the purview of two regional water quality control boards. These boards, which answer to the state, issue and approve discharge permits as well as manage large-scale pollution control programs. In 1993, industry and dischargers joined with environmental interests and government to create a Regional Monitoring Program. The program conducts ongoing assessments of whether local and national water-quality objectives are being met for the bay. The San Francisco Estuary Institute runs this program, evaluating pollution in water and sediment at about 40 locations around the bay on an annual basis. Citizen groups such as BayKeeper, DeltaKeeper, and Communities for a Better Environment also keep a keen eye on pollutant issues. The state Coastal Commission conducts beach cleanups, and a number of Bay Area pollution-prevention groups collect used medications, dental mercury, thermometers, and motor oil, as well as recycle paints, chemicals, and fluorescent lightbulbs (for more information, see p. 320, "Learning More, Helping Out").

Looking back on his time as a regulator with the San Francisco Bay Regional Water Quality Control Board, former director Steve Ritchie says the bay is slowly and surely growing cleaner. "The first decades after the Clean Water Act were the era of command and control environmental protection, and we made great strides in cleaning up conventional pollution. Next we started to deal with toxics, which had more diffuse sources than sewage, which made it tough to create useful water quality standards or discharge permits. Now we're getting close to the end of what we can do with command and control, both in water quality and on the endangered species front, and more is being accomplished for the health of the estuary outside the regulatory arena than within."

The region has long moved on from viewing bay waters as a dumping ground for all things unwanted and dangerous. More and more residents are beginning to evaluate what they add to aquatic environments via toilets, sinks, gardens, garages, and flameproof furniture. Equally important to bay health are all of the products residents buy, the hours they drive, the lawns they fertilize, and the pests they exterminate. With wild and urban areas in such close juxtaposition around the bay, actions that seem insignificant in isolation add up fast when repeated by the Bay Area's seven million residents.

Curing the Throwaway Habit

A yellow metal claw dangles from the crane on the deck of the U.S. Army Corps vessel *Raccoon*, ready to snatch from bay waters floating logs, construction materials, and garbage that might prove a navigational hazard. Two such cleanup vessels ply the bay every day. Retired captain Eric Carlson remembers an average daily haul of about 80 tons of garbage 30 years ago but says the waters have gotten much cleaner since. The *Raccoon* is more adept at pulling out big debris than small bits of trash. Sometimes it takes the helping hands of an army of volunteers to handpick the trash out of bay environs. In 2005, Coastal Cleanup Day volunteers picked up 173,000 pounds of trash and 30,000 pounds of recyclable materials from creeks, rivers, and shorelines in the Bay Area alone.

The presence of so much human refuse takes a major toll on the environment. Most insidious of all, however, is plastic trash. Plastic's primary offense is its longevity. These petroleum products can take many decades to decompose; any breakdown that does occur typically involves flaking into ever smaller pieces. Once gone from land, plastic trash is not forgotten. A gull that pokes its head into a six-pack ring, or a sea lion snared by fishing line, will almost certainly die before its plastic necklace degrades. Many marine animals mistake floating plastic for edible jellyfish. Laysan Albatross chicks and adult sea turtles alike have been found dead or starving, stomachs bloated with nothing but plastic bags.

The organic surfaces of plastics also tend to accumulate pollutants such as PCBs, DDT, and other chemicals. Anything that eats these ragged bits absorbs both these chemicals and the plastics themselves—and might itself wind up in the contents of a tuna sandwich. A 1997 study showed that at least 267 marine species worldwide ingest, or are at risk of entanglement and drowning due to, plastic trash. Closer to home, a 2007 assessment of trash in Bay Area creeks found that more than half of the refuse consisted of plastic and Styrofoam. The survey's results led regulators to declare 28 water bodies and bay segments "impaired" due to the presence of trash—an entirely preventable impairment. Because plastic trash floats, it tends to

Marshes and shorelines such as this one on Yosemite Slough near San Francisco's Hunter's Point have long been dumping grounds for all manner of refuse. (Jude Stalker)

travel in the layer of fresh water at the surface of the bay right out of the Golden Gate.

So much plastic has entered the oceans over the last 30 years that the Pacific now includes a feature called the Great Pacific Garbage Patch. Located northwest of the Golden Gate and halfway between Oregon and Hawaii, this region of refuse sprawls over an area twice the size of Texas. Others have described these waters as a plastic soup that extends as deep as 100 feet. In some parts of the patch, plastic outweighs even plankton by a ratio of six to one. Its tons of garbage are fed by ocean currents from as far away as Japan and California. Ocean currents act like relay runners in a race until, over the course of several years, trash from the Bay Area ends up in the patch.

Bay Area governments are taking steps to keep the estuary and the oceans clean. Cities around the region sweep their streets to remove trash from roadsides and gutters. Oakland charges businesses that produce disposable products a fee that goes toward litter pickup, and it bans the use of Styrofoam and plastic utensils in favor of compostable food service-ware made of potato and other starches. And San Francisco limits the use of ubiquitous grocery store plastic bags. Over time, these efforts should help stem the tide of trash that threatens the health of the bay and the oceans alike.

Last of the Fishing

While catching and canning fish from San Francisco Bay no longer occupies the lives of many Bay Area residents, as it did a century ago, a hardy few still make half a living at it. Most have other jobs and fish seasonally until they've reached the quota on their annual state fishing permits. The times of plenty, when salmon paved the rivers and sardines made a mirror of the bay, may be gone for good. But there is hope that with careful management the last remaining fisheries may be sustained, if not restored to their former glory.

The years between World War II and the arrival of the twenty-first century saw many fisheries go through boom-and-bust cycles—due both to fluctuating ocean and estuarine conditions and to the toll taken by human nets and lures. Some fisheries crashed, some waned, and some moved farther offshore. Primary remaining fisheries in the bay and coastal region between 1950 and 1990 were Dungeness Crab, Pacific Herring, rockfish, and salmon.

In this era, salmon fishers began traveling out the Golden Gate for the ocean harvest of adults. Over the years, an ever larger share of their catch consisted of hatchery fish, as dams and water diversions increasingly took a toll on wild salmon. "Until the 1970s, few people worried about the loss of the different runs, the distinct life histories. A salmon was a salmon," says UC Davis's Peter Moyle, a scientist who has dedicated decades of study to the health of the estuary's fish species. "The prosperity of California depended on the dams, and the implicit promise was that fishing would continue despite the dams."

As commercial fisheries declined and markets for certain fish changed, sport fishing for Striped Bass, sharks, and other fish increased in the 1960s and 1970s. Over the same period, the region sustained more than 200 duck clubs covering almost 70,000 acres, and tens of thousands of Bay Area and Sacramento residents regularly traveled to Suisun and delta marshes to shoot duck. Sport fishing and hunting continue to contribute to the Bay Area economy to this day.

As of the 2010s, only a handful of commercial fisheries still work the waters inside the bay, and some hover on the brink of viability. These catch herring, live bait (sardines, anchovies, Bay Shrimp, and other organisms larger fish find delectable), and Brine Shrimp. A few boats still drop lines for halibut, croaker, rockfish, and surfperch, while the delta supports a small crayfish fishery. Interestingly, though, these are among the few remaining urban commercial fisheries in the nation—testimony to efforts to keep the bay clean and the fisheries sustainable.

Just outside the Golden Gate, those trolling for salmon and trapping

TABLE 3. San Francisco Area Catch: Landings in Pounds

	1996	**2000**	**2004**	**2008**
Anchovy, Northern	231,772	256,796	23	91
Crab, Dungeness	10,049,844	794,394	4,042,902	1,872,916
Halibut, California	353,770	284,389	534,265	200,985
Herring, Pacific	10,472,969	7,276,197	2,974,318	1,379,997
Salmon, Chinook	1,359,687	1,952,945	2,659,737	fishery closed
Sardines, Pacific	no data	996	815,938	1,102,104
Shrimp, Bay	113,312	82,816	66,424	45,873
Shrimp, Brine	979,832	890,703	843,388	no data

Source: California Department of Fish and Game, Marine Region, Table 10.

crab are still surviving in the twenty-first century, though the salmon fishers are just barely hanging on. Annual crab landings reached a high of more than four million pounds in 2004, but salmon populations hit such abysmal lows in 2008 and 2009 that the Pacific Fishery Management Council banned commercial fishing entirely for both seasons. Even sport fishermen in Central Valley rivers were given a zero-bag limit. In the years ahead, the council hopes the ban will yield a recovery of sorts.

The bay's herring industry, meanwhile, offers a sense of what it takes to sustain a modern-day urban fishery. To catch these slim fish, local fishers are required to get a license and a permit from the California Department of Fish and Game, and limit themselves to a quota. The state sets this quota based on intensive field work by boat and from shore, as well as lab work on the fish specimens themselves—work that has endured for more than 30 years. Each year's quota is based on the previous year's "spawning" biomass, among other things. Just how many herring come to the bay to spawn from one year to the next depends on the age and number of herring documented in prior years, as well as on ocean conditions offshore. During El Niño years, when waters in the Gulf of the Farallones warmed significantly, the herring—a coldwater fish—temporarily disappeared. More recently, the fishery has teetered on the brink of closure.

State biologists like Ken Oda begin the research work needed to set each year's quota in October, committing themselves to a biomass assessment process that can last up to six months, across the long herring spawning season. After climbing aboard the research vessel *Triakis* (named after the Latin genus for Leopard Shark), the state's crew begins hunting up and down the bay, gazing at the screen of an echosounder bouncing sound waves off the bay bottom. When the sound waves get deep enough to bounce off the fish, the visuals look first like a few specks at 40 feet, or "salt and pepper," says Oda, and deeper down like a solid

State vessel conducts herring survey near the Bay Bridge. (Ryan Bartling)

mass. When a sea lion chases the herring, they can spin into a cyclone or contract into a sphere, which appears as a dancing red ball onscreen.

"Any footage of schooling fish shows they almost act as one when they move," comments Becky Ota, who worked on the herring project for 10 years. "Once they spawn, they typically leave the bay within two tidal cycles. It can be just a continuous revolving door through the Golden Gate, with these schools coming in week after week through March."

Once they find herring, the crew trawls a net through the school to bring up samples. Back in the lab, scientists test the fish for ripeness (for spawning), record length and sex, and remove otoliths (ear bones) to confirm a specimen's age. Most schools contain fish 2–6 years old. The otolith is about the size of a kernel of rice and grows a new ring every year, just like a tree. The strength of each year class is indicative of the potential number of future spawners returning to the bay.

State crews also monitor where schools of herring go in the bay, and they look at acoustic data to figure out which school spawned where. How do they tell different schools apart? Each is dominated by one or two year classes, associated with a specific location, and can be distinguished from other schools by ripeness and how far along they are in the spawning cycle.

The work does not all occur on the big boat. Biologists also climb into the smaller skiff *Ronquil* (common name for a bottom fish) to survey where and how much spawn—or roe—is being deposited. The crew first maps a school's spawning episode, then samples it by working their way at low tide out from the shore wielding a long rake. The raking and sampling is a race against time, as seabirds and fish find herring eggs especially tasty. The skiff might also nose around eelgrass beds, dragging a modified rake behind it to retrieve clumps of vegetation and eggs to take back to the lab.

Most herring fishermen pay careful attention to the ripeness of the schools in order to land the ripest individuals. But fishing for herring eggs is not as lucrative as it once was, nor is the fishery as predictable. A permit for a single vessel once cost $40,000–$60,000 but was worth much less in recent years. In the last decade, the herring quota for all of San Francisco Bay averaged around 3,000 tons. Only about 25 vessels remain to land these fish, using gill nets, in the bay today. Market demand keeps changing. In the meantime, the state continues to invest in the annual biomass surveys and research that may keep this fishery sustainable in years to come.

Of course, some people still fish just for fun. Locals continue to seek out bayshore piers to spend a peaceful afternoon amid the seabirds, sun, and waves. In the last few decades, however, new arrivals to the region have started fishing to feed their families off these same piers and breakwaters.

A Save the Bay survey found that most of these fishers ate more bay-caught fish per month than the amount recommended as safe for human health by state health agencies. The five most frequently caught and eaten fish species were Topsmelt, salmon, Striped Bass, White Croaker, and perch. Testing of a variety of bay fish indicates that most fish are contaminated with multiple chemicals, including DDT, dioxin, PCBs, and mercury. Different fish concentrate different contaminants: White Croaker and Shiner Perch collect more PCBs; and Leopard Shark, Striped Bass, and White Sturgeon collect more mercury. Less than 5 percent of fish harbor excessive pesticides.

In general, bigger, fatter, longer-lived fish are more likely to accumulate contaminants over their life spans—which is why health advisories now recommend that people eat less than two meals a month of bay-caught fish, and children and pregnant women even fewer. From the bay, White Croaker is the fish to avoid, because its habit of feeding on the bottom, as well as the way it stores fat, make it among the most contaminated species. State advisories also recommend avoiding Striped Bass over 35 inches in length.

As in all things, moderation is the key to bay fish consumption. It's not that bay-caught fish should be avoided, but no one should eat too much of it (see chart on next page). Since these fishing surveys, local agencies and groups have worked hard to notify the fishing public of potential health hazards via signage, advertising, and education in communities of concern.

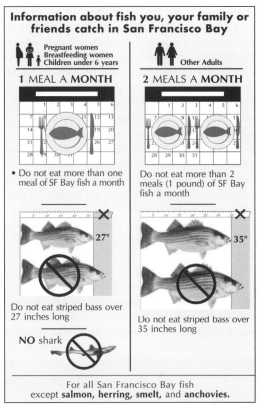

Fish consumption advisory poster. (California Department of Health Services)

Maintaining Ports and Shipping

The massive container ships and oil tankers plying the bay embody the strength of the local maritime economy. Everyone crossing the Bay Bridge, meanwhile, knows the shape of the Port of Oakland's gigantic cranes, which call to mind the long-legged imperial vehicles in George Lucas's movie *The Empire Strikes Back*. The region has a long history as a maritime and naval hub—a world-class port and center of seagoing commerce. This transportation infrastructure promoted economic growth but also affected the environment, especially as larger and heavier ships sought to enter a naturally shallow bay.

The Port of Oakland invested in hulking dockside and rail-mounted cranes in the 1960s. It also dredged deeper berths, hired more crane operators and longshoremen, and embraced its future as one of the top five intermodal ports in the nation, moving shipping containers among boats, trains, and trucks. The Ports of San Francisco, Richmond, and Redwood City also continued to expand and modernize their maritime facilities, as did the navy, on 21 bases around the bay.

Traffic on the bay grew busier. Tugs and dredgers worked to keep the ports and marinas from silting up. Bar pilots guided giant oil tankers, container vessels, and cruise ships in through the narrows, fogs, and shoals of the Golden Gate, and longshoremen loaded and unloaded containers and cargoes. Coast Guard crews rescued vessels, surfers, and swimmers in distress, and responded to oil spills and wayward whales. Local marinas and yacht clubs grew to support a spurt in recreational boating and sailing.

Today, the bay floats vessels of every stripe. More than 1,000 commercial fishing boats consider the bay home port. Speedboats, sailboats, kayaks, and windsurfers also ply these waters for pleasure, steered and paddled by some 225,000 recreational boaters. Four thousand commercial ships move in and out of the bay's harbors annually, and cruise ships often brighten San Francisco's piers with their white flanks and twinkling lights.

The bay and delta's reliance on water for commerce, recreation, and transportation endures to this day. But in the 1960s, associated maritime

A ship equipped to load diverse cargoes—"breakbulk"—in its holds. The port of San Francisco hosts the bay's primary breakbulk facilities. (Francis Parchaso)

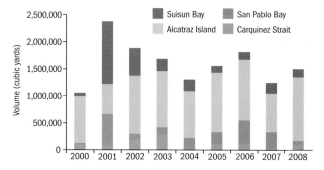

Figure 11. Annual volume of dredged material disposed of in the bay between 2000 and 2008. In recent years, more than one million cubic yards of material have been deposited by bay dredgers at four disposal sites, while more is taken out to the ocean. (S.F. Estuary Institute)

dredging activities began to generate some serious environmental problems. At that time, operators dredged whenever necessary to prevent vessels from running aground in at least 17 locations around the bay. Most of the dredge spoils were dumped back in the bay somewhere else.

With the Clean Water Act and the creation of the San Francisco Bay Conservation and Development Commission, local regulators began to examine the environmental impacts of dredging more closely. They calculated that in the 1980s, two million to five million cubic yards of sediment were being cleared from the bay bottom each year for maintenance purposes alone. Surveys also showed that a lot of the material cleared from channels was simply washing right back into them.

To get a better handle on the problem, the U.S. Army Corps of Engineers decided to centralize disposal at three sites: one in San Pablo Bay, one in the Carquinez Strait, and one off Alcatraz Island. They chose sites in the main channels of the bay, thinking that high-velocity flows would sweep the dredged material out the Golden Gate. The approach seemed fine until the mid-1980s, when an inbound ship suddenly found itself grounded in the middle of bay, its depth finder flashing "0." A 72-foot-high mound of dredge "spoil" had accumulated just 30 feet below the water surface at the Alcatraz dump site.

Planner Steve Goldbeck, who worked on bay commission permitting for dredging and disposal at the time, speculates that the mound may have been the result of a shift in dredge spoil types. Instead of the "fluffy" sediments generated by maintenance dredging, dredges were now biting into the denser, heavier material that makes up sediment bedding planes—sediments that were far more difficult for waves to disperse. These were generated by a spate of port and military deepening projects.

The hidden mound ignited a local firestorm, Goldbeck says. "Dumps from all the big projects just kept piling up at Alcatraz, one on top of the other, with no time for dispersion and lots of turbidity. So we had a disposal capacity problem right when Oakland needed deepening for the bigger ships, with fishermen getting upset about turbidity, and environmentalists worried about toxics in the material getting back into the bay."

John Beuttler of United Anglers commented at the time: "They were dumping in the Bay every 30 minutes. Even charter fishing boats with the most sophisticated electronic equipment couldn't find bait fish or Striped Bass or halibut. . . . Party boat captains consistently reported [brown outs] blanketing Central and San Pablo Bays . . . for days."

A "mudlock" developed—no one could agree on the right place to put the dredged material without hurting somebody or something. Various management initiatives failed. The big carriers grew impatient with the dredging impasse, dubbed the bay an "inefficient harbor," and started looking for deeper harbors to accommodate their maritime mammoths.

Eventually, however, warring mudslingers worked out a strategy that continues to this day. Most of the dredged material is now dumped outside the Golden Gate in deeper waters off the continental shelf, at much higher transportation cost. Much of the rest of the material is being put to greener use. These include caps for old landfills or brown fields, as well as new material to raise the elevation of lands subsided behind dikes and restore wetlands (see p. 252, "The Marin Shore"). And dredging can only occur during specific windows of time when schools of herring and other sensitive species are not around.

With the military retiring many of its shoreline berths and shipyards, and less sediment coming into the bay from upstream, the need for dredging has diminished. At the same time, scientists project that the region's wetlands will be needing more, rather than less, sediment to keep up with future rising sea levels. Thus the practice of taking what remains of the bay's sediment supply out to ocean dump sites may change (see p. 246, "Key Ingredients: A Wetland Recipe" and p. 285, "Climate Change and the Bay's Future").

A Place for Wetlands and Wildlife

Barbara Salzman, a seasoned Marin Audubon Society activist with a gruff Philadelphia accent, has been saving wetlands long enough to know just about everyone who owns a scrap of marsh, hayfield, or open space along her county's shore. Her stories evoke the first eras of the wetland crusades, when most people still thought of baylands as swamps—better off drained than left to the tides. She shakes her head over one recalcitrant rancher who wouldn't sell, and kept pumping away the ponded rainwater on his grazing fields rather than leaving it for birds and wildlife. She remembers acquiring another small marsh with two phone calls. She has cleaned invasive water hyacinths out of freshwater pools and handpicked pellets of Styrofoam out of a newly created slough channel where the backhoe disturbed some old garbage. And she has probably read thousands of pages of environmental impact reports to save wetlands from being transformed into waterfront condo complexes, malls, and golf courses. She has won these battles by bringing to light how many Clapper Rail nests or acres of foraging grounds or pickleweed would be lost if the bulldozers were to be let loose on various historic baylands.

"Back in the 1970s, everyone wanted to save the pretty ridge tops, so most of the priority areas for preservation were uplands. We felt the bay shore and wetlands were being neglected, and decided to do something about it," says Salzman.

With so little left of them around the bay and in the delta, wetlands certainly needed the attention. By the 1970s, shorebirds and waterfowl, Harvest Mice, and Clapper Rails had lost 90 percent of their historic wetland habitats. Foxes, rats, raccoons, and cats began to invade their habitats via levee tops to hunt birds and mice. Hawks found new perches on power pylons from which to scout the marsh for delicacies. Contaminants began to concentrate in wetlands and waterways draining agricultural

Arrowhead Marsh on the East Bay shore. (Drew Kerr)

fields and urban landscapes. Indeed, birds associated with water seemed to be suffering most from the onslaught of development all around the bay and in the Central Valley. Bay waterfowl populations dropped to a record low of 89,863 birds in 1995 (far below pre-1900s highs in the range of 300,000).

Concerned about waning wildlife and fisheries nationwide, the federal government passed legislation to preserve endangered species in 1966. California followed with its own version in 1970. Clapper Rails, terns, and trout were among the first bay species listed as at risk in California. Since then, state and federal laws have continued to protect species from extinction in tandem. Between 1970 and 2010, the number of listed plant and animal species found within or around California's coast grew from 32 to 177 (see also p. 183, "Mini Guide: Species in Peril"). Wetlands sustain 23 of the 32 species of wildlife declining in the estuary basin.

Around the bay, the fight to save the Salt Marsh Harvest Mouse and its neighbor the California Clapper Rail has eclipsed all others. Three hundred years ago, these animals lived in tidal marshes that stretched broad and unbroken all around the bay. Uniquely adapted to this salty environment, the mouse evolved to become an agile swimmer and to eat the seeds and shoots of halophytes. Whenever possible, it stayed dry by clambering from stem to stem within its knee-high forest and weaving grass nests within pickleweed boughs. Only the highest tides and lush summer grasses could draw it into adjacent meadows.

The rail, meanwhile, stalked through the marsh in search of worms and clams, mussels and snails, spiders and the mouse. It disappeared easily into the thickets of cordgrass and pickleweed. At dawn and dusk, its clattering call mixed with the cries of gulls and shorebirds.

Today, the daily activities of these two species may be the same, but their environment is quite different. A jumbled matrix of salt ponds, dikes, condos, roads, and riprap now surround and divide the remaining marshes. Once-wide stretches of pickleweed and gum plant are now narrow strips along the steep sides of levees. Avenues of escape, dispersal, and cover for both species during high tides are scarce. In some areas, treated sewage discharge has freshened this once-salty world and shifted its vegetation mix. The mouse cannot use these freshwater plants as habitat.

The mouse can still be found in the marshes around Mare Island and the sloughs east of Palo Alto and Mountain View, though sightings are unlikely at best. The rail has hardly fared better. Between 1971and 2008, their estuary populations dropped from as many as 6,000 to as low as 500 birds. The decline stems from a combination of habitat loss and intensified predation. The rail can still be seen and heard every day off the wooden boardwalk at Martin Luther King, Jr. Shoreline, though it also lives in other bay marshes.

Bay Area species on state and federal threatened and endangered lists.

Not all species of concern can be covered here, and the list changes with political and environmental conditions. Other sensitive bay–delta species currently include the Sacramento Spittail, Longfin Smelt, the Suisun thistle, and the San Francisco Garter Snake, to name a few.

Black Rail. (Danika Tsao)

California Black Rail (*Laterallus jamaicensis coturniculus*) A diminutive black bird with a round, red eye and cinnamon back dotted with white speckles, the California Black Rail is on California's list of threatened species. In the estuary, it is primarily found in San Pablo and Suisun bays in large marshes closer to water a good distance from urban areas. Fragmentation and degradation of its salt marsh habitat have substantially reduced its original range. YEAR STATE LISTED: 1971 SIZE: 6 inches POPULATION IN SF BAY, 1988: 600 CURRENT POPULATION IN SF BAY: 600

California Clapper Rail. (Max Eissler)

California Clapper Rail (*Rallus longirostris obsoletus*) This stocky shorebird picks its way through stands of cordgrass, gum plant, and pickleweed in search of snails, mussels, and other invertebrates. Both individuals and groups may emit bursts of the clattering calls for which it is named. Sturdy dun-colored legs and rust-red cheek plumage distinguish this species from its smaller relative, the Virginia Rail. The elimination of much of its marsh habitat has drastically reduced the rail's populations. YEAR LISTED: 1970 SIZE: 14.5 inches POPULATION AT LISTING: 500 POPULATION TODAY: 500–1400

California Freshwater Shrimp (*Syncaris pacifica*) The only 10-legged shrimp in California that occurs in nonsaline waters, this shrimp camouflages its translucent body with chromatophores that help it blend into the streambed environment. It appears to frequent areas with undercut stream banks, exposed roots, or overhanging woody debris or vegetation. Currently found in 17 perennial stream segments within Sonoma, Napa, and Marin counties, its limited range puts it at risk of extirpation. However, it can still be found in selected reaches of Lagunitas and Olema creeks. YEAR LISTED: 1988 SIZE: 2.2 inches POPULATION: unknown

California Least Tern (*Sterna antillarum browni*) Orange-yellow legs and bill plus a black cap with white forehead distinguish this bird from other terns diving into surface waters to catch smelt and anchovy. Though human disturbances have spoiled many of the open beach areas where these members of the gull family prefer to nest, a well-protected breeding colony on the Alameda Wildlife Refuge now hatches up to one-half of all Least Tern fledglings in

California Least Tern. (Max Eissler)

the state. YEAR LISTED: 1970 SIZE: 9 inches POPULATION AT LISTING: ~300–1200 pairs POPULATION TODAY: 2,500 in 1995; as many as 13,000 today

California Red-legged Frog (*Rana draytonii*) In "The Celebrated Jumping Frog of Calaveras County" by Mark Twain, a California Red-legged Frog outjumps the competition thanks to a little skullduggery and buckshot. This largest of North America's native frogs once inhabited cool, deep pools throughout the mountains and foothills of the Bay Area as well as up and down the state. How-ever, heavy harvesting for San Francisco

California Red-legged Frog. (Chris Brown)

dinner tables in the late nineteenth century, the loss of foothill ponds and wetlands to cattle grazing and city blocks, and the arrival of new predators including non-native fish and the North American Bullfrog have drastically reduced their former range. YEAR LISTED: 1996 SIZE: 1.75–5.25 inches POPULATION: unknown

Chinook Salmon, winter-run (*Oncorhynchus tshawytscha*) Also known as King Salmon for their majestic size—up to 85 pounds—most winter-run Chinook generally return from the ocean from November through April to fight their way up the Sacramento River and reproduce. As recently as the 1960s, more than 100,000 winter-run Chinook Salmon returned to the mainstem Sacramento River to spawn; by 1991, degraded stream habitat and migration obstructions such as dams had reduced the run to just an estimated 211 fish. YEAR OF FEDERAL LISTING: 1990, listed as threatened; 1994, uplisted to endangered YEAR OF STATE LISTING: 1989, listed as endangered SIZE: averages 33–36 inches, up to 58 inches POPULATION WHEN LISTED: 696 POPULATION IN 2009: 4,500

Chinook Salmon. (Doug Killiam)

Delta Smelt (*Hypomesus transpacificus*) (Photo, p. 206) Once among the most abundant fish in the San Joaquin–Sacramento Delta, populations of these slender blue-grey smelt have crashed to the point where they face imminent extinction. A combination of factors—including altered freshwater releases through the delta, entrainment by pumps moving water to southern California, competition with alien fish species, and even falling plankton populations—are all suspected to have hastened this fish's decline. However, they can still be found in surface and shoal waters from the lower reaches of the Sacramento River below Isleton out into Suisun Bay. YEAR LISTED: 1993 SIZE: 2–3 inches POPULATION AT LISTING: 8.2 fish per trawl on average POPULATION 2009: 0.3 fish per trawl on average

Greater Sandhill Crane (*Grus canadensis tabida*) A crimson cap, pearly grey body plumage, and long, long legs make the elegant figure of the state's tallest bird unmistakable during winter breeding season. They are most commonly seen in the open fields of the San Joaquin Delta, often in large flocks. Their exuberant courtship dance involves reciprocal leaps, wing flaps, and trilling cries. Loss of

Greater Sandhill Cranes. (Max Eissler)

wetlands due to agriculture, water diversion, and other development projects is the primary cause of their population decline. YEAR LISTED (STATE THREATENED): 1993 SIZE: 46 inches tall POPULATION AT LISTING: unknown POPULATION TODAY: 6,000–6,800

Green Sturgeon (*Acipenser medirostris*) This largest of California's freshwater fish looks every inch the Jurassic era throwback it is. Bony plates of armor on its back and a vacuum-hose mouth only add to the alien specter of its man-sized frame. Yet 200 million years of evolution were not enough to prepare the Green Sturgeon for its encounter with industrial-age humans. The one-two

Green Sturgeon. (Matt Manuel)

punch of overfishing and dams installed on its spawning streams reduced the southern distinct population segment, which spawns solely in the Sacramento River system, by 96 percent between 2000 and 2006. YEAR LISTED: 2006 SIZE: 6.5–7.2 feet STATUS: threatened POPULATION SIZE: unknown POPULATION TODAY: unknown

Lange's Metalmark Butterfly (*Apodemia mormo langei*) With fiery orange forewings and black dorsal wings speckled with white, Lange's Metalmark Butterfly cuts a dashing figure as it flits above the sands of the Antioch Dunes National Wildlife Refuge. Adults feed on nectar from several types of dune wildflowers, but they lay their eggs exclusively on leaves of naked stemmed buckwheat—the only food their larvae will eat. A century of sand mining and

Lange's Metalmark Butterfly. (U.S. Fish and Wildlife Service)

industrial development at the confluence of the Sacramento and San Joaquin rivers has diminished the butterfly's habitat, while nonnative vegetation has stabilized the shifting sands its host buckwheat needs to propagate. Today, Lange's Metalmark Butterfly is found almost exclusively within the dunes' refuge borders. YEAR LISTED (FEDERALLY ENDANGERED): 1976 SIZE: wingspan of 1–1.5 inches POPULATION IN 1986: <200 POPULATION TODAY: several thousand

Salt Marsh Harvest Mouse (*Reithrodontomys raviventris*) About the length of a human thumb and weighing less than a nickel, the Salt Marsh Harvest Mouse eats the salty leaves and seeds of tidal marsh plants, then washes it all down with sips of brackish seawater. Secretive and almost never seen, it prefers the dense cover of pickleweed stands and generally emerges only at night. Its numbers have

Salt Marsh Harvest Mouse. (Department of Water Resources)

declined due to the destruction of its salt marsh habitat, which may be contributing to genetic stagnation among the predominantly smaller populations. YEAR LISTED: 1970 SIZE: 4.6–7 inches, including tail; body, 2.4–3 inches POPULATION: unknown

Soft bird's beak. (Jude Stalker)

Soft bird's beak (*Cordylanthus mollis ssp. mollis*) A member of the snapdragon family with red-tinged greyish foliage, and pointy clusters of white to yellowish flowers, soft bird's beak is semiparasitic and can obtain nutrients from the roots of other marsh plants. Freshwater withdrawals upstream from the delta have made much of the plant's former habitat in Suisun Marsh too salty for this plant to tolerate, a problem exacerbated by development, habitat fragmentation, and the spread of invasive plants. YEAR LISTED: 1997 SIZE: 10–16 inches tall POPULATION SIZE: fluctuates considerably from year to year. One population on Joice Island had 1,000 plants in 1991, 7,650 in 1993, and 150 in 1999 SITE OCCURRENCES: 14 occurrences in Solano County, but one since extirpated at Mare Island

Western Snowy Plover. (Caitlin Nilsen)

Western Snowy Plover (*Charadrius alexandriunus nivosus*) Grey or black side patches rather than a full band around the throat, grey legs, and a thin black bill distinguish this federally threatened plover from its North American relatives. In the estuary, it frequents the mudflats, salt ponds, levees, and evaporation pond edges of the South Bay, where it snaps up small crabs, Brine Flies, and other invertebrates. Its habit of nesting in pebble-lined scrapes on beaches has left it vulnerable to predation and nest disturbance by dogs, joggers, and hikers. YEAR LISTED: 1973 SIZE: 6.25 inches POPULATION AT LISTING: unknown POPULATION TODAY: 2,300

Tidal flat
Tidal marsh
Salt pond
Deep bay/Channel
Shallow bay/Channel

~1850

Map 9. Map of historic wetland habitats around San Francisco Bay, circa 1850.
(Data from S.F. Estuary Institute, redrawn courtesy of S.F. Bay Joint Venture)

Efforts to save these and other species from extinction—and to support remaining bird, fish, and mammal populations around the watershed—eventually evolved into a battle to preserve their last remaining wild habitats, and later to restore and create new ones (see pp. 209 and 237, "Restoration Frontiers"). In the North Bay, the first sparks in the wetland preservation battle came from duck hunters, who favored dabbling ducks

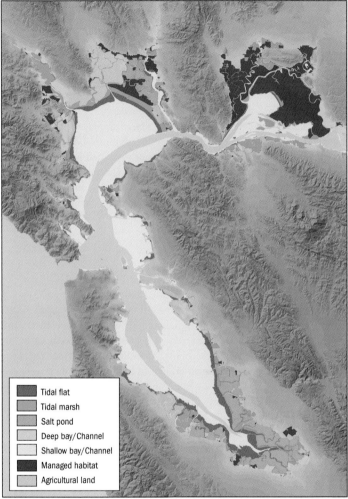

Tidal flat
Tidal marsh
Salt pond
Deep bay/Channel
Shallow bay/Channel
Managed habitat
Agricultural land

~2000

Map 10. Map of current wetland habitats around San Francisco Bay, circa 2000. (Data from S.F. Estuary Institute, redrawn courtesy of S.F. Bay Joint Venture)

and seasonal ponds over tidal marshes, and who eventually succeeded in state lobbying to create a Suisun Marsh protection area in and around 150 private clubs.

Elsewhere around the bay, as Save the Bay's campaign against fill gathered steam, concerned residents began trying to stop construction on the bayshore and to defend tidal marshes. Championed by Congressman Don

Edwards, these early initiatives helped create the country's first urban wildlife refuge in 1974 and fueled its eventual expansion. It now consists of six areas and 40,000 acres that encompass open bay, salt pond, salt marsh, mudflat, upland, dune, and vernal pool habitats. Eventually, the refuge was named in honor of Edwards.

In addition, dozens of local park districts, open space groups, land trusts, and nonprofits have collaborated with the California Department of Fish and Game, the U.S. Fish and Wildlife Service, and the California Coastal Conservancy to acquire and maintain the last remaining open spaces and vestigial habitats along the estuary's shores. As a result, there are currently over 121,000 acres of wetlands protected by parks, refuges, and preserves in the estuary basin. Within all these habitats, regulators also set "no-work windows." During sensitive times, such as when endangered species are reproducing, these windows forbid construction activities or disturbance.

Warring over Water

Since its postwar population boom, California has never had enough water to go around. By the 1960s, demand for water had grown so great that the vast federal and local water project infrastructure built before World War II (see p. 138, "Controlling Water Supply and Floods") had to be much more closely managed. So as not to run short, engineers and water districts had to juggle water supplies, maintain levees, and work to accommodate seasonal fluctuations in supply and demand. California's daily manipulation of nearly every drop of fresh water that fell from the skies or melted into reservoirs from the snowpack had begun.

California decided that the federal Central Valley Water Project—and smaller municipal projects built on the Mokelumne and Tuolumne rivers in the 1930s and 1940s—did not provide enough water for the growing Golden State. In 1959, it gave the official go-ahead for the largest state-built, multipurpose water project in the United States. The resulting State Water Project (SWP) now delivers over two million acre feet of water in an average year, gathered from the Feather River in the Sacramento Valley and piped to urban, industrial, and agricultural consumers as far as 600 miles away from its three Sierra reservoirs and the Oroville Dam. When full, this 770-foot-tall dam—which looms taller than the towers of the Golden Gate Bridge—can trap up to 3.5 million acre feet of water spread over 15,000 acres. That's a cubic mile of water behind one dam.

Since 1960, SWP has built 29 dams, 18 pumping plants, 5 hydroelectric

Water pumps at Tracy. (Department of Water Resources)

power plants, and 600 miles of canals and pipelines. These include the 444-mile-long California aqueduct, a straight blue ribbon that crisscrosses the golden grass and desert along Interstate 5. The SWP went on-line between 1968 and 1972. The project delivers water to two-thirds of Californians today.

Seeking still more supply and efficiency, California expanded the other water management behemoth in the heart of the state. Between 1950 and 1990, California added hundreds more miles of aqueducts to the Central Valley Project, and in the 1970s covered 25,000 acres with two huge new reservoirs (New Don Pedro and New Melones). By the late 1970s, there were 1,251 reservoirs in California, many on rivers or creeks that drained into the bay.

Altogether, the state's largest diversions—as well as 1,800 smaller agricultural diversions in the delta—remove about two-thirds of the fresh water that had historically flowed out through the bay and to the sea each year. With all of these facilities to catch and move water, California's landscape became a patchwork of startling green orange groves next to semi-arid deserts, turquoise swimming pools amid hot sand and cactus, grey freeways snaking through palm-lined malls, and red-roofed homes with backyard koi ponds, where coyotes can eat Japanese every night.

"California's very existence is premised on epic liberties taken with water—mostly water that fell as rain [and snow] in the north and was diverted to the south, thus precipitating the state's longest running political wars," wrote author Marc Reisner in *Cadillac Desert*. "Virtually every drop of water in the state is put to some economic use before being allowed to return to sea." Indeed, many people still think that fresh water allowed to make its way all the way through the delta to the bay and Pacific is "wasted."

With all the new water facilities on-line, feuds began to brew between historical water rights holders upstream who had been taking water out of neighboring creeks and rivers for decades, and downstream users who wanted to divert more water elsewhere or out of the system altogether. These conflicts and increasing demand inspired more public scrutiny of water projects. Rivalries developed between major state and federal agencies over control of the water. Fishermen and environmentalists began fighting to claim part of the water supply for salmon and other estuary species.

The extent of California's water diversion system was bound to affect the fish. Not only did the dams block salmon from returning to their historical spawning grounds in stream and river headwaters, but upstream

---

LEVEES UNDONE

Levees surround and make much of California's critical water-supply infrastructure possible. These ramparts also prevent flooding of subsided delta and bay lands. But no matter how strong or how tall the levees, floods continue to overrun the Central Valley. In 1982–1983, more than four times the average volume of runoff passed through state rivers, bursting through levees on three islands. In 1986, 650,000 cubic feet per second of water surged past the city of Sacramento, enough in one day to meet the household needs of three million to five million people. The surge breached levees on five islands. During that year floods on all the major tributaries forced 50,000 people to evacuate their homes in the valley, caused $150 million in damage, and killed a dozen unfortunate people who happened to be in the wrong place at the wrong time. Since 1990, winter floods have caused several major levee breaches in the delta. Today, maintenance of delta and riverfront levees has evolved into a Herculean responsibility, one that flood control agencies have been unable to keep up with. Any day now, an earthquake—or, in the coming years of sea level rise, a storm surge from runoff or tides—could leave many low points in the watershed looking like New Orleans after Hurricane Katrina.

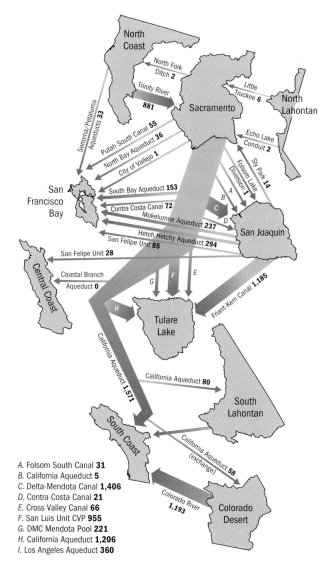

North Coast

North Fork Ditch **2**

Trinity River **881**

Sacramento

Little Truckee **6**

North Lahontan

Echo Lake Conduit **2**

Sonoma/Petaluma Aqueducts **33**

Putah South Canal **55**

North Bay Aqueduct **36**

City of Vallejo **1**

Sly Park **14**

Folsom Lake Diversion **1**

San Francisco Bay

South Bay Aqueduct **153**

Contra Costa Canal **72**

Mokelumne Aqueduct **237**

Hetch Hetchy Aqueduct **294**

San Felipe Unit **85**

A

B

C

D

San Joaquin

San Felipe Unit **28**

Central Coast

Coastal Branch Aqueduct **0**

G

F

E

Friant-Kern Canal **1,185**

H

Tulare Lake

California Aqueduct **80**

South Lahontan

California Aqueduct **1,571**

California Aqueduct (exchange) **58**

South Coast

A. Folsom South Canal **31**
B. California Aqueduct **5**
C. Delta-Mendota Canal **1,406**
D. Contra Costa Canal **21**
E. Cross Valley Canal **66**
F. San Luis Unit CVP **955**
G. DMC Mendota Pool **221**
H. California Aqueduct **1,206**
I. Los Angeles Aqueduct **360**

Colorado River **1,193**

Colorado Desert

Map 11. Regional water imports and exports in thousands of acre feet per year as of 1995 level of development. (Redrawn from California Department of Water Resources 1998, and Carle 2004)

areas now lacked enough water and gravel for the salmon to build their redds (a gravel "nest"). Elsewhere in the watershed, salmon and other fish suffered from high water temperatures, reversed flows on rivers as the state sent water south, and "entrainment" (getting caught up and/or killed) in pumps and unscreened water diversions. More than twenty million fish are drawn into state and federal pumping plants every year.

In the first half of the 1990s, Chinook Salmon and Delta Smelt were both placed on the federal threatened and endangered species list. The listings brought the needs of fish into conflict with big cities and big business. Californians of every kind went to war over water. In general, the war has raged among a triangle of three powerful interests, according to author John Hart: "On one side of the triangle are the demands of San Joaquin Valley agriculture, which seeks always to have as much water as possible pumped south. . . . On the second side are the state's burgeoning urban regions. They need water too, and in the past have often lined up alongside farmers in support of more dams and diversions. . . . On the triangle's third side are people whose interests somehow lie with a healthier bay–delta estuary [including fishermen, scientists, environmental groups, hunters, recreationists]. . . . These various people want more water, or anyway not one drop less, to flow westward toward the

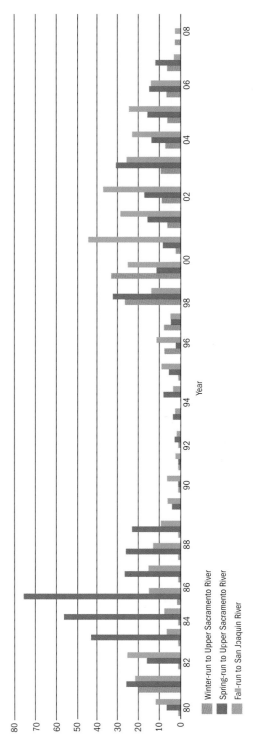

Figure 12. Salmon runs of concern in thousands of adult fish returning to spawn. (S.F. Estuary Partnership)

sea. They want diversions out of the watershed in general—and out of the Delta in particular—to be curtailed."

The question of whether the Endangered Species Act could trump farmers and cities concerned about their water supply came to a head in the early 1990s. The debate roared around whether the state should issue a "flow standard," specifying a certain amount of water to be released at sensitive times of year for fish, and whether the federal government would force the issue. Adversaries eventually came to agreement through a series of accords, lawsuits, and legislative initiatives. Among these was the Bay–Delta Accord of 1994. The accord, which created the interagency CALFED Bay–Delta Program, required that those managing water supplies and enforcing fish protections shepherd supplies for the benefit of all uses. The accord also set a state water standard that would maintain certain levels of salinity in a critical estuarine mixing zone around Suisun Bay, in lieu of mandating specific quantities of flow out to sea (see p. 219, "Water Rights for the Ecosystem").

Another milestone in the water wars, the Central Valley Project Improvement Act of 1992, forced the giant federal waterworks to dedicate a certain percentage of its annual yield to the restoration of fisheries and wetlands. It also called for a doubling of anadromous fish populations by 2002, though implementation was delayed by years of lawsuits.

"This is a starved estuary," says Gary Bobker of The Bay Institute, whose organization has been a tireless champion of the most dewatered and disenfranchised parts of the watershed. "We've radically altered its hydrograph. And even larger scale changes are being planned upstream. If we make changes upstream, there will not only be consequences for the delta but also in the bay, the ocean, the rest of the ecosystem. It all comes down to the connectivity of an estuary."

The larger-scale changes Bobker refers to include the latest version of a peripheral canal. Water managers have long proposed such a canal to connect the upper Sacramento River and its fresh water directly to the giant supply pumps at Tracy, bypassing the delta and all its fish, tidal incursions, and turf wars. Californians rejected several versions of the canal, most recently a 400-foot-wide trench version proposed in 1982. A stumpier minicanal was proposed in 2007 and, more recently, some pipelines and tunnels that might be less disruptive to local landowners. Whatever the physical format, engineers claim it will not only solve saltwater intrusion problems once and for all but perhaps even help the fish.

More delta visions and conservation plans seem to get created every year. Politics, as always, drives water management in California in cycles far too short to ever fully embrace the longer cycles at play in the state's climate, rivers, bays, and ocean waters.

Caring for Urban Creeks

The quest to pave streets, build houses, control flooding, and provide safe drinking water has changed many Bay Area creeks almost beyond recognition.

Once, interactions among soil, water, and vegetation helped creek watersheds absorb the flood flows produced by storms. In some areas, for example, live oaks and other perennial trees held raindrops in their canopies for many hours. The leaves held rain like a sponge, preventing the surge of water from overwhelming streambeds. Fungal filaments and the roots of native grasses held soils together and leaf litter roughened the surface, slowing flows. Overflows pooled in freshwater marshes.

Changes began when the Spanish introduced ranching to the California landscape. As densities of cattle, goats, and horses expanded under American management, they trampled the riparian vegetation holding creek banks in place, compacted the ground with their hooves, and devoured the fallen leaves that once sheltered the soil.

Wetlands engineer Jeff Haltiner of Philip Williams Associates recalls visiting gulches in Monterey County where only deer had ventured for at least 150 years: "There was a foot of duff, pine needles, and oak tree leaves. When it rained, you'd never see the water run off the surface of the ground. It just went into this whole matrix like a sponge." By contrast, he says, the

A rain garden at Brisbane City Hall funnels urban runoff laden with oil and contaminants into a living filtration system made of plants and soil. (Matt Fabry)

cattle-grazed grasslands of Contra Costa County "are like walking on concrete. The water runs off the landscape like it's practically pavement."

Settlers made conditions worse by diking the marshes that once absorbed overflows. Then urbanization began paving over soils, leaving water fewer places to slow and seep into the ground.

Overloaded creeks incised (cut deeper) or burst their banks to accommodate the torrents from storms, setting off a domino effect of further erosion, bank undercutting, and channel deepening. This damage sent the network of trees and other riparian plants that once held the soil in place tumbling downstream. Stream waters filled with dirt and debris, muddying fish spawning habitat and clouding the bay. Alarmed at their crumbling stream banks, both individuals and communities sought to armor creeks against the water's assault.

By the twentieth century, local flood control districts and the Army Corps of Engineers were routinely demolishing natural stream reaches in favor of earthen or concrete channels, which were thought to reduce the risk of flooding to neighborhoods and businesses built on natural floodplains. Smaller versions of the Los Angeles River setting for car chases in movies like *Grease*, these channels were designed to deliver water downstream in the fastest, most efficient manner possible.

Unfortunately, poorly planned projects that put creeks in artificial channels and armor their banks tend to worsen rather than prevent flooding. Development has virtually eliminated places for rivers to spill over their banks and spread out. The construction of dams and reservoirs at the headwaters of local creeks has further altered water flow patterns. In a storm, natural creeks experience a gradual increase in flows that peter out over many hours. But creeks encased in artificial channels swell rapidly to torrent strength in heavy rains, then slacken to nearly average levels within a brief span of time. Gone is the "sustained tail" seen in natural creek flows that may have mediated flooding, pushed out channel obstructions, and rinsed the mud from gravel beds used by spawning salmon and trout.

Summer conditions along creeks are equally distorted from their original state. The region's Mediterranean climate, marked by a long stretch of rainless months, once dried up many creek reaches from midsummer to late fall. Now, many previously intermittent streams receive reservoir releases (for fish) and urban runoff all summer long—remodeling vegetation and stream ecology.

"The Bay Area is very diverse in terms of geology, rainfall, and climate. So it's not a surprise that streams would look so different in different places, but this variety is masked by urbanization and homogenization. Every stream winds up being, at best, a narrow channel with some trees along it," says historical ecologist Robin Grossinger of the San Francisco Estuary Institute.

Virtually all of the estuary's historic tributaries have been modified, some almost beyond recognition. In Berkeley, at least two waterways— Derby and Potter—have disappeared entirely. No visible surface traces remain of these "ghost" creeks. "All of their topography was bulldozed flat," according to aquatic biologist Christopher Richard of the Oakland Museum of California. What little remains of Derby Creek today is a short reach on UC Berkeley's Clark Kerr Campus, and intermittent seeps and springs.

Residents once cared deeply about the health of their local creeks because they were essential for human survival. Creeks supplied all of the water needed for drinking, washing, livestock, or industry. As Bay Area populations swelled, cities and counties secured faraway sources of water to slake their thirst. Access to these distant water supplies nearly severed the age-old connection between creeks and communities.

In recent decades, people have begun to rediscover the value of their local creeks to humans, wildlife, and the health of the bay. Starting in the early 1980s with the "daylighting" of culverted Strawberry Creek in Berkeley, an increasing number of ordinary people have become activists on behalf of their creek and its watershed. Today, nearly every creek has a nonprofit friends group that defends creek interests. These organizations conduct regular trash cleanups, replace invasive exotic plants with native species, and help return neglected waterways to central importance in their neighborhoods. Friends of creeks groups also agitate to daylight buried streams and remove dams that stymie Steelhead runs, as well as negotiate for more ecology-friendly flood control or erosion projects.

Within the next two decades, scientists say, the historic links between the bay and its creeks will become increasingly important. As sea level rises with global climate change, storm surges and overflows in the bay will find their historic inlets, inundating creek mouths, shoreline culverts, and sewer outfalls in the process. Restoring the absorbent qualities of natural creek mouths, alluvial fans, and wetlands may play a pivotal role in the Bay Area's ability to adapt to sea level rise, and underscores the need to reconsider urban creeks as a part of the larger watershed (see p. 225, "Reviving Bay Creeks").

Preventing Invasions

The language of biological invasions mimics that of primetime police dramas. Rapid response teams armed with bioweapons scramble to tackle alien species. Such scenarios are an unfortunate reality in the bay. Foreign species of every aquatic kind—from Chinese Clams and Japanese Snails to

Brazilian plants and Black Sea Jellyfish—continue to arrive and settle in San Francisco Bay. Some do little harm or never gain a foothold in the local ecosystem, but others can wreak havoc and spread quickly from the point of introduction. A single individual of these species may produce thousands of seeds, yield masses of larvae, or reproduce from bits of roots and stems. Whatever their origin, they aren't likely to find their natural predators in their adopted home.

Bay Area locals first noticed how devastating a bioinvasion could be as early as 1913, when the wood-boring Naval Shipworm arrived from the Atlantic Ocean. The worm (actually a clam), riddled 50 major wharves, ferry slips, and other structures in the North Bay with its thumbtack-top-sized holes. Other exotic organisms had already arrived in Gold Rush ships, and locals had begun farming eastern oysters and introduced Striped Bass and American Shad for sport fishing. But the Shipworm was one of the first exotics to cause significant damage to human property around the bay.

Scientist Jim Carlton was the first to raise the alarm about bioinvasions in the Bay Area in the 1970s. Carlton, a marine ecology professor, came from Williams College in Massachusetts. By 1998, he and local scientist Andrew Cohen had identified a total of 234 exotic species and 125 crypto-genic species (of unknown origin) that had established themselves in the bay–delta ecosystem. According to their work, the rate of invasions had accelerated from an average of one new species every 55 weeks between 1851 and 1960 to one every 14 weeks between 1961 and 1995.

As the most invaded estuary in the world, San Francisco Bay is now struggling not only with the Overbite Clam from Asia but also with Large-mouth Bass from the Mississippi eating the young of endangered salmon and Atlantic cordgrass hybridizing with its Pacific cousin (see p. 268, "Weeding by Satellite"). Meanwhile, upstream reservoirs, islands, rivers, and creeks are being choked out by invasive plants, and suffering from aquarium keepers dumping their former charges into the water.

Whereas the oysters and bass that early entrepreneurs ordered for aquaculture purposes traveled by rail, most accidental introductions have arrived by ship. Vessels taking up ballast water in one port and discharging it in another have delivered thousands of hitchhikers to San Francisco Bay, not to mention whole colonies of barnacles, mussels, limpets, and other species clamped to their hulls. Recreational boats also carry hitchhikers on travels from inland lakes and rivers to launch ramps in California. Fishing gear, surfboards, kayaks, and wetsuits often harbor exotics as well. The young larvae of many aquatic organisms are too small for the human eye to detect.

It took until the 1990s for concerned legislators to pass the first of a series of federal and state laws to regulate ballast water releases and to edu-

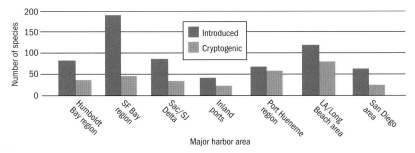

Figure 13. Number of nonindigenous taxa in seven major ports of California. *Cryptogenic* refers to unknown origin. (Office of Spill Prevention and Response, California Department of Fish and Game)

cate aquarium purveyors and buyers about not releasing their pets into the wild. Even the Clean Water Act classifies exotic organisms as biological "pollutants." But scientists say it is unclear whether these legislative measures, and subsequent vessel monitoring and public education, have made any dent in the problem. No studies have been done to confirm any change in the invasion rate. But more plans with good intentions have been completed in the form of California's first statewide aquatic invasive species management plan.

Invasive species displace, disrupt, and in some cases even consume the natives in their new habitats. Nationwide, about 400 of 958 species listed as threatened or endangered are considered at risk due to the impacts of non-native species. Non-natives contributed to 68 percent of fish extinctions in the United States in the past 100 years.

"If we care anything about having some semblance of native biodiversity or natural ecosystems, then this ongoing and almost wholesale re-

---

BALLAST EXCHANGE

Ships take on and discharge ballast water to balance their loads and control how high they ride in the water. When released, ballast water often introduces live organisms from one port into another. To prevent such alien imports to California waters, large vessels are now required to flush out and replace their ballast in the open ocean, typically beyond 200 nautical miles from land. Far fewer organisms live in the open ocean than in coastal waters, and those taken up in ballast are unlikely to thrive in the very different environmental conditions of the bay. Ships must document and report these "ballast exchanges," but only limited resources are dedicated to follow-up and enforcement. In the future, onboard or onshore treatment to kill alien organisms may become the preferred option.

placement of the native organisms in the bay with exotic organisms is probably the biggest threat we face, outweighing the threat from pollution, fishing, and climate change," says Andrew Cohen.

At this point, San Francisco Bay will never go entirely native—it would be impossible to rid the bay of its established invaders. Any attempt would involve poisoning the entire bay, and eradicating all of the natives in the process.

But parts of the bay ecosystem still sustain a fair number of their original native species. Some locales, habitats, or taxonomic groups may be completely dominated by exotic organisms, but others are not. For example, says Cohen, the nonanadromous fishes that most people catch with their fishing poles from bay piers are largely natives. Likewise, zooplankton communities in the Central and South Bay are much less altered than their counterparts in the fresher, lower-salinity waters around Suisun Bay. In terms of fish, the northern reaches of the delta retain more of the natural mix of species than southerly waters. So parts of the estuary ecosystem are still worth defending from invaders.

A Few Bad Actors

The delta's longest lived and most expensive invaders are exotic plants that clog waterways, snag propellers, and block fish passage. Perhaps the most familiar of these is the water hyacinth, *Eichhornia crassipes*. The hyacinth was introduced into the United States in 1884 as an ornamental plant for water gardens, where its floating, showy, lavender-blue flowers attracted many admirers. Able to double in size every 10 days in hot weather, water hyacinth is the world's fastest growing plant. Recent surveys indicate that by early summer, California's infestation can cover up to approximately 4,000 acres of the Sacramento–San Joaquin Delta.

To clear a path for boaters, the state Department of Boating and Waterways sprays the hyacinth with herbicides every year. The treatment kills about half of the hyacinth mass, but costs millions of dollars. Similar control programs are undertaken by the state Department of Food and Agriculture to kill hydrilla, purple loosestrife, giant salvinia, and alligatorweed, among other aquatic and wetland weeds. But the most insidious plant invader, likely introduced via an emptied aquarium, is *Egeria densa*. Also known as Brazilian elodea, this aquatic plant now infests approximately 12,000 acres of submerged delta habitat. *Egeria* changes the architecture of shallow water ecosystems, erecting walls between deepwater and intertidal habitat.

Invasive aquatic plants such as water hyacinth (shown here) and hydrilla (*Hydrilla verticillata*) clog waterways by growing in dense mats. The state sprays infestations to keep channels open. (Department of Boating and Waterways)

The battle against these and other plants is less about getting rid of the invaders than about containing and controlling them. Timing the sprayings to the plants' seasonal growth cycles, while minimizing side effects on sensitive species, is a fine art tweaked anew every year. The battle against exotic crabs, clams, and other critters is a tougher fight. Even targeted poisons don't seem that effective at fully eradicating problem species.

It has taken the construction of "Crabzilla"—an 18-foot-long traveling screen—to declog South Delta fish salvage facilities of the Chinese Mitten Crab, for example. But it will take much more than a big piece of metal to combat the Zebra Mussel, a native of the seas of Eastern Europe. After arriving in the Great Lakes region, this tiny invertebrate quickly spread to 20 states. Worse, it clogged water pipes, intakes, and cooling systems, shutting them down right and left. As a result, water managers from California to New York now view the Zebra Mussel as a "superorganism" that can live anywhere and survive anything.

No one really knows how the mussel got to a secluded reservoir near Hollister in Central California in 2008, though it probably came overland in the bilge water or hull crannies of a small boat towed behind a trailer from another state. The year before, the state had begun pulling out all the stops to prevent this from happening—setting up incident command posts, border inspections, traffic breaks, and quarantines—because biologists had discovered Quagga Mussels in the Colorado River aqueduct, and soon afterward in San Diego and Riverside counties using Colorado River water. Quagga Mussels are a close relative of the Zebra Mussel and almost equally feared as California invaders. Despite the state's measures, an angler fishing in the San Justo reservoir near Hollister reported landing a clump of Zebra Mussels in January 2008.

As luck would have it, this early detection of a small infestation was easily isolated and quickly quarantined. That would not be the case for invaders traveling down the Colorado River. If the response is rapid, enclosed reservoirs, lagoons, and lakes can be treated to eradicate offenders. Each target species and location may require a different approach. For the Northern Pike, a big fish, officials detonated underwater explosions and poisoned Frenchman Reservoir in the Sierra Nevada; for *Caulerpa taxifolia*, a type of algae from the aquarium trade, a combination of hand removal and bleach injections under floating tarps were needed to rid two southern California lagoons of the pest; for Zebra Mussels in a small reservoir, it was hoped that drawing the water level down and adding potash (a common fertilizer) would do the trick.

So far, no mussels have been found in the delta or the State Water Project, which delivers water all over California. According to Andrew Cohen, the Zebra Mussel, a fresh water organism, needs certain calcium and pH levels to survive—conditions that make most Sierra Nevada reservoirs inhospitable to the mussel, but that also might make the South Delta and San Joaquin River more vulnerable. Every organism, super or not, has its limits, according to Cohen.

While the Zebra Mussel could prove a big pain in water pipelines, Bay Area residents have been feeling another kind of irritation from an exotic invader—swimmer's itch. In recent years, kids and adults wading and swimming on one East Bay beach have been coming home with red rashes akin to poison oak. Scientists say the rashes are an immune response to a parasitic Trematode Worm hosted by an exotic Japanese Snail, and they hope to study the local outbreak.

Some exotic organisms are bad and others may be good, but most of them change or challenge the relationships and functions of the ecosystem. "We rely on these ecosystems for many different things, including fresh water, food, sport, and commerce. We've also invested a lot of research time learning how these ecosystems work so we can manage them for our benefit. These exotic organisms come in and change ecosystems virtually overnight, so they become completely unpredictable. These dramatic changes, coming one after another after another, have real costs to human society. We can do better. We just have to decide to focus on the problem before another 100 species colonize the bay," says Cohen.

Synergistic Problems

Invasive species are simply the latest in a series of assaults on the bay's native flora and fauna. First there was the wave of mining debris, then the rush of sewage and algae blooms, followed by the construction of all manner of barriers and channels with hard edges, as well as the pressures of heavy industry and urban development. Humanity even put a cherry on top—plastic.

Estuarine species might have withstood one of these assaults, or a couple, or perhaps even a mild dose of everything. But scientists no longer seem to feel sure about this causing that, or one thing leading to another. With water being the great connector, synergistic effects on the last remaining species and habitats are inevitable.

"There's a bunch of stressors out there naturally, like climate, and a bunch of stressors we've added, like toxins and invasive species and water exports," says EPA's fish czar Bruce Herbold. "If resilience has disappeared

---

WATER AND PARTNERSHIPS: THE GREAT CONNECTORS

A system as complex as the San Francisco estuary and delta cannot be managed without strong science and an open mind. There came a point in the bay's history when managers realized they needed not only local data gleaned from fieldwork in the region's own ecosystem but also input from diverse interests to tackle conflicts between water supply and environmental health. As a result, dozens of collaborative, multi-interest, or interagency initiatives emerged in the 1980s and 1990s. One of the first times public and private interests—from farmers to industrialists to environmentalists to water engineers—came to the same negotiating table to hash out some solutions was in 1988. The hundred-member group, gathered through the U.S. Environmental Protection Agency's San Francisco Estuary Project, did not shrink from the wars over wetland fill, species extinction, and development in sensitive floodplains and shorelines. The project was among the first to bring the term "estuary" into wide local usage, to fill gaps in the scientific study of human impact on the estuarine system, and to craft a comprehensive 145-action plan for the Sacramento–San Joaquin Delta and San Francisco Bay. This early collaborative groundwork nurtured other constructive initiatives, as well as many on-the-ground restoration projects. It also spawned a network of environmentalists, anglers, politicians, ports, birdwatchers, industries, farmers, utilities, and regulators with the best interests of the bay and delta at heart. In 2010, the project was renamed the San Francisco Estuary Partnership to reflect its ongoing commitment to the health of the estuary.

from some of our species, it's because all the stressors are now operating at a high level all the time."

Take the case of the Delta Smelt, a small silver fish no longer than a finger. It lives in a narrow zone of the estuary between the two pumping plants that supply millions of Californians with drinking water. The smelt should be adapted to very variable conditions, yet it seems to be losing its ability to bounce back.

The droughts of the 1990s, shrinking habitat, and untimely flows were all bad for the fish. Water exports slowly changed what was once a dynamic fresh and salt water mixing zone into a warm, giant lake. Those fish wandering upstream in search of better habitat, or in response to sudden changes in turbidity, got ground up in the pumps. Too often these "takes" occurred before the fish were ready to reproduce—a grim scenario for a fish that seldom lives past its first birthday. Smelt can't rely on younger or older generations to buffer the species against environmental catastrophes.

Delta Smelt, a native fish that once spawned in shallows associated with tidal rivers and sloughs throughout the delta. Today's population is a tiny fraction of its historic size due to human changes to its habitat, including the export of water. Consequently, this small, short-lived fish is frequently blamed for big, long-lived conflicts over who gets how much of California's fresh water. (René C. Reyes)

On top of these stresses, the food supply for smelt isn't so plentiful anymore in the estuary. Their staple, plankton, is being eaten by the Asian Clam, or has become more difficult to catch. The hungry smelt end up chasing copepod species they never used to eat, using more energy to catch these aquatic morsels than they gain from the meal. Smelt habitats, meanwhile, are now tainted with ammonia from sewage outflows, or with toxic blue-green algae, or with mats of Brazilian water weeds full of predatory Largemouth Bass. These changes have turned the entire world of a smelt upside down.

The tragedy is that this story isn't limited to the Delta Smelt. A similar tale can be told for three fish species—Longfin Smelt, Striped Bass, and Threadfin Shad—although each has a different life history and set of stressors in the estuary, and two are long-established non-natives. Water managers grew so concerned about the rock-bottom populations of all four of these species between 2002 and 2005 that they gave the phenomenon a name—Pelagic Organism Decline (POD)—and assigned a bevy of scientists to pinpoint the causes and a bevy of engineers to suggest some fixes.

For Delta Smelt, however, it may be too late. The POD involves multiple species in a highly variable and heavily modified environment with multiple and often interacting stressors. As scientist Andrew Cohen put it: "It's the idea of the perfect storm, a number of things come together and give you something that's beyond all imagining in terms of impact from individual causes. It tells us something about the difficulty of trying to manage these systems. With so much uncertainty, we need to really commit to adaptive management, and continually reassess and rethink whether and how we should proceed."

Conclusion

At the end of the twentieth century, many of the military bases lining the bay closed and returned their shorelines to the people. Large, formerly walled-off parts of the shoreline were opened up to the public. People began visiting the bay not just to shoot ducks or dry shrimp, but to walk dogs, fish off a pier, paddle a kayak, or watch birds.

From these new access points to the bay, anyone who has seen the region change over the past 20 years knows the water is getting cleaner and clearer, and the shorelines prettier. Many more people take to the water to swim, surf, sail, or board, and parents take their children to splash in the knee-high waves without a second thought. Few get sick from sewage contamination in the bay, and if a spill or a storm compromises water quality, state and local authorities now post helpful warnings. Between 2005 and 2009, the average number of Bay Area beach closures for Alameda, San Francisco, and San Mateo counties combined was about 30 per year, and the number of postings 200, according to the state authorities.

Every few years, The Bay Institute issues an ecological scorecard called the San Francisco Index. The index uses more than 36 science-based indicators to grade the condition of San Francisco Bay and the effects of human uses on its health. Among other things, the scorecard recently gave the bay a grade of B– for water quality, an F for food web health, and a C– for stewardship due to little perceived progress in conserving water, reducing pesticide use, and restoring freshwater flows.

The bay also earned a C– for a special index called "fishable-swim-mable-drinkable." The index combines measurements of the fishing success of recreational anglers, the edibility of the fish caught (essentially a

Urban art at the Albany Bulb on the East Bay shore, a former landfill site. "Our lady of the trash" continues a half-century-old tradition of shoreline sculpture made of driftwood, trash, old tires, discarded construction materials, and household casta-ways. (Max Eissler)

measure of contaminant levels), the frequency of beach closures due to bacterial pollution or other factors, and the quality of local drinking water sources. An update to the scorecard was slated for 2011.

Over the long term, the scorecard—just one form of measurement among many—suggests that most bay health indices are getting worse rather than better, save in the realm of water quality. But compared to where the region was a century ago, many scientists and activists see a sea change in public attitudes—from a time of degrading the bay to a time of cherishing it.

"Whether it's the most altered estuary in the world or not, it has enor-mous potential for restoration and revitalization and the support of the public. And we in turn have deep cultural ability to change and remake ourselves as a community that's a healthy part of the California coast," says Save the Bay's David Lewis.

I have regularly surveyed, hiked, and canoed the same 10-mile reach of the Tuolumne River near LaGrange since 1994. In the summer, I've stood in 50 cfs [cubic feet per second] of water baking in 100F+ degree Central Valley heat, and my shoes barely got wet. In spring, I've tried to stand in a 9,000 cfs roar of icy snowmelt. In fall, I've seen the cottonwoods color the river canyon yellow, and drop their leaves on the spawning Chinook Salmon. Even though this reach of the river is so familiar, there is always something different each time I return: a riffle shifted, a tree fallen, creating a new pool; a mining pit filled, or spawning gravels added to help rebuild river habitats. These things give me a glimpse of a working river, a dynamic ecosystem still struggling to survive despite the large dam upstream. It's the same river—whether you put your toe in at Tuolumne Meadows or Modesto or any place in between—but the river is never the same, and that gives me hope.

TIM RAMIREZ, NATURAL RESOURCES DIRECTOR, SAN FRANCISCO PUBLIC
UTILITIES COMMISSION (FORMERLY WITH THE TUOLUMNE RIVER TRUST)

AS PART OF AN ESTUARY, the bay's health is inextricably connected to the health of its watershed. Everything that happens on the lands upstream, and on the banks of the rivers and creeks flowing into the bay, affects the quality of its waters and quantity of its salmon, waterfowl, and other wildlife. The rivers and streams of the watershed connect inland California to the coast, and the bay to 40 percent of the state.

"In the last 20 years, one of the best things we've done from an ecological perspective is recognize the value of landscape-level restoration, such as restoring flows to a dewatered section of the San Joaquin River, and re-introducing tides to the South Bay salt ponds," says Tina Swanson, who once ran The Bay Institute. The institute was one of the first groups to make the case that the health of the bay was dependent on the health of its watershed. "Unlike smaller projects, which mostly provide locally isolated refugia, the scales of these projects reconnect habitats across the watershed landscape and restore ecological function," says Swanson.

Central Valley wetlands. (Department of Water Resources)

Restoring ecological function is the best that can be done in a watershed as built-up and replumbed as that of the San Francisco Bay Estuary. The idea of "restoration"—humans returning a degraded landscape to some more pristine historic state—is inspirational but romantic. What people are really doing is not restoration but "renaturalization," according to Stanford hydrologist David Freyberg. He says natural systems aren't fixed—especially not highly variable estuarine systems—so restoration targets are indistinct at best. At most we can reintroduce more natural flow patterns in the watershed, and then monitor whether these changes result in healthier species.

But knowing what is "natural" and deciding what to aim for in the future still requires finding out what ecological functions and habitats were like in the past. This is the specialty of historical ecologist Robin Grossinger and colleagues at the San Francisco Estuary Institute. They study aerial photos, lot surveys, Spanish-era maps, and other archival sources to reassemble a landscape's historical geography. The aim is not to return every creek to some former historical state but to bring back what the institute calls the "broad ecological palette" of original habitats.

This region's commitment to creating a palette of riparian and marsh habitats, on a scale that dwarfs almost every other watershed project nationwide, promises to revive the health of the bay and its tributaries. What follows are two chapters on the history and frontiers of restoration. The first is on the rivers, creeks, and floodplains of the watershed, and the second reports on efforts in San Francisco Bay.

"It's time to put the picture back together," says Josh Collins, a biologist with the San Francisco Estuary Institute. "The bay is the bottom of local watersheds, and local watersheds are the top of the bay."

Historical Milestones

The earliest documented restoration efforts in the bay's watershed focused on specific gravel beds, riverbanks, waterfowl habitats, and creeks. These early efforts occurred on a piecemeal, site-specific basis that was later dubbed "gardening-style restoration." Managers paid little attention to the flow of water from one part of the landscape to another, or to the role of water in connecting ecosystems.

In the 1970s and 1980s, state water planners found themselves pressed to protect California's irrigation and drinking water supplies from saltwater intrusion and environmental challenges. They took a harder look at the connection between the ocean tides and river flows, and started thinking about estuarine processes.

True landscape-level restoration arrived with watershed-wide planning in the 1990s. Legislation to better manage storm-water runoff spurred the formation of dozens of planning groups. In these groups, local landowners, along with representatives from utilities, water districts, and special interests concerned with specific creeks or rivers, grappled with common challenges. For the first time, these stakeholders began thinking about adjacent land uses and environmental quality all along the flow line—from headwaters to major rivers and the ocean.

But work within single watersheds failed to address larger state water conflicts. Urban and agricultural water users still refused to relinquish

Scientist Carol Digiorni collects organic carbon samples in floodwaters produced by a levee breach on Staten Island in the Delta. (Department of Water Resources)

their annual allotments of snowmelt, forcing wildlife managers to try other means to improve the lot of failing fish populations. The main tactic, and the most politically palatable one, was to make physical improvements to fish habitats.

In the 1990s, this endeavor began with a fund for habitat restoration, to which major urban water districts from the Bay Area and southern California contributed. The fund later morphed into the interagency state–federal CALFED program. Among myriad habitat improvements, CALFED placed gravel in scoured-out riverbeds so salmon could better dig their redds; re-created river bends long straightened by levees; set levees back so that riparian plants could sprout on their edges; and left delta islands flooded by levee breaches to become sheltered shallows for fish.

In the seven years between 2000 and 2007, agencies spent $957 million on projects that fulfilled the objectives of the CALFED Ecosystem Restoration Program. The program installed or improved 82 fish screens, protected or restored 55,000 acres of agricultural lands and 130,000 acres of habitat, and removed numerous dams and barriers to fish movement. Plans developed by the water supply community and a governor's task force called for another 65,000 to 100,000 acres of tidal restoration over the next 50 years.

More recent planning efforts for the delta have continued to emphasize restoration. A 2008 strategic vision made the goal of restoring the delta ecosystem coequal to the goal of creating a more reliable water supply for California. Then 2009 biological opinions about what should be done to save endangered smelt and salmon—issued by U.S. Fish and Wildlife Service and the National Marine Fisheries Service—called for the restoration of 8,000 acres of intertidal and subtidal habitats in the delta and Suisun Marsh. And a new delta stewardship council will for the first time have land use permitting authority.

Despite the focus on physical habitat in the 1990s and 2000s, CALFED and other concerned stakeholders also made some effort during this period to put more water into the watershed's creeks and rivers to benefit fish and the ecosystem, and to conserve water so that more might be available for this purpose.

Key Ingredients: A Riparian Recipe

Restoring a river, or even a creek, is not as easy as breaching a dike to convert a salt pond back into a wetland. The biggest obstacles standing in the way of restoration on 95 percent of the watershed's rivers and creeks are dams. While dams may help farms and cities collect water, they also withhold essential ingredients rivers need to build fish and forest habitats.

"If there is a deficit in people's understanding of creeks and rivers, it is that they have two jobs: to transport water and to transport sediment," says Christopher Richard of the Oakland Museum.

Other obstacles to restoration are the levees and riprap lining riverbanks and the homes and farms standing in old floodplains. Controlling rivers via engineering may not be sustainable, according to restoration engineer Philip Williams. Levees continue to fail, floods continue to swamp homes, and dams never seem to be able to store enough water to slake California's thirst. Young trees are not growing up to replace old ones along riverbanks, and the new hatchery-raised salmon are not as resilient as their wild cousins.

"The hardest question, if we commit to restoring our rivers, will not be how to do it, but how long to continue investing resources in perpetuating obsolete river engineering works that prevent us from managing rivers in a way that allows them to restore themselves, " said Williams in a 2003 article in CALFED's *Science Action*.

Healthy rivers and creeks need room to move and meander, areas to flood, and vegetation along their banks. They need gravel added below their dams and adequate flows to distribute that gravel downstream. Garden-variety gravel may not be good enough, either, because it won't smell right to salmon. Indeed, salmon may not use a gravel bed until it has

Rivers make new land such as this point bar on the Sacramento River. As the channel moves away from one bank, gravel collects on the other, allowing cottonwoods and other plants to take root. (Eric Larsen)

been "seasoned"—the small rocks having rolled around, interacted with the water, released minerals, and accumulated algae.

With so much concrete lining their shores, rivers and creeks also need new spaces for vegetation to grow, trees to rise, and logs to fall. They need setbacks to invite water onto old floodplains, or bulldozing to re-create a long-lost meander or bend.

"People have historically thought that a migrating, eroding channel meant something was wrong, that a raw riverbank was a bad bank," says UC Davis's Eric Larsen, a fluvial geomorphologist who is one of the "go-to" guys for Sacramento River restoration. In reality, rivers create new land by eroding and redepositing sediments. "The river is not alive unless it's migrating. All its ecological processes are built on the basis of the river moving across the floodplain."

Riparian specialists concocting restoration recipes are now thinking big. They seek to re-create river processes across entire landscapes. They are looking beyond the need for a new riffle here or a better fish screen there, to how best to sustain 10 mile to 100 mile reaches of river. It is only on such broad scales that riparian processes—in which water, sediments, seeds, and fish interact—come into play. And it is only on these scales that the pitfalls of gardening-style restoration, where benefits are highly localized and often short-lived, can be avoided.

Beyond adding good ingredients in the right quantities, any recipe must also keep bad ingredients out of the mix. Poor water quality from agricultural and wastewater discharges, harmful invasive species, and high water temperatures can all too easily negate the value of restoration, or impede its intended purpose.

The Big River Projects

In the last few decades, more than $100 million has been spent releasing Central Valley rivers in the bay's watershed from their straightjackets. Their channels and sandbars are being allowed to move and change, and their banks to overtop, erode, and re-form. Still more effort has gone into restoring the trees, brush, and plants associated with riparian habitats.

Along the 100 miles of the lower Sacramento River—between Red Bluff and Colusa, where early settlers in centuries past fought so hard for so long to control floods—public interests have secured more than 9,000 acres of "inner river zone" for an experiment in re-creating meander function and regenerating forests. This was no easy task in a river reach where more than half the cut banks—the clifflike outer bend of a meander—are lined entirely with concrete. They have also been working to revegetate the riverbanks and former floodplains, which once sustained over 500,000 acres of riparian forest, but of which only 25,000 acres now remain. As of 2009, they had cleared weeds, planted new trees, simulated natural flooding conditions, and reintroduced riparian species to more than 5,800 acres.

One species adapted to ever-changing river paths is the cottonwood tree. Cottonwood evolved to take advantage of eroding banks and the flash floods of natural flows in spring, which swept away old vegetation and created fertile seedbeds. Generations of these trees once lined the great waterways of the valley, ranging from silver-barked octogenarians on the upper banks to middle-aged saplings and young seedlings closer to the water. But on the Sacramento River in the 1990s, riparian ecologists noted the seedlings weren't growing up. Modern dam operations and shoreline riprap had changed river conditions until the light, hairy seeds germinated too low on the riverbank and in places susceptible to winter storms. In the last few decades, the Nature Conservancy has been working

NOT SO GOLDEN GRASS

California's summer hills were not always golden. Exotic, annual turf grasses introduced by Spanish ranchers to benefit cattle are what dry up and turn yellow; the original native grasses stayed green all summer. The state has more than 300 species of native grasses—most are perennial bunchgrasses that leave space in the soil for other plants and wildlife. Conversion of native perennial grassland to non-native turf has increased erosion, runoff, fire danger, and weeds, and it has reduced water retention in the soil. Efforts to restore native grasslands are now gaining ground with the help of fire and herbicides.

with state water managers to re-create healthier conditions for cotton-wood growth along the Sacramento.

Along smaller rivers, Californians have been busy mending some of the damage created by the mining of sand, gravel, and gold. The Tuolumne River—one of three large Sierra tributaries of the once-mighty San Joaquin—had worked itself into a particularly deep rut since it was dammed for hydropower in the 1800s, and then again for San Francisco's water supply in 1923. It was also heavily mined for gravel. Restoration projects have since filled huge offshore lakes and in-stream pits left by mining, and reintroduced some natural river topography.

River restoration in the bay watershed has also involved the removal of dozens of small dams, poorly designed culverts, bridges, and other barriers. The organization American Rivers estimates that in the last decade, 15 barriers between five and ten feet high have been removed from Bay Area streams, and about the same number in the Central Valley. The largest removal to date may have been the demolition of the 20-foot-high, 184-foot-wide McCormick-Saeltzer Dam on Clear Creek, a Sacramento River tributary, in 2000.

To get an inkling of how rivers might have functioned before dams, scientists study the Cosumnes River. It is the only completely free-flowing river left in the bay's watershed. Here, they've been experimenting with reconnecting rivers to their historic floodplains. Researchers have found that floodplains once varied in elevation by as much as three yards, contrary to the laser-level flat topography of today's surrounding farm fields. These natural nuances may be important in restoring variety to riverine habitats.

If the Cosumnes is distinctive as the last free-flowing river in the system, the San Joaquin is known as the river with little or no flow at all. For decades, so much of the San Joaquin's natural flow has been diverted that the riverbed runs dry for many miles between the Friant Dam and the confluence of the Merced River.

After a 20-year legal battle, the river and its extirpated salmon may get a chance at rebirth. In 2006 a settlement of the litigation was achieved, and in 2009 Congress approved federal funding for the next major landscape-scale restoration in the system. "It will turn what is a dead river into a live one, and reintroduce salmon to the state's second largest river," says Tina Swanson, whose organization helped the Natural Resources Defense Council champion the cause in court. "Neither winter-run nor spring-run Chinook Salmon will recover from the brink of extinction until we establish additional populations in other rivers." The San Joaquin got its first official restoration flows under the settlement in 2009–2010 and, as of this writing, salmon were to be reintroduced in 2012.

The Delta and Shallows

Downstream of these rivers in the delta, very little natural marsh or river floodplain remains in today's network of canals, cutoffs, and diversions built to deliver water. "Historically the delta had very diverse habitats, and any organism adapted to living there had a lot of choices," says Stuart Siegel, a scientist who has contributed to many generations of delta restoration visions. "If you were a fish, you could always find more than one spot that worked for you."

Scientists and resource managers are bringing variety back to the delta in two ways: improving the "shallows"—shoals, dead-end sloughs, seasonally flooded areas—that grow food and nurture fish, and connecting improved habitats.

Migrating birds over Central Valley wetlands. (Courtesy of Natural Resources Conservation Service)

Even temporary and artificial shallows can be a magnet for fish. Take the example of the 84-square-mile Yolo Bypass. The bypass is a vast area of farmland on floodplain into which the Sacramento River can overflow during winter storms, and then rejoin its main stem via Cache Slough (see Map 12, p. 220). Scientists view the Yolo–Cache Slough complex, and the two already-flooded islands at its heart, as one of the delta's most promising candidates for restoration. After floodwaters broke through the Liberty Island levee in 1998, 500 acres of tule marsh grew on the site. Here, in the least-subsided edge of the delta, scientists envision creating a landscape-scale habitat corridor that is a mosaic of riverine habitat, tidal sloughs, sinewy channels, shallows, and floodplains—the kind of habitat mix most needed by salmon and splittail. According to a recent sampling, more prespawning adult Delta Smelt lingered in Cache Slough than anywhere else in the delta in 2007.

Unfortunately, some of the shallows already restored in the delta have ended up harboring more non-native bass—predators that eat young salmon and smelt—and the Brazilian aquatic weed *Egeria,* than native species. More successful, perhaps, were efforts to remake a few of the delta's levees into mini-habitats—widening them and setting them back from the river so they could nurture narrow bands of riparian and wetland vegetation.

Other restoration targets for the future are those areas with the fewest private landowners and expensive standing infrastructure. These areas include the Mokelumne and Consumnes river corridors, the McCormick–Williamson Tract, and Suisun Marsh, where the delta merges into the greater San Francisco Bay.

Water Rights for the Ecosystem

Extensive as the physical habitat improvements have been, they have not provided what native fish populations may need most: more water. Native fishes rely on ample flows of fresh water in certain seasons and places in the watershed to rear, migrate, and spawn. "In all our delta conservation plans and visions, we've placed heavy emphasis on habitat and some emphasis on stressors. But there's been a big battle over the need for water. If you don't do all three things, no one thing alone is going to work," according to Stuart Siegel.

The battle over water has resulted in a few concessions for beleaguered fish. Restoration advocates have managed to negotiate releases from upstream dams to re-create some elements of the natural annual flow pattern. Yet these flows have been so small that some refer to them merely as "life support." But eventually, stakeholders and government managers agreed to three landmark allocations of water for the benefit of fish, wildlife, and the estuarine ecosystem.

The first allocation came about in 1994, when California created a unique water quality standard designed for fish. The standard required that a special zone of low-salinity habitat be maintained in the region of Suisun Bay. The zone moves up and downstream with tides, freshwater withdrawals, and seasonal shifts. When the zone occurs around Suisun Bay, however, aquatic organisms—and the fish that eat them—are particu-

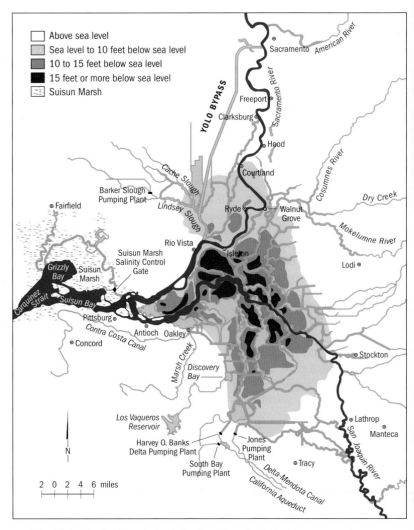

Map 12. Land subsidence in the delta. (Department of Water Resources, redrawn from Ellen Hanak et al., 2010)

larly abundant. As such, the state requires enough fresh water to be released in certain seasons to keep this low-salinity habitat in the most nurturing place in the estuary.

In a second landmark dedication of water to fish, Congress redefined the purpose of the federal Central Valley Project (CVP) in 1992, allocating 800,000 acre-feet per year of water specifically for salmon recovery.

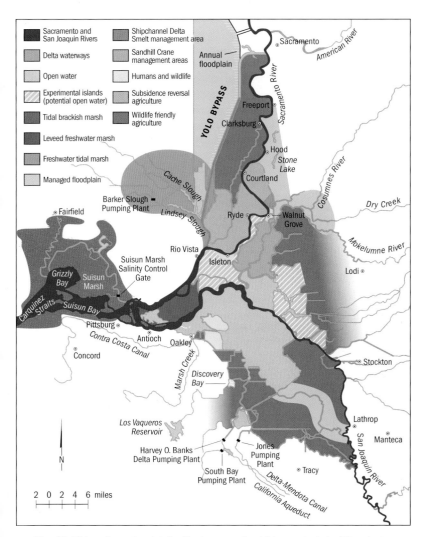

Map 13. Vision of a restored delta. The key aspects of this map include: (1) protecting levees in the western delta to allow for opportunistic through-delta pumping; (2) large expanses of pelagic, open water habitat; (3) large areas maintained for environmentally friendly agriculture; (4) Suisun Marsh re-created as brackish water tidal marsh; (5) large areas of freshwater tidal marsh; (6) the Sacramento ship channel and deep areas of Cache Slough managed for Delta Smelt spawning; (7) large expanses of floodplain, with annual floodplain created along the eastern edge of the Yolo Bypass; (8) the Stockton ship channel maintained through a larger area of open water (shown here as the San Joaquin River); (9) the integrity of the Sacramento River maintained through the delta for salmon migration; and (10) islands reserved for experimental use, including flooding. (Public Policy Institute of California, 2010)

In practice, however, this allocation has helped more lawyers—arguing about it in court—than fish. Critics say the allocation is now more often used to meet the state salinity standard described above than as an additional dollop of water for salmon.

The third landmark allocation of water for fish was more unusual, and involved the creation of an environmental water "account." For the first time in California, fish had money to buy and bargain for their own water. "Part of this was motivated out of the structure of water rights in California, and the fact that nonhumans don't have water rights," says David Freyberg, who helped review the performance of the new account. Part of this was also motivated by visionary environmental leaders like Tom Graff of the Environmental Defense Fund, who argued that market forces must be brought to bear on resource conflicts.

As a result of this new accounting system, water projects reduced pumping at key times during the biological and migratory cycles of several species of fish. The account then bought water on the statewide market to cover the shortfalls. State and federal fish biologists teamed with water-supply engineers to decide where to send the water, and adapted their decisions to the ongoing uncertainties of a naturally variable system and changing fish behavior. Having engineers and biologists team up together, Freyburg says, was novel for government restoration initiatives.

The account gave the "environment" some crucial buying power. But neither the account, nor the CVP's 800,000 acre-feet, nor the estuarine salinity standard really improved conditions for fish. Instead, these tools simply guaranteed flows at a level designed to prevent extinction. Some think these tools actually paved the way for more diversions.

"Since then, the ecosystem has gone into the tank," says Tina Swanson. "We've got multiple species of fishes with populations at record low levels, more species being listed as endangered, commercial and recreational salmon fisheries closed several years in a row, and recognition that these species are in really big trouble. Clearly the steps we took weren't enough."

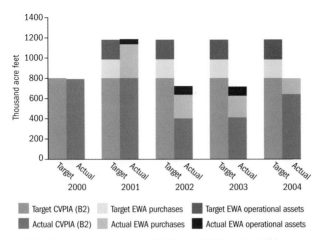

Figure 14. Gap between target (set by CALFED and CVPIA) and actual (measured or released) amounts of water dedicated for environmental uses, 2000–2005. EWA refers to environmental water account; CVPIA to the Central Valley Water Project Improvement Act. (Environmental Defense Fund)

Production or Conservation Hatcheries?

Any attempt to restore native populations of Sacramento and San Joaquin River Salmon must consider that the few remaining fish aren't so native anymore. This issue came to a head in 2005, when poor ocean conditions killed nearly all of the juvenile fall Chinook that reached the sea.

Peter Moyle of UC Davis puts the problem squarely at the doorstep of the hatchery system: "These fish have been having hard times in recent years because of their uniformity in life history and genetics. Those that make it to the ocean tend to be the same size and to do the same things because of their hatchery parentage, so if conditions are bad, most die. Under natural conditions, the wild salmon in each stream would have differed from salmon in other streams, and had more variability in size and time of ocean entry. This allowed large numbers of fish to avoid unfavorable conditions. With hatcheries, we have taken away this resilience."

The traits needed to thrive in a hatchery are very different from those required to survive in the wild. "If a fish is trying to defend its territory in a trough with 50,000 other fish, it's wasting its time. But in the wild, that's the path to success," says the U.S. Environmental Protection Agency's Bruce Herbold. Studies show that selection for hatchery traits can occur among Steelhead within just two generations. Even if both of the parent fish used to sire new hatchery fish were born and raised in the wild, their

Fish raceways during feeding time at a trout hatchery on the American River. (John Staiti)

offspring cannot help but be affected by the sheltered, concrete world of the hatchery. In other words, though hatchery fish look wild, in truth they are every bit as domesticated as a chicken or cow.

In a stream, hatchery fish are easy to spot, and just as easily eaten by predators. "Hatchery fish are pale and sitting in the middle of pools waiting for chow to drop out of the sky. Wild trout are hidden, skilled in the arts of remaining unobserved," Herbold says.

An estimated 99 percent of all hatchery fish die after their release from the facility. Those that manage to return to the wild do so thanks to their sheer numbers. Hatchery fish that wander into different streams and breed with local strains merely dilute the genes of wild populations. Called *introgression*, this phenomenon reduces the fitness of future generations. The presence of bigger, better-fed hatchery fish can also disrupt the social structure of wild salmon, because the more massive males can intimidate their wild brethren in the competition to find a mate. Hatcheries can also be a source of contagion for disease and parasites to antibiotic-free wild fish.

To address such problems, hatcheries are now exploring new practices. These include breeding nonhatchery parent fish, releasing fewer fry into rivers to avoid overwhelming natural populations, and acclimating fish to wild conditions by holding them temporarily in cages placed in brackish water.

Hatcheries are not going to go away. For one thing, they have sustained the commercial salmon fishery in California for more than 50 years. For another, they have preserved the genetics of fish runs otherwise blocked from breeding by dams.

Scientists are now weighing whether to use conservation hatcheries as last-ditch attempts to preserve other species. One such hatchery could be built to sustain the endemic Delta Smelt. Scientists originally learned the ins and outs of raising smelt to produce fish for experiments. That know-how may be all that stands between the smelt and eternal oblivion, says Moyle. "It is not outside the realm of possibility that the only smelt around will be in that rearing facility."

Reviving Bay Creeks

When people think about salmon runs, the rural rivers and creeks in the headwaters of the Sacramento and San Joaquin rivers are what generally come to mind. But the bay is surrounded by 85 smaller watersheds where salmon and Steelhead once thrived. These urban creeks often pose different restoration challenges.

Creek restoration has been occurring around the Bay Area for decades. Local waterways tend to be smaller in scale, and their banks are more accessible than mudflats or marshes, making them prime candidates for rejuvenation by volunteers with strong backs. Some form of restoration has been done on about half of the bay's named creeks over the last 40 years. This work has taken many forms, such as clearing trash from channels, removing small dams, and ripping out invasive ivy coating banks. To strengthen crumbling creek banks, people have bundled willow and other vegetation into living walls, and reshaped stream channels and floodplains to restore their ecological function. More than 50 creek groups are active in the East Bay alone. A few have been responsible for sparking interest in creek restoration not just in the Bay Area but across the country.

The "watershed moment" of creek restoration occurred at Berkeley's Strawberry Creek. In the early 1980s, creek activist Carole Schemmerling, Berkeley parks architect Doug Wolfe, members of the nonprofit Urban Ecology, and others exhumed a stream buried beneath an old rail yard in central Berkeley, then turned the area into a park. They dug up the culvert encasing the creek, smashing the concrete pipe with sledgehammers. The darker soil saturated by groundwater meandering along the old stream channel helped activists re-create the original creek meanders.

This 350-foot section of Strawberry Creek marks one of the first recorded instances of creek daylighting in the United States. According to the Oakland Museum's Christopher Richard, it was "a hugely influential event which engendered creek consciousness in the population of the Bay Area."

An equally important battle was fought over Wildcat Creek 10 miles to the north. Wildcat is one of the few completely open streams left in the Bay Area. More than half is protected within the East Bay Regional Park District.

During storms, Wildcat Creek used to flood North Richmond every other year or so. Despite the regular arrival of mud and water in their homes, community leaders for decades held fast to their dream of a green and healthy creek lined with bait and bike shops and an environmental magnet school. Then, in the 1980s, fluvial geomorphologist Ann Riley, as well as engineers and community leaders, introduced a radical new concept to river engineering: reducing floods by restoring streams.

Embraced by the community, the project became the Army Corps of Engineers' first-ever attempt to build a natural flood-control project. It brought back Wildcat Creek's naturally active channel and permitted overflow into a floodplain. The project's stellar performance in rainy conditions has caused a sea change in Corps attitude toward flood-control design.

Wildcat Creek remains a work in progress. Its floodplains are hemmed in by development, as well as besieged by trash dumping, industrial pollution, and urban blight. Yet community groups are employing at-risk youth and high school students to remove invasive plants and restore creekside greenbelts there. Meanwhile, the county flood-control district plans to buy and demolish houses remaining in the floodplain, to give Wildcat Creek the space to flow and flood again.

The hamlet of Martinez off Suisun Bay also suffered from chronic flooding every two to three years. Its downtown buildings belly right up to the banks of Alhambra Creek, with several spanning the creek itself. The town asked wetland engineers at Philip Williams & Associates to tame these floods. The engineers realized that the town's old railroad bridge blocked stream currents, and they built a new bridge nearly four times wider and slightly higher. They removed town levees and, at the creek's outlet, excavated a tidal marsh along the shore, then directed bulldozers to cut tidal channels. The marsh allows creek water to spread out sooner, lowering water pressure upstream. In town, workers widened the channel wherever possible, and planted the banks with riparian vegetation. Completed in 2003, the design has held its own during storms that have left many other Bay Area towns underwater.

As if to demonstrate the project's ecological value, a pair of beavers

Volunteers rebuild and replant a bank along Cordonices Creek in Berkeley. Here they have installed, among other things, a natural coir fiber erosion-control blanket and a brush mattress made of willow branches. (Courtesy of the Urban Creeks Council)

paddled into town in late 2006. The big rodents built a dam and lodge right next to the creek's downtown pedestrian walkway. Their arrival caused a sensation, attracting wildlife tourists from miles around. Subsequent generations of beavers have made the most of the renovated habitat, and have been joined by River Otters, muskrats, turtles, a tule perch, and even mink, a species of weasel rarely seen in urban areas.

Ann Riley, now with the San Francisco Bay Regional Water Quality Board, calls the removal of creek constrictions such as the Martinez railroad trestle the most important urban stream restoration remedy of the future. "These undersized crossings back flood waters into many communities. Letting the stream flow freely under trestles and roads avoids flooding and allows for the restoration of habitat," Riley says.

Like the railroad bridge in Martinez, many of the Bay Area's bridges, culverts, sewers, and overpasses will reach the end of their functional life spans within the next few decades. This presents planners with a golden opportunity: the chance to help streams function for both people and wildlife. "We haven't really tried to design our cities and infrastructure to support natural processes. We are only just making our first attempts. Just think what we could do if we tried," Robin Grossinger says. "We've worked to protect the hills and the bay. The streams are a critical piece connecting them."

MIGRATIONS: TWO SALMON TRAVEL BUTTE CREEK

Stream restoration has produced the most visible results for migrating fish at Butte Creek. This creek originates in the mountains of Lassen National Forest, 15 miles northeast of the town of Chico. From its headwaters in a volcanic canyon 7,000 feet above sea level, it flows through mountain meadows into flats planted with fruit trees and rice, then empties via the Sutter Bypass and a slough into the Sacramento River. Efforts to restore fish habitat on this creek have vastly improved conditions for migrating Chinook Salmon, whether they are adults headed upstream to spawn or juveniles moving downstream to a new life in the ocean.

What are these journeys like? Imagine it is late February. A 20-pound, 30-inch-long male salmon chasing sardines out in the Gulf of the Farallones catches a whiff of something. That something—a smell, a taste, a specific chemical signature—has arrived in the ocean via the winter outflows of his natal stream. All of his senses now tell him it's time to return to the place of his birth and spawn.

He begins swimming purposefully toward the Golden Gate, and doesn't stop to eat or rest on his way through San Francisco Bay. At the confluence of the Sacramento and San Joaquin rivers he chooses the former. For 100 river miles he follows the thread of outflow that seems to grow ever stronger until he enters a ditch near the Sutter Bypass. The ditch is thick with other salmon—spring run numbers have more than doubled here due to restoration in upstream stretches. A few weeks after leaving the Pacific, he arrives in Butte Creek, the stream of his birth.

Before 2000, the going would have gotten rough here. Along the 90 miles of creek ahead, he'd have had to find his way over or around more than a dozen small dams and diversions, each one delaying his progress for days or weeks. If he got stuck, state fish and game trucks might have given him a ride upstream. But since 1998, four dams have been demolished and removed from his path. And on this day in early March, as he pumps his powerful tail against the surge of water going the other way, the only thing that disturbs him is a Red-breasted Merganser diving for a meal.

At Willow Slough he encounters the first of 11 new fish ladders, each tailored to site-specific flow and elevation conditions. Willow Slough's ladder isn't made of rungs climbing over a dam or weir. It's what's known as a "pool and chute," offering fish a chute-style passage through a hole in a step up in the river into a resting pool. Today, most ladders are designed to move fish under and through obstacles, rather than over them. The only thing going over the dam these days is what biologists call "attractant" flow.

Past the Parrot–Phelan Dam, before 1996, this male might have ended up short on water or sidetracked into the M&T Chico Ranch water intake. Today, however, M&T diverts less water here than its rights allow, leaving more water in the creek October to June when the spring run salmon need it most. Buoyed by these waters and barred from entering the intake by one of seven new exclusion barriers, this salmon moves safely upstream.

Salmon in Butte Creek. (Allen Harthorn, Friends of Butte Creek)

Swimming into the tree-shaded pools of Butte Creek's headwater canyons, the male lingers through the summer months preparing to spawn. Come September, he teams up with a female. As she digs a redd and lays eggs in the gravel, he fertilizes them with his milt. A few weeks later, he dies in the waters of his birth.

By the following February, one of his offspring has grown big enough—one and a half inches in length—to head downstream. Her clock is ticking. She has to get through the delta and into the bay and ocean before freshwater flows taper off.

Heading down through the upper creekshed she occasionally encounters a screen that prevents her from getting pumped onto an adjacent orchard or field. These new screens now cover five water diversions. Irrigators carefully manage pumping rates through these perforated steel sheets so that fish don't get sucked against them and hurt. When the female reaches the Sutter Bypass, swollen into a lake by rain and snowmelt, she lingers in this food-rich, historic floodplain of the Sacramento River. By late April, she is fatter and longer, having grown to three inches.

Once out of the bypass, she's swept along by the powerful currents of the Sacramento River. She moves safely by another screened intake supplying water to California's capital city, and by the giant concrete gates of the Delta Cross Channel. The gates to this man-made shortcut to the pumps of the state and federal water projects are now closed February to May, increasing her chance of survival.

The islands, channels, and sloughs of the delta are a maze, and finding a route downstream is often challenging. One minute the tide pulls her off course; the next it swamps the freshwater pulse signaling the way. Later, an agricultural water diversion draws her under a bank dangerously near a hungry Black Bass. Luckily, the water is too murky for the bigger fish to see her. By the time she exits the delta and enters Suisun Bay she's a smolt six to seven months old, big enough and physiologically able to survive the next stage of her life out in the ocean. ARO

Common Mergansers, which frequent freshwater creeks, lakes, and other areas with waters clear enough for them to hunt fish and aquatic insects by sight. (Richard Bohnet)

Bringing Back the Steelhead

Alameda Creek is a strange modern hybrid of a stream. Its waters are among the most intensively replumbed in the Bay Area, and lands around it are becoming increasingly urbanized. Yet Alameda Creek has the potential to be the most productive Steelhead habitat in the entire region. Its watershed covers more than 700 square miles, and its banks contain some of the most complete collections of native fish and amphibians in the region. At the same time, its flows have been so drastically manipulated that the waters in its three subwatersheds now seldom mix.

Indeed, only a fraction of the water that once naturally flowed from Alameda Creek's extensive watershed enters the bay. What little isn't put to human use flows into the creek's 12-mile lower reach, which runs through a concrete channel into downtown Fremont and shoreline salt ponds. Built to handle massive floods, the channel is almost devoid of tree cover, with sluggish flows that heat up easily in the sun. Yet upstream of the Fremont flood-control channel, a good portion of Alameda Creek and its tributaries run through rural cattle ranches, parklands, and publicly owned watershed, constituting some of the most promising spawning grounds for anadromous fish in the entire Bay Area.

"The big systems are forever changed. The Sacramento, the San Joaquin and the Tuolumne rivers: they're never going to be what they were. The smaller systems are places with more potential," says Tim Ramirez. The former director of the Tuolumne River Trust, Ramirez manages the natural resources division of the San Francisco Public Utility Commission (SFPUC), which owns and operates the largest dams and reservoirs in the Alameda Creek system. Under his leadership, the SFPUC has ceased to stonewall Alameda Creek's restoration.

Big dams owned by the SFPUC at Calaveras and San Antonio reservoirs have prevented Steelhead and Chinook Salmon from reaching upstream spawning areas on their own for decades. Yet since 1996, creek activists have documented more than 100 Steelhead and three dozen Chinook Salmon that have sniffed their way up Alameda Creek from the bay, through the maze of shoreline salt ponds and past the exposed flood-control channel, where they are stymied by a weir that protects the railroad and BART track piers plus three inflatable rubber dams. Beyond stretches an estimated 15 miles of potential fish spawning grounds.

The question of whether these would-be spawners deserve protection has alternately driven and stalled restoration in the lower creek. Central Coast Steelhead were listed under federal law as threatened species in 1997, a status finalized in 2006. The ruling about which fish are considered Steelhead is based on the circumstances of an altered landscape: all *Onchorhyncus mykiss* Trout still able to migrate between inland spawning grounds and the ocean are Steelhead protected by the Endangered Species Act, whereas resident fish unable to access the ocean due to blockages are unprotected Rainbow Trout. That means none of the *O. mykiss* in the Alameda Creek watershed are protected by law until a ladder permits the fish to bypass the BART weir and access the ocean.

Tales of frustrated fish drew environmental activist Jeff Miller to Alameda Creek in 1996. He spoke with local anglers who recalled fishing the creek's abundant Chinook and Steelhead runs in the 1950s and 1960s, and who continued to hand-carry returning spawners over the rubber dams. Miller created the Alameda Creek Alliance to bring down these obstructions.

Over the years, the alliance has needled agencies into removing one barrier after another between fish and the upper reaches of Alameda Creek. These include two swimming hole dams in Sunol Regional Park, two abandoned dams from Niles Canyon, and the lower rubber dam. As early as 2012, fish ladders at the BART weir and remaining rubber dams will be installed. And plans to restore the salt ponds at the creek's mouth should help juvenile fish make the physiological adjustment to salt water. Thanks to these efforts, Steelhead and salmon may soon reach Little Yosemite—a natural waterfall in Sunol Regional Park—under their own power.

All that's needed now is water, made available at the right times for Steelhead to enter, live, and leave the watershed. In early 2011, the SFPUC reached agreement with government agencies on a flow schedule for water

Jeff Miller and helper rescue and rerelease trapped Steelhead in Alameda Creek. (Alameda Creek Alliance)

releases for fish as part of a project to rebuild seismically vulnerable Calaveras Dam.

"Here in the Bay Area, people will be able to go to Alameda Creek and see the salmon spawning in the fall and Steelhead leaping upstream to spawning grounds in the winter. That's huge, because there's no way we're going to pass future bonds for restoration unless people see benefits from all the previous ones," Ramirez says.

Conserving and Recycling Water

Restoration will require not only releasing more water for fish but also reducing human demand for the same water. California's water supply is finite. It is difficult and costly to engineer more supply (by building dams) and to make that supply reliable. Reducing water demand via conservation by agriculture, industry, and urban users is an essential component of any California water budget and restoration plan.

The motivation for conservation, however, has historically come from water shortages and droughts—not goodwill and government mandates. "Any time it starts raining for awhile, or we get an El Niño year, people forget about the importance of conserving and recycling water," says

Rachel Wark of RMC Water and Environment, an environmental consulting firm. Rain or shine, what few people realize is that recycled water is often cleaner than garden-variety tap water from the delta.

A 2008 Pacific Institute report indicates that water conservation can make a real difference in reducing demand, and yield as much new water as 3 to 20 modest-sized new dams. The report also concludes that the absolute volume of water exported from the delta is too high, especially at critical times for ecosystem health.

The average Californian uses 154 gallons of water per day, but the lion's share of the state's water doesn't go to urban taps and toilets—it waters crops. On the upstream farms and orchards using more than three-quarters of the state's water supply, steps to improve efficiencies have been modest. Farmers and their water districts have been encouraged to shift to less water-intensive crops, to replace flooding between crop furrows with drip and sprinkler irrigation, and to monitor and manage irrigation more carefully. Little accounting of the extent to which these conservation measures have been implemented on the ground has been done to date.

Cities have made similarly modest progress in conserving and recycling water. During droughts in the 1970s and 1990s, urban water districts—particularly in southern California—started installing low-flow toilets and recycling water to irrigate golf courses. In the early 1990s, the Irvine Ranch District experimented with running recycled water through toilet flushing systems in new high-rise office buildings. The dual plumbing systems reduced the use of drinking-quality water by up to 75 percent.

Diverted irrigation water sustains Central Valley agriculture. (Department of Water Resources)

Over the last quarter century, Los Angeles's Metropolitan Water District has paid out $220 million worth in incentives, leading to the production of 1.2 million acre-feet of recycled water. In recent years, the six counties at the heart of the district recycled about 155,000 acre-feet annually.

The temperate Bay Area also undertook conservation and recycling projects during droughts, but at a less urgent pace than hot, dry southern California. The Bay Area isn't an egregious water waster. Between 1986 and 2004, the region's population grew by almost 21 percent, but total water use only increased by 3 percent. Since then, conservation measures have included weather-based irrigation management, public outreach to urban gardening groups, water saving messaging, washing machine rebates, and landscape surveys to help schools and businesses better budget their water. More recently, interagency partners have been examining opportunities for regional conservation across city and county borders, including ways to reduce the miles water must travel from supply to demand. Because two-thirds of the Bay Area's water comes from outside the region, and California uses a lot of energy redistributing water, reusing local supplies can save gallons, gigawatts, and greenhouse gases.

"Recycled water is a drought proof source of supply," writes David Carle, author of *Water in California*. Unfortunately, recycled water only accounted for about 3 percent of Bay Area water supplies in 2007. To date, around half of the 40 wastewater treatment facilities in the Bay Area are recycling a portion of their flow for beneficial uses, according to RMC's Randy Raines. He estimates that, as of 2010, about 35,000 acre-feet of recycled water were being delivered via purple pipes to golf courses, parks, soccer fields, and car washes every year.

In 1999, Bay Area agencies produced a regional master plan for recycling. In a recent update, Raines estimated the regional approach could generate 150,000 acre-feet per year of new supply by 2030. The more recycling done, the more the bay and the fish in its watershed will benefit from both reduced demand on "pristine" source water and cleaner wastewater discharges. "In today's world no one thinks twice about recycling solid waste, but recycling water just isn't there yet," says Raines. "Growing public support of environmental quality will make it happen soon."

Conclusion

Restoration on a watershed scale demands multifaceted projects conducted over hundreds of square miles. Connecting the dots between cool rapids upstream and warm shallows downstream; between cottonwood stands and underwater weeds; between fish hatcheries, dam removals, and low-flow toilets, requires a broad mind and a powerful computer. It also requires a willingness to revisit long-standing assumptions.

So far, progress in the struggle to renaturalize the watershed and the bay remains intangible. For decades now, scientists and resource managers have been trying to measure whether their work has resulted in healthier species or a healthier ecosystem. But trying to figure out what works and what doesn't, and changing course accordingly, has been an uphill battle prolonged by the lack of funding for long-term monitoring, bureaucratic inertia, and political shifts.

Without the will or the consistency to effect major changes, "We're faced with essentially retrofitting a fundamentally damaging system to create a different balance between human and nonhuman activities," says Stanford's Freyberg.

Whether called retrofitting, restoration, or renaturalization, the value of reviving long-absent connections between the watershed and the bay is clear. In this altered waterscape, designers must piece together the best of what's left of nature with a lot of other ingredients: steel and jute, concrete and mud, garbage and purple pipes filled with recycled water. As engineers blast holes in river levees and bayshore dikes, and add plumbing and pumps to return water to the land, new hybrid habitats are growing up from the Sierra headwaters to the salt ponds near San Jose.

RESTORATION FRONTIERS
The Bay

Looking for birds in tidal marshes can be dicey. The older marshes are almost entirely covered with pickleweed, and the channels beneath often invisible. You have to poke your way along in your waders—you're always optimistic that today is not the day you're going to get wet. But inevitably, when you're out there all alone, you get distracted—you hear something or see a bird or write something in your journal—and suddenly you fall in a six-foot-deep channel. It's easy to get stuck down there, with the bay mud almost like quicksand, and the channel banks sloughing off while you try to get a foothold. Plus, you're already handicapped because you're busy trying to save your scope or binoculars or books. Some marshes are so dicey we carry a 10-foot piece of PVC pipe horizontally as we walk, so we have something to pull ourselves out of the muck with.

JULES EVENS, AVIAN ECOLOGIST, AUTHOR, *CALIFORNIA BIRD LIFE*,
CALIFORNIA NATURAL HISTORY GUIDE

CALIFORNIANS ACCUSTOMED TO majestic redwood giants, lofty Sierra peaks, and golden hills dotted with oaks took some coaching to appreciate the beauty of a flat, wet swamp. But in the end, they voted to spend millions reviving the bay's shallows and shores. In the process, they committed to restoring a ring of wetlands around the bay roomy enough to ease wilder inhabitants off the endangered species list.

Though the bay has lost almost 90 percent of its historic wetlands, the tides are now being invited back onto half of them. Engineers who once scraped eelgrass beds off harbor bottoms and buried creeks in culverts are now reversing such disruptions. Where barbed wire once prevented access to the shoreline, visitors will now find bike paths, flowering bushes, and park benches.

Low tide reveals intricate drainage networks on baylands. (Invasive Spartina Project)

The catch, of course, is that no modern wetland works the same way it did 300 years ago. "No land can just manage itself anymore. We've changed too much; we're a part of the system now. We can't go back to what once was on the baylands," says Christy Smith, a U.S. Fish and Wildlife Service refuge manager.

Smith is among the latest of several generations of land managers, scientists, engineers, and activists who have been working to restore some of the natural functions of bayland habitats for the last 50 years. This chapter touches on the biggest milestones in local restoration history. It describes how engineers and biologists have arrived at their restoration recipes and highlights the perils of greening the resulting mudflats in a hurry. It also introduces some of the larger landscapes of restoration projects on the rocky Marin shore, the rural North Bay rim, and the South Bay's patchwork of salt ponds and wildlife refuges.

The baylands present obstacles both similar to and different from those faced along the flow lines of a river or creek. But infrastructure such as dikes, walls, weirs, and dams remain ubiquitous up- and downstream, forcing planners to work around hard edges while creating soft habitats.

Climate change makes shoreline restoration experiments even more vital. Resilient living wetlands will be crucial in regional efforts to adapt to the advance of water over the lowest parts of the shoreline, and into areas filled long ago to create airports, railroad beds, and downtown waterfronts. Rising sea levels promise to change the shape and size of the bay once again, and regional planners are counting on new wetlands and reconnected floodplains to help absorb some of the shockwaves.

"We're not restoring the bay anymore; we're designing it," says San Francisco Bay Conservation and Development Commission (BCDC) director Will Travis.

Historical Milestones

Without the foresight of conservation-minded duck hunters, there might not be any marshes left in the bay today. Private duck clubs bought up most of Suisun Marsh in the North Bay, for example, and were the first to begin "managing" their marshes—regulating flooding to improve habitats for their winged quarry. But legislation is what allowed the business of "restoration" to begin in earnest. The California Environmental Quality Act of 1970 required developers to assess potential environmental impacts of their projects, followed soon afterward by the Clean Water Act's establishment of a no-net-loss policy for wetlands. Waterfront developers who destroyed tidal acreage were soon required to replace them with marshes of equal or greater size.

While legislators and planners were crafting this new legal framework for wetland management, biologists and engineers were busy experimenting with the building blocks of restoration—plants, tides, and mud. In the late 1960s, Tom Harvey, a biology professor at San Jose State University, planted a clump of native cordgrass (*Spartina foliosa*) in the Faber Tract at Palo Alto before dikes were opened to the bay. Until this time the general belief was that, once gone, wetlands were lost forever. Harvey's plants lived, kindling the notion that marshes might be restored in the Bay Area. At the time, the nation's only models of healthy wetlands were the cord-

Scientists turn to old marshes as reference points for wetland restoration. Marin's China Camp Marsh is one of the few remaining ancient bay marshes with a completely intact watershed; its fresh to brackish saline gradient supports diverse native plant species. (Jude Stalker)

grass marshes of Georgia described by scientist Eugene Odum, so everyone looked east to re-create marshes out west.

In the 1970s, local action around wetlands focused on dredged material disposal sites, with engineers seeking ways to speed the transformation of these sites from glistening fields of mud to green marsh. The U.S. Army Corps experimented with methods of promoting cordgrass growth to stabilize banks and vegetate mudflats along Alameda Creek in the East Bay. They considered several options: sowing seeds, planting sprigs, or transplanting whole clumps. According to Phyllis Faber in a 2000 *Coast & Ocean* magazine article, the Corps's experts noted the poor seed set of the local native cordgrass and opted instead for a hardier, more productive cordgrass stock from the Atlantic coast. Though they meant well in choosing the most prolific species, they had little idea that they were introducing a destructive alien that would cost millions to get rid of decades later.

Most of the early restoration projects in the 1970s and 1980s involved no more than an acre or two, and most were done as mitigation for the paving over of wetlands for shoreline development. New, postage stamp–sized wetlands sprang up here and there as a result. "Developers wanted to claim that they were immediately creating the same value in wetlands that they were destroying," says Philip Williams, who has been building wetlands in the Bay Area for nearly 30 years.

In the rush to create instant wetlands, the bayshore regained few of the functional benefits of natural, mature wetlands, which include absorbing floods, filtering pollutants, cycling nutrients, producing the basic foodstuffs of the aquatic ecosystem, and providing warm, quiet, shallow nurseries for fish, birds, and other wildlife.

In these early decades of experimentation, automated helpers such as modern tide gauges, radar, and global positioning system (GPS) units weren't included in project budgets. Williams remembers running one early project for the Coastal Conservancy using human, rather than electronic, brains for monitoring. He organized a system in which volunteers at various marsh stations would record the changing level of the tides every 15 minutes over the course of 30 hours by observing measuring sticks stuck in the mud. Though the plan looked fine on paper, Williams didn't quite think through every detail. "We set up a nice base camp on Black John Slough with coffee and everything, and we rotated everyone every four hours, shuttling volunteers out to their stations through these small sloughs in canoes. Then it got dark, the tide dropped, and I realized we couldn't get to all these people because it was too shallow," he says. "They had to sit out in the marsh all night."

After a while consultants like Williams began specializing in creating bay wetlands and learning from their experiences. Some began to monitor the results of their efforts and adjusted accordingly. Others benefited from the critiques of neighbors and environmental watchdogs.

Corte Madera's Muzzi Marsh was one of the bay's first large-scale and most continuously monitored restoration projects. The Golden Gate Bridge District began the project in 1976, breaching the outer dike in four places as mitigation for building the Larkspur Ferry Terminal. In 1980, managers increased the amount of water flowing to the landward portion of the marsh via a remedial channel. By the late 1990s, plant expert Phyllis Faber noted that cordgrass grass and pickleweed had spread throughout the new marsh.

Another milestone project got its start 10 years after Muzzi, when engineers breached a slough levee and opened up a deep borrow pit at Warm Springs in the South Bay. Here, researchers learned how the depth and characteristics of the substrate play an important role in the rate of vegetation. Over the following two decades Faber observed the site evolve from supporting salt marsh vegetation to growing brackish species nurtured by the swelling flow of fresh water out of the discharge pipe of the San Jose treatment plant.

In the 1980s and 1990s, the region restored wetlands at 34 sites. Of these, 70 percent were for mitigation purposes and included Cogswell,

Martin Luther King Jr., and Robert's Landing projects. In 1983, the University of California's Margaret Race conducted the first scientific critique of wetland mitigation banking and restoration. She wasn't impressed.

Eventually, local activists began arguing for restoration in its own right—and for the good of the ecosystem—rather than just for mitigation. Projects such as Ora Loma, La Riviere, and Outer Bair Island marshes were the first products of this different perspective. Carl's Marsh, breached in 1994, set a record for the rapidity with which it became a home to plants and wildlife. And efforts to revive the Napa salt ponds, bought in 1994 with a settlement from a Shell oil spill in the bay, set a record for size. At 10,000 acres, this project shifted the bay's restoration frontier to a landscape scale.

While biologists and engineers experimented with plants, tides, and backhoes, government agencies overseeing the no-net-loss policy began discussing ways to improve their haphazard permitting process for mitigation projects. And resource managers charged with recovering the endangered Salt Marsh Harvest Mouse and California Clapper Rail, as well as other wetland advocates, began to call for some kind of regional approach or plan. They also began fighting about the ecological pros and cons of converting seasonal wetlands with existing habitat values into tidal marshes with different habitat values.

Eventually, a collaborative push from the U.S. Environmental Protection Agency and the regional water quality board, among other groups, got an

Volunteers helping with restoration planting. (Jude Stalker)

ambitious planning endeavor off the ground in the 1990s. They asked 100 top scientists to figure out what kinds of wetlands, in what amounts, the fish and wildlife that once thrived along the bayshore needed in order to thrive again, and where these wetlands should be located.

The science team selected 120 species representative of the complexity of the bayland ecosystem, and then explored the habitat needs of these species. For reference, they drew on an *EcoAtlas* of the bay's past and present habitat mix, which was being researched and digitized by the San Francisco Estuary Institute. The atlas provided snapshots of historical ecology, a critical reference point for the regional vision of the future.

After three years of work, the team published 300 pages of recommendations for the kinds, amounts, and distribution of wetlands and related habitats required to sustain bayland species. They entitled this opus the *Baylands Ecosystem Habitat Goals*. The thrust of the goals was to more than double the region's expanse of tidal wetlands. The experts agreed that at least 100,000 acres were needed baywide to support higher ecosystem functions. A second objective was to connect large new patches of 1,000-plus acres with areas already sustaining mice and rails. The goals recognized the need for seasonal and saline ponds, as well as upland refuges from the tides. By making specific acreage recommendations for four different subregions of the bay, the goals provided scientific agreement about what a healthier bayshore would look like.

"The goals report really made the case for large-scale restoration around the bay, for projects orders of magnitude greater than anything

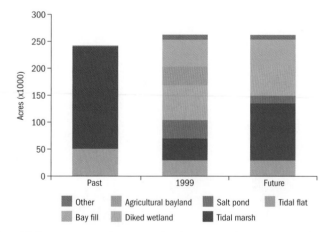

Figure 15. Past, present, and recommended future bayland habitat acreage for the San Francisco Bay region. (Data from *Habitat Goals*, redrawn by S.F. Estuary Institute, courtesy of S.F. Bay Joint Venture)

we'd done before, and for what mix of new tidal wetlands and existing managed ponds we needed," says Amy Hutzel, manager of the San Francisco Bay Area Conservancy, a state agency that has since played a key role in securing properties for restoration. This mix had been a sticking point for many earlier projects.

The region then launched a new organization to help coordinate implementation of the goals. The San Francisco Bay Joint Venture would consist of a partnership of on-the-ground wetland, wildlife, and shoreline managers from both government and nonprofit organizations. Its work also embraces national U.S. Fish and Wildlife Service efforts to sustain the wetlands, coasts, and waterways that ducks and geese depend on as they migrate through the United States and Canada.

But the real impetus behind bay wetland restoration sprang from Californians' growing support for clean water. "People liked projects that made the water environment better, that gave them clean, safe, reliable water—whether they were drinking it from the tap or touching it on the bay shoreline," says Steve Ritchie, who once oversaw regional water quality and supply programs and later ran major restoration programs both up- and downstream. "Everyone thought restoration was a worthwhile investment." Voters overwhelmingly approved money for delta restoration in 1996 with Proposition 204, and for bay restoration in 2000 with Propositions 12, 13, 40, and 84. "It was a sea change in our approach to clean water and environmental quality, the beginning of the serious age of restoration," says Ritchie.

Since then, every region of the bayshore has benefited from new science, new partnerships, and new funding for restoration. According to the

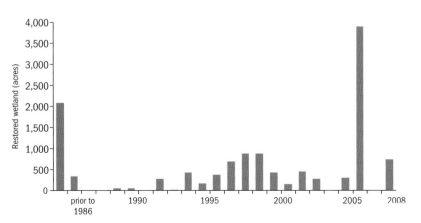

Figure 16. Acres of salt pond and other habitat opened to tidal action since the 1980s. (S.F. Estuary Institute)

joint venture, between 1996 and 2010 the region acquired more than 39,000 acres of bay habitats, restored nearly 10,000, and enhanced close to 5,500 (seasonal wetlands got a 5,000-acre boost on these three fronts). Another 13,390 acres of bay habitats were in the throes of final restoration permitting or construction as of this writing. Because it will take years for many projects to evolve into mature marshes, experts differ as to how close the region is to meeting its 100,000-acre goal for tidal marsh. But progress in the tens of thousands of acres is tangible.

"Twenty-five years ago, when I was working for the Audubon Society, we were just battling one development project after another that impacted bay wetlands," says Beth Huning, coordinator of the San Francisco Bay Joint Venture. "Now, instead of focusing on stopping things, we're re-creating ecological functions, re-establishing natural hydrology, and re-connecting habitats and open spaces around the bay. Momentum is on our side. Landowners are contacting us now, instead of developers. They want to work with us to protect their lands, rather than build on them."

Key Ingredients: A Wetland Recipe

Building a wetland from scratch requires more than just taking a piece of land and adding water. Over time, techniques have ranged from "guerrilla restoration"—knocking over a weir or blasting a hole in a levee—to the careful engineering of new landscapes, with detailed attention to the planting of vegetation, the creation of upland refuges for wildlife during high tides, and the digging of sinuous channels that mimic their natural counterparts. Every site presents unique characteristics. For engineers trained to create stability, the challenge is to design for complexity, variability, resilience, and long-term change.

According to Phil Williams, "We've gone through successive generations of restoration projects, where we can actually see how well they did. We are learning from our experiences by going back, monitoring, assessing, being accountable for the work we've done. It's a learning curve unprecedented in any other major estuary."

Through generations of projects around the bay, wetland planners learned a number of key lessons about what makes a good wetland recipe. First was that it didn't have to be green to be good, at least not at the start. Designers of large projects soon stopped planting plugs of cordgrass and other marsh species in favor of letting tides import seeds.

The second lesson was that in order to foster the natural growth of a vegetated marsh, the base elevation of the site must be exactly right. Engineers experimented with adding mud until elevations were just above and

THE GULL PROBLEM

Where there are landfills there are gulls, and lots of both can be found all around the South Bay shore. The grey-and-white-feathered California Gulls are the most obvious garbage grazers among bay wildlife species. These birds pose a big threat to shorebird populations. In recent surveys, gulls ate 61 percent of Avocet chicks and 23 percent of Stilt Chicks, and they preyed on 50 percent of Snowy Plover nests in South Bay salt ponds. In 1980, 24 gull nests were counted in the South Bay; by 2008, the gull population had exploded to an estimated 46,000, and the gulls had expanded their breeding range to Alcatraz and the Farallon Islands. But by far the most gulls are found in the South Bay. Biologist Jill Demers notes that the salt ponds offer great breeding habitat for gulls—they are similar to inland saline lakes such as Mono Lake that the gulls prefer. How can other species be protected from gulls? Biologists say culling individual gulls doesn't work, nor does addling their eggs because it is too labor-intensive. Hazing—with fireworks, dogs, falcons, ATVs, and trucks—reduced gulls at one landfill, but they just moved to another one. A regional plan may be needed to control them.

Gulls love landfills. (Max Eissler)

just below tide levels, with grading and not grading, and with creating and not creating topography. Then they studied the results in places like the Muzzi Marsh.

Phyllis Faber, who has been monitoring Muzzi for more than 30 years, sums up the take-home message: "We've learned to give more careful consideration to final elevations, to allow tidal drainage channels to form, promote good tidal exchange, and establish diverse salt marsh flora." Faber

Carving out a hole in a levee, whether with a backhoe or dynamite, allows the bay to surge back into former wetlands and drain farm fields such as this Bahia restoration site in the North Bay. At one South Bay breach, engineer Philip Williams rode the first wave into the Warm Springs restoration site, 20 feet below sea level, in a canoe. As such, Williams claims he's the only person who has ever ridden a Class III tidal rapid in San Francisco Bay. (Jude Stalker)

showed that most common flora species established naturally within a 10-year period at Muzzi—thus allowing marsh restorations to proceed with local seed, rather than expensive planting programs. "After 35 years of experimentation, we now think it might take more than 50 years to develop all functions of a mature tidal salt marsh," she says.

The final lesson seems to now be not to try to engineer every detail in advance. Planners now talk of creating "templates" for wetlands—sending in bulldozers to push the land to the desired elevations relative to sea level, and perhaps digging out a historic slough or building up an island. Upon this template, nature is left to work her magic.

Letting the new landscape evolve slowly over time also brought another important ingredient to the recipe—change. Instead of one fixed type of wetland habitat with set ingredients, designers aimed for evolving habitats with different ingredients. It was okay, for example, to breach a levee and create a shallow pond until enough sediment accumulated to support vegetation, because this provided interim shorebird habitats. Phil Williams calls this a significant shift in the thinking process: planning for the evolution of a landscape over 50 years or more.

"We recognize we're no longer creating a snapshot of historical ecology, but rather a new trajectory for how the bay will evolve. We have to decide where we are going to keep the shoreline where it is, where we will let the shoreline retreat, where we will restore marshes, and where we want the sediment to come from and go to," he says.

Sediment may be the most challenging wetland ingredient for planners to obtain. The bay's sediment supply comes from many sources, ranging from the sand and silt already lying on the bay floor, to particles eroded off headlands and coasts, and imported by ocean tides and river runoff. Once in the bay, sediment is easily moved by wind, waves, and other disturbances.

In the past, the biggest source of sediment to the system was Central

Valley rivers and the mining debris they carried downstream. As early as 1914, mining had increased the amount of sediment coming into the bay by tenfold over natural baseline levels. But in the late 1990s, U.S. Geological Survey (USGS) scientists discovered that instead of absorbing a steady supply of new sediment, the bay floor had actually started eroding. More recently, they've noticed the water growing clearer. "Of course there is still erodible material in the bay, but the huge excess from mining may now have worked its way out of the system, or is no longer available for resuspension by winds and tides," says the USGS's David Schoellhamer, the bay's chief sediment accountant. As a result, erosion of existing mudflats may be the most significant source of sediments to build marshes with in the future (see also Figure 3, pp. 42–43).

To help restoration planners accommodate this change, Schoellhamer calculated a series of sediment budgets for the entire bay system. He tracks what comes in, what gets resuspended, and what escapes out the Golden Gate via tides or dredge barges. His calculations suggest that sediment inflows from the delta have decreased over the second half of the twentieth century, and sediment inflows from local tributaries are now greater than what comes in from the delta. Despite these inputs, the annual net loss of sediment from the bay to the ocean has almost doubled, from 1.4 million metric tons (mmt) between 1955 and 1990 to 2.4 mmt, during normal water years, since 1995.

Though the Bay as a whole is now eroding, some areas continue to have strong deposition, says Schoellhamer, making them prime spots for wetland restoration. The Petaluma River, for example, exhibits some of the largest sediment concentrations measured around the bay: the river channel traps a lot of sediment because flows and tides aren't strong enough to carry it out into San Pablo Bay. This explains why just four years after a Petaluma River levee near the Highway 37 bridge was breached, Carl's Marsh had gained six vertical feet of sediment.

SUBSIDENCE: HOW IT HAPPENS

When landscapes are separated from the tides that once flooded them by building dikes, their elevation subsides. The spongy soils, once expanded with water and vegetation, dry out and contract. Initially, decomposing organic matter in once water-logged peat soils cause subsidence. Subsidence can be further accentuated by agricultural tilling and groundwater withdrawal, depending on land uses in the immediate area. As a result, many delta islands now lie 10–25 feet below sea level (see Map 12, p. 220). Former bay tidal marshes have also dropped below tidal levels due to diking and loss of local aquifers, but not to the same extent as their delta counterparts.

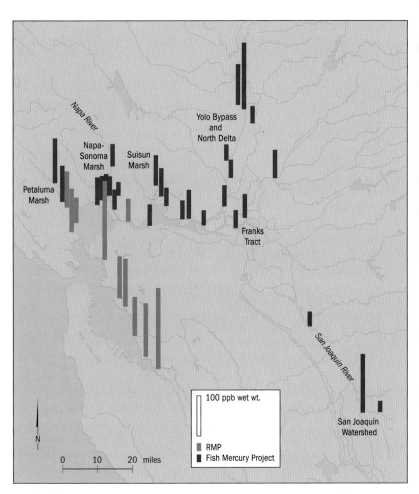

Map 14. Levels of methyl mercury (parts per billion, wet weight) in small fish throughout the bay and delta in 2007. Heartening are the lower levels found in the Napa–Sonoma Marshes, a major restoration site. (Regional Monitoring Program, S.F. Estuary Institute & UC Davis Fish Mercury Project)

Another area that collects a lot of sediment from local creeks is the South Bay below the Dumbarton Bridge. This bodes well for the area's ambitious salt pond restoration project. Project planners asked Schoellhamer to budget sediment requirements for a variety of restoration designs. After examining the elevations of 65 different ponds, he found that some were much lower than others. In a design converting all of the ponds to tidal marsh, he projected that the vast majority of sediment would be needed to

TABLE 4. Methyl Mercury Biomagnification (ng/g dry weight)

	Mukooda Lake, MN	Ryan Lake, MN	Almaden Reservoir, CA
Mercury source	Atmospheric	Atmospheric	Mining
Water (wet weight)	0.000018	0.00019	0.00037
Seston (mostly algae)	3.5	8.3	4.1
Zooplankton	17	197	640
Young fish (age 1)	181	943	4,830
Northern Pike (55 cm)	1,130	9,725	

Note: Methyl mercury biomagnifies in aquatic food webs. In Voyageurs National Park, Minnesota, concentrations in young Yellow Perch were more than one million times greater than those in water, and in adult predatory pike more than ten million times greater. In the South Bay's Almaden Reservoir, near a historic mercury mine, concentrations were higher in the water than in the Minnesota lakes, which is reflected in the elevated transfer up to zooplankton.

Source: MN from Wiener et al., University of Wisconsin-La Crosse; CA from Kuwabara et al., USGS.

fill only five ponds. Scientists call such holes in the bay floor "sediment sinks." The project design took his calculations into account, focusing tidal restoration plans on higher elevation ponds.

The bay's sediment budget will also determine whether the new marshes will survive or be obliterated in coming decades. Though sea level has been rising slowly for decades, USGS experts project a much faster rise of between four feet and five feet by 2100. Wetlands must rise too or they will become inundated. Scientists estimate that to keep up with the projected rise over the next century, bay marshes would need more than half a billion cubic yards of material (sediments, decomposing plants, and organic matter) but that only about 30 percent to 60 percent of this may be available from natural erosion and runoff processes.

Though sediment is a key ingredient in bayland restoration, it may harbor another ingredient that isn't so welcome: mercury. Numerous restoration projects include monitoring of how reintroduced wetland processes are interacting with the region's mercury legacy, and the San Francisco Estuary Institute has been trying to identify mercury hot spots in the bay.

The chemical interactions and bacterial and decomposition processes occurring naturally at the mud and water interface of wetlands can convert innocuous inorganic mercury into toxic methyl mercury. In general, methyl mercury tends to be higher in sediments closer in to shore. At low tide, damp mud baking in the sun fuels bacterial activity in the oozes that may boost methylation. Unlike many other contaminants, methyl mercury gets hundreds and thousands of times more concentrated each time it moves up the food chain (see Table 4). Though mercury may not hurt a small fish, it can harm the offspring of the larger animals that eat them—hence the warning labels on cans of tuna.

Whether restoration promotes methylation, and exactly how it affects the species that live in the baylands, is an open question. Studies so far suggest that seasonal wetting and drying cycles in bay margins and floodplains, rather than tidal marsh processes, may trigger spikes in methylation. Areas with larger plankton blooms may pump more mercury into the local food web. New studies suggest, however, that birds and fish frequenting restoration sites will have levels of mercury similar to, not higher than, those from other areas around the bay.

Mercury, sediments, politics, and design are all factors that will influence future restoration projects around the bay. In the following sections, some of the on-the-ground, nitty-gritty challenges of restoration are explored in more detail.

The Marin Shore

Head up Highway 101 from the Golden Gate Bridge, and the marvels of the bayshore are quick to materialize. At low tide, the mudflats of Richardson Bay sparkle with dappled light. Along the verge, egrets stalk in the soggy spots. Here and there between Marin's condo complexes and malls, flashes of green marsh, blue water, and rough ground catch the eye.

What may not be so apparent is the fact that Marin also sports the bay's rockiest shores. Three peninsulas jut out into the bay between the Golden Gate and San Rafael, restricting wetlands to a few coves and the inlets of Gallinas, Corte Madera, and Coyote creeks. North of the rocky hills and cliffs of San Pedro Point, near the town of Terra Linda, Marin's shores open and soften. Marshes here once filled the landscape between the bayshore and Highway 101, and they once fanned out all along the lower reaches of the Petaluma River.

Over the years, many restoration projects on this shore were championed by the Marin Audubon Society, which owns 509 acres of baylands and has restored and enhanced 53 acres. In Southern Marin, at the state's Corte Madera Ecological Reserve, Audubon used fees from water-quality violators to restore a one-acre field to tidal marsh and create an island for Clapper and Black Rails. Sewage spill funds helped Audubon and state agencies restore tides to the slough at the mouth of San Clemente Creek. And at nearby 31-acre Triangle Marsh, they reconnected ancient wetlands with new ones, and planted gum plant, creeping wild rye, coyote brush, and coast live oaks.

Audubon's hardest-won projects lie along the Petaluma River in Northern Marin. Fighting off golf courses, plans for more lagoon-style homes with private boat docks, and landfill expansions at places like Black Point, Bel Marin Keys, Bahia, and Novato, Audubon partnered with others to protect a 3,000-acre corridor of baylands reaching from the former Hamilton airfield all along the Petaluma River into remote ranchlands.

Saving the marshes along the Petaluma River was a great triumph, because it helps connect Marin County habitats with the much wilder 55,000 acres of wetland open spaces of the North Bay rim. Restoring these rural ranchlands and seasonal wetlands involved little more than straightforward dike breaching and revegetation. A far more difficult landscape was Marin's Hamilton Air Force Base, with its old runways and antenna fields to transform, its regiments of abandoned buildings to tear down, and its oil spills and landfills to mop up.

As part of a multiuse redevelopment of the base into a new community adjacent to shoreline habitats, the California Coastal Conservancy and the U.S. Army Corps of Engineers have been trying to implement one of the most complex wetland restoration designs undertaken in the bay to date. The design is complex because it uses material from harbor dredging projects to bring the long-subsided landscape up to tidal elevations, and because the 2,500-acre project re-creates the entire spectrum of shoreline

Hamilton wetland restoration site in Marin County, where dredged material is being beneficially reused to raise subsided lands to appropriate levels for new habitats. (Courtesy of the U.S. Army Corps of Engineers)

habitats, from mudflat and outboard marsh all the way up to seasonal ponds and upland buffer zones.

"We're taking areas diked off by man and converted to agricultural use, and then to military use, and restoring them back to what nature had here originally," explains Eric Polson, consulting civil engineer on the Hamilton project. "It's going full circle, a 360-degree turnaround."

Most sites in the midst of restoration look lunar, and Hamilton is no exception. For a long time there were just miles of bare dirt, crisscrossed by levees, and dotted with the bent elbows of backhoes. On a visit during the construction period, the levees and ponds trembled with the passage of yellow trucks with snouts, called "haulers," as well as the rumblings of half a dozen mudcats. These special bulldozers have a wider track than most, enabling them to operate in mud and fluid environments without slipping.

Before the military could hand over its airfield for restoration, the Army Corps had to do a fair amount of cleanup. Luckily, Hamilton served as an operations center—rather than a weapons or aircraft or shipbuilding factory—and there wasn't too much contamination.

The lowest hanging fruit for cleanup were the landfill and the shooting range. Like many of the bay's landfills, Hamilton's mound of washing machines, car tires, tree trunks, and old fuel drums was capped, greened, and plumbed with vents to off-gas methane. Just as in other hunting areas around the bay, lead shot and bullets had to be scraped off the ground on the shooting range. In the end, workers removed 5,000 cubic yards of soil from the range, which was filled mostly with the spent firepower of the Thompson or "Tommie" machine gun.

These were small cleanups compared to the work that had to be done on the marsh plain outside the outboard levee, where the base's sewage and storm-water outfalls once discharged to the bay, and where the military also had a burn pit and debris pile. Here, the corps scraped down five acres and moved 30,000 cubic yards of soil and sludge.

Army Corps environmental manager Ed Keller says the most serious contamination at Hamilton came from leaking fuel tanks, both those used for household heating oil and those employed for aviation gas and jet fuel. In the airfield's heyday, jet fuel supply tankers hooked up to a pipeline that extended three miles into the bay. Keller had that pipeline flushed and plugged with concrete. On the landward side, he had thousands of feet of leaky fuel line removed, as well as lots of surrounding soil. Keller believes he got lucky because the base was built atop some very fine silt and clay soils. "The soils were extremely tight. Water could not move through them at all, so we had no contaminant plumes," says Keller. "Even in a firefighting training area, where soldiers basically poured fuel on trash and set it on fire, we only had to go 7 feet down and 10 feet beyond the concrete pad in each direction to get all the contaminants. In 40 different wells we sampled on the base, there was no contamination."

Once the base was clean enough, the restoration engineers moved in. Initially, one of their most critical tasks was to build a rather unusual pipeline from the shoreline out to a spot five miles into the bay where it was deep enough for tugs and barges to maneuver. Without the pipe, engineers could not import the key ingredient in their design: dredged sediment. But with the help of the pipeline, 10 million cubic yards of sediment—offloaded from barges out in the bay and mixed with water into a slurry—could be pumped through the pipeline and onto subsided areas. In some places, land levels were more than eight feet below sea level. Even better, the project was putting sediments that harbors and marinas wanted removed from their channels and berths to good use elsewhere in the bay—fulfilling a regional "beneficial reuse" goal.

To lay the section of pipeline crossing the soft wetland surface, workers made a temporary road for their heavy equipment out of huge wooden timbers and rafted-up rubber mats. As Polson remembers, "We built that over Christmas during bad weather with tides so high our mats were floating. It was pretty dicey." Once built, however, the pipe allowed crews to work year-round in the marsh, instead of pausing between February and August, when Clapper Rails and Salt Marsh Harvest Mice might be raising young. The pipe is much less disruptive than alternative methods of moving sediment: haulers, backhoes, and other noisy, smelly machinery.

On the site itself, the pipe snakes in and out of various giant pits. Workers can move the slurry spray around as they prepare each unit. One day, the units will be a mix of seasonal wetlands, wildlife corridors, tidal wetlands, tidal pannes, and ponds. "We're setting a template for a functional wetland, so species can move back in and propagate," says Polson. "We're trying to give them the right set of conditions—elevation, sediment, substrate, water, hydrology—to get things going in the right direction. You look at natural analogs and do your best to copy them."

By 2050, visitors should be able to see a pretty good copy of the 2,500 acres of wetlands that historically covered the Hamilton shore.

North Bay Hayfields

Drive along Highway 37 across the rim of the North Bay between Vallejo and Novato and three qualities describe the scene: it's wide open, flat, and often wet. This shoreline is a world away from the high rises of San Francisco or Oakland. It's rural. Fields of hay bristle and wave in every direction. Bay waters beckon from every overpass and through the occasional break in the railroad levee, then disappear from view for long stretches. Only by squinting at the far distance does anything resembling a big building materialize.

The fields of water on the north side of the highway are only knee-deep, and most are former salt ponds flooded to provide better habitat for shorebirds and waterfowl. On the south side of the highway a tawny tapestry rooted in mud and salty water reaches out into the bay, breaking into the occasional wide slough. Indeed, apart from the highway and a few ranch buildings, there's not much on the San Pablo Bay rim but wet open space. This is the bay's largest remaining undeveloped shoreline—a 55,000-acre landscape preserved by a federal wildlife refuge, a state wildlife area, the Sonoma Land Trust, various other land conservation interests, and a few cattle ranchers and hay farmers (see Map 15).

"We've all worked to create a continuous wildlife corridor, without fragmentation, around the North Bay, and up into Sonoma Creek, the Petaluma River, and the Napa River. Our goal is not a monoculture of salt marsh but rather a mosaic of wetland and edge habitats," says senior wildlife biologist Larry Wyckoff of the California Department of Fish and Game, which owns 15,000 acres of habitat, mostly north of Highway 37.

"We're here to manage these lands for wildlife first," says Wyckoff's federal neighbor in the corridor, Christy Smith, who ran the adjacent 13,190-acre San Pablo Bay National Wildlife Refuge until 2010. "The inherent nature of marshes makes them perfect for wildlife and pretty inaccessible for people."

In the North Bay, most visitors are drive-bys. The few who do pull off Highway 37 and venture out into this wilderness are carrying a gun, a fishing rod, or a bag of garbage they'd rather not pay dump fees to drop. Anglers come year-round both for fun and to feed their families; hunters come when the season's open for waterfowl and pheasant. Most of the area can only be reached by boat, kayak, or canoe, and only by those who really know the tides. Despite the patches on their shirts, Smith and Wyckoff aren't rangers. Those whose vessels get stuck in the mud and call for help via cell phone, are more likely to be asked about their sunscreen and water supplies than rescued before the next high tide. In any case, the first thing

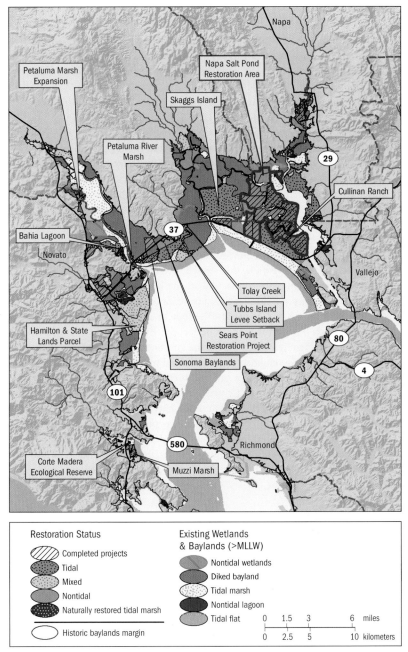

Restoration Status

- ⊘ Completed projects
- Tidal
- Mixed
- Nontidal
- Naturally restored tidal marsh
- ⬭ Historic baylands margin

Existing Wetlands & Baylands (>MLLW)

- Nontidal wetlands
- Diked bayland
- Tidal marsh
- Nontidal lagoon
- Tidal flat

0	1.5	3	6	miles
0	2.5	5	10	kilometers

Map 15. Existing, restored, and planned wetlands in the North Bay. (Stuart Siegel)

they'll say is not to try to leave the boat: those who do face sinking to the waist in bay mud.

Restoration in this vast diked area of farm fields and salt ponds has taken many forms. In the arc of bayshore between the Petaluma and Napa rivers lie examples of nearly every kind of wetland and restoration technique.

Under the Petaluma River Bridge, the first high point on the highway east of Novato, drivers can see beautiful S-shaped sloughs through the marshes. The closest of these looks likes it's been there for centuries but was only created in 1994, when a backhoe carved two 50-foot holes in the levee and let the tides in under the guidance of the California Department of Fish and Game's Carl Wilcox. Wilcox championed and oversaw many of the earliest restoration projects in the North Bay, and the new wetland was called "Carl's Marsh" in his honor. Wilcox remembers the moment of the breach in a 2001 *San Francisco Chronicle* article by reporter Jane Kay: "It immediately started to fill up, and black-and-white Western Grebes flew overhead fishing for the Yellowfin Goby that came in on the tide."

From a grebe's-eye view, this stretch of river branches off into thick wetlands and eventually connects with the bay's finest historic natural marsh a short distance upriver. This upstream reach of the 4,000-acre Petaluma River Marshes, managed by the state, is one place where scientists come to study how nature makes a perfect wetland.

Farther along Highway 37 east of the Port Sonoma marina lies a restoration project where engineers experimented with ways to speed natural sedimentation and vegetation processes. Here, in 1996, designer Philip Williams used 2.5 million cubic yards of material dredged from the Oakland harbor to raise 300 acres of subsided hayfields closer to tidal levels. The project accomplished two goals at once: providing a place to reuse dredged material and elevating the land decades faster than nature could. The design also included some engineered wetland topography, some low peninsulas to buffer wave action, and a few plugs of planted cordgrass. Years later, the Sonoma Baylands are growing into a complex, functional

---

TOUR WETLANDS BY PODCAST

Download a private tour of the wetlands, wildlife, and restoration projects along Highway 37 from the San Francisco Bay Joint Venture website, www.yourwetlands.org. This audio tour narrates what can be seen along the highway via an iPod or mp3 player. Other visual and audio tours of the Sonoma Baylands and South Bay salt ponds are also available via the Internet (see "References").

San Pablo Bay's northern shoreline: in the foreground, from left to right are Tolay Creek, Tubbs Island, Sears Point, Sonoma Baylands, and the Petaluma River. The Sonoma Land Trust will restore nearly 1,000 acres of Sears Point to tidal marsh beginning in 2012. (Stephen Joseph, courtesy of the Sonoma Land Trust)

wetland, one that visitors can walk and bike around all the way to Tolay Creek on the Bay Trail.

The Bay Trail will also run past the old Clementino dairy farm at Sears Point, where locals and feds have teamed up to create a new wildlife refuge and land trust headquarters. The site both preserves the farm buildings and cattle that graze the surrounding fields, and offers visitors a window into the complexity of the wetland ecosystem. "People relate more easily to the farm culture than they do the wild. When they come to the baylands, they're often not sure what to do, or how to be here," says Christy Smith. "At the refuge, we can connect them to both, give them a sense of belonging to nature right in their backyard."

The only place visitors could connect with these baylands before this new hub came into being was Tubbs Island. The island lies midway across Highway 37, and for a long time it was the only place on the North Bay shore offering picnic tables, interpretive displays, bathrooms, and sign-posted trails.

Beyond Tubbs and the roar of the Infineon Raceway, Highway 37 crosses Sonoma Creek, and there's a clear view through the refuge marshes all the way out to the open waters of the bay. To the north stretches Skaggs Island, once a top-secret communications center for the navy. The restoration fate of this fallow farm, added to the wildlife refuge in the 1990s, is still being decided. In the meantime, it offers seasonal wetland habitat and hosts an antenna array used by pilots to triangulate their position as they fly into regional airports.

Most of the land north of the highway between the Sonoma Creek and Napa River bridges is part of state-owned Napa–Sonoma Marsh. These 10,000 acres of old salt ponds came to the people of California via an oil spill settlement in 1994, and another 1,400 acres of ponds were added in 2003. Among the 12 ponds slated for restoration, Pond 2A proved a simple one-man job. As the story goes, Carl Wilcox simply chose a good spot on the levee to blast a hole and "presto," he created a wetland. But nearly every other pond was more problematic. Too much salt had built up in the ponds to permit simple breaching. If flushed out into the Napa River, the saline slurry would kill fish or violate water-quality standards. One pond even contained bittern, a byproduct of salt production toxic to fish and aquatic life unless extremely diluted.

By 2003, the state had come up with a plan for converting three ponds adjoining the Napa River to tidal marsh and leaving five inner ponds as the kind of open water favored by diving ducks. During a wet winter in 2006, when sloughs were full of freshwater runoff, managers undertook "salinity reduction breaches" on the three ponds slated for tidal marsh restoration. In the future, urban wastewater from Sonoma County will help dilute the bittern pond until it can be converted into marsh.

The levee at this former salt pond near the Napa River, breached several years ago as part of a restoration project, is now just visible above the water line. Such projects form shallow-water shorebird habitat at first, then evolve into vegetated tidal marsh. (Jude Stalker)

Farther along the highway beyond the state salt ponds and just before the bridge to Vallejo lies Cullinan Ranch, among the most eastern lands in the San Pablo Bay wildlife refuge. Soils on the diked ranch lost their original wetland sponginess long ago, and now lie five to seven feet below sea level. Breaching the dikes all at once will quickly immerse the ranch in three feet of water, and thereby drowning a lot of animals.

On Cullinan Ranch managers face challenges now nearly universal for Bay Area restoration projects. "No-work" windows designed to protect endangered species don't always coincide with periods best for construction. Christy Smith says that, at Cullinan, such restrictions mean work can be done for only two or three weeks out of an entire year. This makes restoration planning a juggling act. "When we breach Cullinan, we have to do it when the salmon are not migrating, but after the breeding season of Salt Marsh Harvest Mice, and in the middle of winter when we already have a sheet of water out there, and the coyotes and rabbits have already retreated to high ground, and it will only take a little more water to flush the remaining critters onto the levees. Then we have to wait for a high tide to dilute that water before we release it back out to the slough, because it'll have been sitting in there for a while, might have turned anerobic, and could pollute the slough."

Whether looking at a map or out from a Highway 37 bridge, it is easy to see the elements of a future landscape that resembles the bayshore's historic mosaic of vegetation, water, mud, and grassland. These future marshes will also help filter out pollutants from runoff, absorb floodwaters from the Napa and Petaluma rivers so they don't creep over sandbags and into town basements, and preserve over 8,000 acres for old-fashioned pastimes. "Because of our agricultural borders, we're more hunting- and fishing-oriented here than the South Bay, which is surrounded by infrastructure, cities, and people who want to walk their dogs, jog with their iPods, or kayak for sport on the bayshore. Our neighbors are farmers who want to do farming things," says Smith.

What really brings a smile to Smith and Wyckoff's faces are the visible signs of wildlife populations returning to healthier numbers. Once salt-making activities quieted down, California Least Terns got busy nesting—laying 96 eggs one year in a new breeding colony (formerly these endangered birds only nested on the island of Alameda). And Harbor Seals recently began poking their heads up in the widening sloughs, curious about their new real estate.

South Bay Salt Ponds Reborn

Concrete hardens most urban shores right to the waterline, but San Francisco Bay's salt-making industry preserved a large area of shoreline in a relatively soft, wet, open state. The opportunity to re-create wetlands on 15,000 acres of South Bay salt ponds—diked and managed for over a century to crystallize salt but never completely severed from the touch of the tides—is unique. No other urban area on the nation's coasts retains such an expansive, seminatural landscape right on its doorstep. And though it may never be the wilderness of salt pannes, cordgrass stands, pickleweed islands, and mudflats it once was, it could get darn close. The plan to restore a mosaic of historic habitats within the network of 65 ponds ringing the bay south of the San Mateo Bridge is one of the largest, most ambitious, and most broadly supported restoration efforts undertaken in the country to date.

"Our region is one of very few places in the world where you have millions of people living adjacent to a natural resource like the bay," says Steve Ritchie, former director of the South Bay Salt Pond Restoration Project. "People can see it changing before their eyes, being returned to some semblance of the state that once was. They're seeing barren salt crusts slowly covered with bay mud, birds and fish coming back in, plants starting to grow, in a place where they can touch it and see it and feel it. When they come to visit this restoration project, they can't believe how extensive an area this is: they stand there with a look of wonder on their faces."

The landscape to be restored is indeed large. If engineers simply bulldozed holes in all the levees, it would double the open-water area of the bay south of the Dumbarton Bridge. After considering whether this

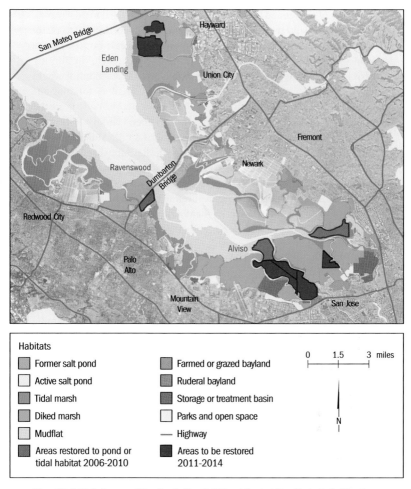

Habitats

Former salt pond	Farmed or grazed bayland
Active salt pond	Ruderal bayland
Tidal marsh	Storage or treatment basin
Diked marsh	Parks and open space
Mudflat	Highway
Areas restored to pond or tidal habitat 2006-2010	Areas to be restored 2011-2014

0   1.5   3 miles

N

Map 16. Initial phases of the South Bay Salt Pond Restoration Project. Putting together a restoration plan for such a large landscape change in the heart of the Bay Area took much more than scientific analysis and professional design. To come up with this plan, the project gathered input from a 30-member stakeholder forum—including conservationists, landowners, local business, and recreation advocates, among others—and held over 50 public meetings. In addition, the project has coordinated its efforts with more than 10 different state and federal agencies, and with 15 local governments and special districts. (Redrawn by S.F. Estuary Institute, courtesy of the S.F. Bay Joint Venture)

patchwork of orange and pink ponds should all be converted to tidal marsh, or a mix of wetland types and shallows, project planners decided to phase in conversions at different times. Not only would this ease impacts on the avian species that frequent the ponds in their current state (by shifting them gently into new and improved habitats over decades) but it would also give managers time to experiment with different restoration approaches, monitor results, and adjust their plans accordingly. If all the ruddy ducks suddenly ceased over-wintering in Eden Landing, if mercury levels spiked in the Alviso Slough food web, or if a critical flood control levee started to erode, the project would have the flexibility to adapt.

The main thrust of the project is biological. Everyone wants to see enough tidal wetlands around the bay to recover native Clapper Rails and Harvest Mice, and enough dry patches around the wetland edge for Snowy Plovers to nest. They want to see verdant new swaths of marsh vegetation and new supplies of plankton, algae, and other fish food to bolster the ecological functions of the bay's marshlands. But the project must also sustain existing bird populations; keep levees strong enough to protect local urban communities from flooding; and provide trails, scenery, and shoreline recreation for the residents of the Bay Area.

Here, nothing could be further from the guerrilla restorations of earlier eras, which involved little more than a well-placed stick of dynamite. Though salt ponds retain more original wetland features than long-tilled farm fields behind dikes—aerial photos reveal branching slough channels beneath their crystalline salt crusts—there's much more to do on many of the ponds than just reconnect them with the bay.

Michelle Orr, an engineer, has worked on restoring more than 30,000 acres of bay wetlands in her 15-year career with the consulting firm Philip Williams & Associates, but she says the South Bay salt ponds are her "most highly engineered" project. Her team's blueprints detail every tide gate and culvert flap, every lowered berm and heightened levee, and every intake and outlet canal. They map out which ponds will get deeper and which shallower, and which will one day grow a carpet of salt-loving vegetation. In some ponds, they specify new islands, to be scraped off the pond bottom and piled up into circular and linear shapes—bird biologists want to see which shape attracts the most nesters. For another pond, they've designed a specialized gate using stacked fiberboards light enough for two people to move, so that they can either allow tides in or keep floods out.

The seeds of this grand project go back decades. Ponds owned first by Leslie Salt, then later by Cargill, have been battlegrounds for as long as the restoration game has been played. When the *Habitat Goals* report threw down the gauntlet in 1999, calling for 100,000 acres of tidal marsh around the bay, Steve Ritchie remembers Cargill's public relations person Jill Singleton looking him hard in the eye and saying: "We're not going to

CONNECTING TO WILDLIFE REFUGES

A landscape-scale restoration in the South Bay is being achieved because the vast properties restored since 2000 fill in bayshore gaps between older restorations and existing wetlands protected by the Don Edwards San Francisco Bay National Wildlife Refuge and the California Department of Fish and Game. Indeed, federal and state land managers were among the first to experiment with how to convert salt ponds back to tidal marsh habitat in the 1980s, and they enhanced large areas around Newark Slough and Eden Landing near Fremont. More recently the U.S. Fish and Wildlife Service is reclaiming more of Bair Island off Redwood City for birds and beasts. Local state and federal rangers, wardens, and park staff will also be the ones in charge of maintaining most of the larger postrestoration landscape, including opening and closing valves to keep ponds at desired water levels.

Willet with crab in mouth. (Edward M. Nguyen)

sell, we'll be in this business forever." But in 2003 they did sell, and downsizing their patchwork of salt-making real estate helped the company become more efficient, according to Ritchie.

Actual restoration work began in 2006 with the opening of 479 acres to the tides in the far South Bay between Coyote Creek and Mud Slough. But the backhoes and bulldozers didn't really get into gear until 2009, when they began Phase I of the long-term plan. Visitors in this first decade of a 50-year restoration process are likely to see more big equipment, bare dirt, and dirty water than marsh. But drivers starting their slow climb over the Dumbarton Bridge from the peninsula's Ravenswood area should get a grand view of long-legged and web-footed birds foraging and paddling in a 240-acre pond and resting on 30 new islands. Some of these islands are designed to go green, offering vegetative cover, whereas others offer secluded mini-mudflats. Doing such delicate habitat construction in mud with a giant bulldozer—each island is no more than a gently sloped mound a couple of feet high—can be difficult, says Orr. But these "managed" ponds are attempts to squeeze as many shorebirds into as little space as possible. They provide more amenities per square foot of wet space than the salt ponds currently offer.

Bird island habitats created in Ravenswood pond (known as SF2 and also pictured on p. 237 post-breach) as part of the South Bay restoration project. Old railroad bridge and water pipelines from Hetch Hetchy reservoir to San Francisco appear in background. (Melisa Helton, courtesy of the U.S. Fish and Wildlife Service)

This 240-acre pond on the western shore of the bay, in the Ravenswood area east of Menlo Park, is one of several spots undergoing Phase I changes over the next few years. Others are on the bay's eastern shore at Eden Landing, and on the far southern shore around the old fishing town of Alviso (see Map 16, p. 263).

At Eden Landing, just south of the San Mateo Bridge, restoration managers have divided two ponds into seven small compartments, each of different salinities. Biologists want to know which salinity birds favor most, and the Eden Landing experiment should produce clues for future phases of restoration. The seven small ponds run much like a salt-production facility, gradually evaporating off more and more water but stopping short of the final crystallization phase. Orr's team had to come up with some convoluted hydraulic systems in order to shunt the saltiest water in the seventh pond through a mixing basin, where it could be diluted before being returned to the bay.

The third Phase I project is taking place at the bottom of the bay, near the old asparagus canning capital of Alviso. This small shoreline town sits about 10 feet below sea level, surrounded by salt ponds, and is home to a historic working class community. Here, the project may give the little town its silt-choked marina back and reinvigorate the local shrimping industry. The plan involves tweaking some of the massive flood-control protections placed here by the U.S. Army Corps in the 1970s. By carefully distributing new tides and runoff flows through the channels and ponds in this complex, Orr plans to slowly scour out the silted-up channel. "We're only going partway toward the long-term solution with Phase I. We need to be able to change our approach in case we get undesirable flooding or more mercury working its way up the food chain," she says.

Whereas the North Bay mudflats include layers of gold-mining debris containing mercury, the South Bay lies at the bottom of a watershed in which mercury itself was mined for over 120 years (see also Map 8, p. 169). During this time, the New Almaden mine extracted over 84 million pounds of quicksilver (mercury by another name) from the Santa Clara Valley foothills. But not all of the mercury left the watershed in flasks.

Avocet being banded on the eastern levee of Pond A8, near Alviso, as part of South Bay salt pond mercury contamination studies. Pond A8 is being carefully monitored due to its location downstream of the New Almaden mercury mine. (Scott Demers)

Some ended up in the Guadalupe River and South Bay sediments draining the mining district, as well as in the Alviso Slough area where so much restoration work is under way.

As each phase of the work unfurls, and as salt ponds of different habitat types are flooded or returned to marsh, scientists will be monitoring mercury impacts. But collaborative studies between 2006 and 2008 by the USGS, San Francisco Estuary Institute, and Santa Clara Valley Water District found that flies, fish, and birds living in South Bay tidal marshes had mercury levels similar to those living in other South Bay habitats. So scientists say the South Bay isn't a bad place for restoration despite the fact that there's more mercury in its sediments.

Tracking mercury movements during Phase I changes to the salt pond landscape is just part of an elaborate restoration plan. The project will begin by restoring 7,500 acres of tidal marsh and enhancing 7,500 acres of managed ponds by 2020–2030. These will be followed by the gradual creation of a mix of 13,400 acres of tidal marsh and 1,600 acres of managed ponds by 2030–2040. At any time, work may be halted depending on how wildlife, public interests, and the bay itself respond to the improvements.

"If we do our job right, Salt Marsh Harvest Mice, Clapper Rails, and Snowy Plovers are not going to be endangered species anymore. How cool is that?" says Orr.

Weeding by Satellite

Every tidal wetland around the bay—whether it's a few tufts of cordgrass, a half-dozen salt ponds, or a vast expanse of mudflats—exists not only in reality but also in virtual space in the computer banks of the Invasive Spartina Project. Click on any computer in their offices, and aerial views of every wet nook and cranny along the bayshore can be called onscreen. Zoom in for a bird's-eye view, or zoom out to the satellite that took the picture. Click again and a digital quilt of tiny pink, red, and purple boxes covers the wetland. Each square has been visited by a Spartina Project biologist with a GPS recorder more than half a dozen times in as many years, and checked for the opportunistic green alien that keeps threatening and mingling with the natives: Atlantic cordgrass.

The project has been battling this wetland weed since 2000, but the invader has been around since the 1970s. Back then, well-intentioned engineers planted it to speed vegetation of bare banks and ponds along the Alameda Creek flood-control channel. *S. alterniflora* spread into adjoining areas fast and, worse, hybridized with native Pacific cordgrass, *Spartina foliosa*.

The resulting genetic variation among spartina plants is astounding, with different hybrids adapting to different salinity, soil, and tidal conditions. Some grow well in high marsh, and others engulf open mudflats. According to the state's aquatic invasive species management plan, "Hybrid smooth cordgrass can produce up to 23 times the seed of native cordgrass, grow taller and/or faster, and tolerate high or low salinity." Hybrids can turn diverse marshes into monocultural meadows, crowd out meandering tidal channels, and transform open mudflats into uniform expanses of green.

This invader is considered such a threat to habitat and ecosystem restoration efforts around the bay that the Invasive Spartina Project's efforts to track down, dig up, spray, and kill both purebred and hybrid cordgrass have widespread public and private support. In 2000, surveyors found 470 acres of hybrid smooth cordgrass, though the original Atlantic parent had become rare. By 2006, when the project began full-scale treatment, they found nearly 2,000 acres of hybrid throughout the region's intertidal baylands—a more than 300 percent increase. By 2009, despite aggressive treatment and the reduction of the most infested areas of the hybrid to just 250 acres, pockets were still peppering the bayshore. Project biologists endeavor to monitor every possible hybrid haven, surveying over 60,000 acres by land, boat, and air. As of 2010, 167 marshes around the bay were still expected to require treatment.

Biologist Jen McBroom documenting, with the help of a yellow GPS unit, invasive spartina spread and hybridization with native species at Coyote Point near San Mateo. (Jude Stalker)

In the early days, the project experimented with eradication techniques until it got the right combination of mechanical and chemical approaches, applied during the most vulnerable stages of the pest's growth cycle. As with any infestation, it's important to keep on top of new outbreaks. According to monitoring manager Ingrid Hogle, annual surveys show that areas treated one year have a 50 percent incidence of reinfestation by invasive hybrids, while treating areas two years running reduces that figure to 10 percent.

How does a patch of non-native spartina hybrid get from the edge of Marin's Corte Madera Creek to a desktop computer in Berkeley? The long way—via space. On a warm June day at Creekside Marsh, for example, biologist Ode Bernstein spends a lot of time trying to stand in the right position so that his small yellow handheld GPS unit can get a connection to a satellite. If it's really poor, he puts the unit on top of his head.

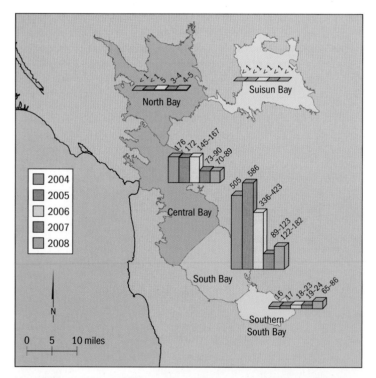

Map 17. Net acreage of invasive spartina by bay region from 2004 to 2008. These data show the dramatic decline in net acreage from the Bay Area total of 776 acres at the height of the infestation in 2005, to less than 300 acres by 2008, largely as a result of monitoring, eradication, and control programs. (Invasive Spartina Project)

Map 18. GPS data loggers from the Invasive Spartina Project record the exact location, species, extent, cover, and treatment of invasive spartina at over 170 sites around the bay on maps such as this one of Creekside Park, Marin (2009). Different colors differentiate S. *densiflora* (purple), *anglica* (yellow), and various hybrids—S. *densiflora x foliosa* (blue) and S. *alterniflora x foliosa* (red). (Invasive Spartina Project)

The patches that Bernstein is monitoring appear on his GPS as polygons, squares, or plot lines. On this day Bernstein's mapping a grid in an area where dense-flowered cordgrass (*S. densiflora*) and its hybrids are found. First he walks around—stepping from bare patch to bare patch in order to avoid vegetation where Clapper Rails may be hiding. Using GPS, he tries to place himself at the center of a predetermined virtual grid square. Then he looks for telltale characteristics such as in-rolling leaves to determine he is among the dense-flowered cordgrass. When he finds some, he eyeballs the grid area, estimates how much of it is covered by the hybrid, and logs the percentage into his yellow handheld.

Bernstein says that being able to identify all the non-native plant species was hard during his first year, but it became easier after several seasons. When in doubt, he'll take a DNA sample. Project workers like Bernstein took 200–1,000 samples baywide per year between 2002 and 2009. In

FIELDWORK: RAIL TELEMETRY

The clock claims it's the peak of the morning commute, but that's hard to judge at Martin Luther King Jr. Shoreline Regional Park. The interstate and Oakland International Airport, just blocks away, emit a muffled rumble here, dampened further by a pearl-grey ceiling of clouds.

I zip my windbreaker high against the mid-April chill and hurry to a boardwalk overlooking a tidal marsh. There, Cory Overton, a wildlife biologist with the U.S. Geological Survey, and his telemetry technician Jeffrey Lewis are observing California Clapper Rails. Overton is managing a survey of how and where these most endangered of Bay Area birds move in the region's marshes. Known as Arrowhead Marsh, this area offers a rare view of the largest and most human-acclimated population of these birds in the state.

Overton has a real fondness for California Clapper Rails. He says of these stocky wetland residents, "Rails are basically chickens, and everything likes to eat chickens—pretty much anything with teeth. But it's the same with the rails; they'll eat anything they can get their beaks around."

Earlier this year, Overton and his team of biologists conducted rail roundups at four marshes. They captured eight birds at Arrowhead alone, outfitting each with radio transmitters. The transmitters are the size of AAA batteries, worn between the wings like a backpack and held in place by Teflon fabric straps.

Clapper Rails are caught by hand and net. Biologists band each bird, then attach a radio transmitter like a backpack between the birds' wings. The radio harness lasts about two years. (Jude Stalker)

It's low tide and an ideal time to take location readings. Jeffrey takes out his telemetry equipment. The set consists of a receiver that can detect the pings emitted by the transmitters, a handheld antenna resembling an old TV aerial, and a set of headphones. Modern electronics miniaturization hasn't affected this piece of equipment; the sturdy metal receiver box, with seven dials and an LCD readout, is the size of a car battery and weighs at least six pounds.

At water's edge, Jeffrey tunes the receiver to the frequency of his target bird, sweeps the antenna in the direction of the marsh, and listens. The pings get louder when the antenna is pointing directly at his quarry, allowing him to home in on the rail's location by moving the antenna in an arc. He refines his position by marking with an outstretched arm where the pings drop off to nothing, then recenters his aerial. When he's satisfied the reading is accurate, he uses a compass and GPS to mark the bearing. He'll repeat measurements for each bird several times as he walks the shoreline paths. Back at the lab, a computer program will triangulate the readings and rate the reliability of each data point. Jeffrey and another technician may take readings several times a day at up to three marshes—once at high tide and once at low tide—to get an idea of the birds' ranges and behavior.

Arrowhead Marsh consists largely of salt-marsh cordgrass, the clumps resembling shocks of hair on a bed-tousled head. Also known as spartina, cordgrass is a mainstay of Clapper Rail life. It offers both cover from predators and building material for nests in a habitat with relatively few other plants.

The success of this cordgrass, a hybrid of native and Atlantic species, is the impetus behind Overton's study. Clapper Rails have been found nesting in the hybrid, and scientists are concerned that programs to eradicate the hybrid could be hurting the birds.

The rail study began in 2006. Census numbers have recorded a sizable recent rise in rail populations in the bay, from a low of a few hundred in the early 1990s to about 1,400 in 2008. The study should help sort out whether the extra cover afforded by hybrid spartina is responsible for the comeback.

Another goal is to determine how many California Clapper Rails local marshes can support. Arrowhead houses a goodly number. Every 20 minutes or so, another bird pops out of the cordgrass or stalks across the expanse of mud alongside the pier. Rails are so plentiful here that it's hard to remember the species is endangered.

The biologists wait for the rails to settle down and nest. According to Jeffrey's tracking, none has laid its clutch of eggs yet, though plenty of birds are showing signs of spring fever. We hear a smattering of the *keck-burr* come-hither calls that females use to solicit males, and we see two of these normally cover-conscious birds bickering in the open mud at the end of the pier. We spot a couple of other resident rails driving intruders from their patch of cordgrass. During breeding season, territory defense attains extra importance because pairs rely on that portion of marsh to support their young.

The birds time egg laying very closely to the tides, to avoid the big surges that can drown their eggs. "Just a few inches higher makes a huge difference if you live in a marsh," Overton says.

The rails' susceptibility to tidal flooding and thus climate change worries Overton and other biologists. But for the moment, these homely avians—the focus of so much human worry and effort—continue to reside in local marshes, thrilling visitors with their boisterous cries. KMW

addition to clipping and bagging a sample for the DNA lab, Bernstein fills out identification questionnaires on his GPS unit, noting, for example, whether the suspect is short, tall, or intermediate in height; dense or sparse at the stem; and which Sherwin Williams paint chip (Strawberry Plains, Lady in Red, Cotton Candy, to name a few) it most closely matches in color. The GPS monitor, meanwhile, pinpoints the exact location and time of the sample. The answers get downloaded into the project's computers and can be updated later as surveyors revisit sites.

The sampling, eyeballing, and monitoring process speeds up dramatically from the air. Instead of having to kayak into the most remote marshes, it is much easier to hover about 10 feet above it in a featherweight helicopter, hopping from point to point or following a line. Helicopters can give biologists access to steep, wet, or roadless places on islands, cliffs, and marshes. The Spartina Project's expert pilot will even touch down in the marsh so the biologist can grab a DNA sample. "Every second you're in a helicopter, the dollars are flying out the window, so you can't hesitate. You have to be real fast, real honed with your spartina inventory—it's speed mapping and super fun," says the project's Jen McBroom. "Even better, though the Clapper Rails sometimes flush and run when we fly over, it's so quick there is very little disturbance."

Underwater Restoration

As projects to restore the wetlands and uplands that ring the bay steam ahead, scientists have been able to turn their attention to a part of estuarine life most easily forgotten by human residents: the area underwater. Including all areas from mean low-tide level and below, these subtidal areas encompass both the water column and the bay floor—essentially, any place a fish can reach. Following the model of collaboration that created the *Baylands Ecosystem Habitat Goals*, scientists recently completed subtidal habitat goals as benchmarks to guide underwater restoration for the next 50 years.

Little scientific information exists about what the bay's underwater surfaces were originally like. This is partly because human activities have wrought substantial changes to these unseen areas, blasting out ship-wrecking rocks, coating oyster beds with mining debris, dredging, dumping, and mining for sand and oyster shells. The federal government conducted the earliest survey of the bay floor in the mid-1850s. They took not only depth soundings but also samples of the bottom. It is these 160-year-old scraps of the bay floor—handfuls of mud, buckets of shellfish beds, sacks of gravel and sand—that scientists dearly want to lay their hands on, but no one knows which archival dungeon they may have ended up in. Until these samples are found, "we don't know how many acres of eelgrass used to exist in the bay, or where native oyster populations used to be," says marine biologist Marilyn Latta of the California Coastal Conservancy and the subtidal goals project.

Scientists aren't letting this lack of historical information hold them back. Major surveys of current subtidal assets are either under way or being mined for data to inform restoration.

Among the top priorities is bringing back the great meadows of eelgrass (*Zostera marina*) that scientists suspect must have once hugged the sandy shallows of bay margins. Expanding eelgrass beds does more than just return a native species to the bay. "We consider eelgrass an ecosystem engineer, a habitat builder," Latta says. Eelgrass blades provide three-dimensional structure to a place that consists largely of featureless mud. Bryozoans and snails settle on and cling to the leaves, sharing space with golden clumps of Pacific Herring eggs. The root bulbs, or rhizomes, of eelgrass can help stabilize bottom sediments, and the long, undulating blades have been shown, in other estuaries, to help dampen the force of waves, ferry wakes, and other turbulence, reducing shoreline erosion. The calmer waters within eelgrass blades offer refuge to salmon smolts, crabs, pipefish, and other organisms too small or fragile to battle the currents. Migrating waterfowl feed directly on eelgrass leaves, which also oxygenate the water.

Scientists venture into the bay to conduct eelgrass research. (Jude Stalker)

Much of what is known about eelgrass comes from studies in other estuaries such as Chesapeake Bay and Puget Sound. Though the species that grows in these estuaries is the same, several aspects of each population are very different. In Chesapeake Bay, where the waters are both clearer and warmer, eelgrass beds tend to be relatively large, extending over several dozen acres. But the plants themselves tend to grow just a few feet long. In San Francisco Bay, the largest remaining bed is 1,500 acres, though most beds are just tens of acres in size. Individual plants often sprout blades up to eight feet long.

Although scientists can't be certain, human activities have likely contributed to the disappearance of these marine meadows.

Central Bay Eelgrass Beds

The most recent attempts at eelgrass restoration began with a loss of habitats. To build the new eastern span of the Bay Bridge, the California Department of Transportation had to sink supports right through an existing eelgrass bed off Emeryville. As mitigation for this damage, the agency paid for a survey by consultant Keith Merkel to map existing and potential eelgrass habitat in the bay. He found that the largest bed, between Point San Pablo and Point Pinole, consists of about 1,500 acres, or about half of the remaining 3,000 acres of eelgrass in the bay. He also mapped two other large beds and a number of smaller ones, mostly in the brisk currents and moderate salinities of the Central Bay. Although this is an improvement over 1987, when just 316 acres of eelgrass were found, Merkel estimates that the right conditions exist to support 10 times more eelgrass acreage in the bay.

Meanwhile, Katharyn Boyer, a professor of biology at San Francisco State University and the Romberg Tiburon Center, has been experimenting with how best to replenish local eelgrass meadows. After a year of laboratory studies, she began planting new eelgrass beds at three half-acre sites in Marin in 2006. One is within San Quentin's watery front yard, one in the next inlet over at the Marin Rod and Gun Club, and the third at Richardson Bay.

Though Richardson Bay appeared the most promising site at first, attempts to establish eelgrass there failed. In retrospect, says Latta, the site may have been too murky, requiring the plants to grow at shallow depths that exposed them to heat stress during low tides. Plants at the other two sites, however, flourished.

Boyer has used four different planting techniques, each designed to take advantage of the plant's natural methods of propagation. The first technique involved digging up healthy plants from existing beds off Point San Pablo and replanting the shoots within plastic frames to provide support against the currents as they took root. As it turned out, few plants took. The second technique involved harvesting eelgrass flowers, and later scattering the seeds by hand over the site. Like transplantation, the technique had only spotty success. The third method required monitoring maturing eelgrass flowers in the wild, collecting the flowers when they were nearly ripe, and bundling several dozen into mesh bags. The bags were then left to dangle from the undersides of buoys. As the seeds ripened, they would break off from the fronds and drop to the bay floor. This last technique, pioneered by researchers on the East Coast, proved the most fruitful. But a fourth technique, affixing an eelgrass shoot directly to a biodegradable bamboo stick with twist ties, and then pushing it down into the mud to cover the roots, is also proving successful. "We have such gelatinous sediment in San Francisco Bay, planting the shoots directly doesn't work well. They can come loose and float away too easily," says Boyer's colleague Stephanie Kiriakopolis, who pioneered this new method.

To trace the rate of plant growth, researchers prick pinholes near the base of new eelgrass blades and return weeks later to find the same plant with the help of a GPS point. They then identify the correct plant, feel along the leaves with their bare hands to relocate the leaf with the hole, and measure how far the pinhole has moved up the stem.

Mesh bags full of eelgrass used in eelgrass bed restoration experiments in the bay. (Jude Stalker)

Experiments to coax new eelgrass meadows out of the mud and water have not been just in the name of science. One day in the 1990s, Jim McGrath, a coastal engineer with the Port of Oakland, went out to the former terminus of the Western Pacific Railroad to oversee some work. While there, he looked out at the water and spotted the telltale green blades of eelgrass. About a quarter-acre of the green fronds waved from atop a sandy ridge separating the 190 acres of Middle Harbor and the main harbor channel.

An avid windsurfer, McGrath had seen plenty of eelgrass habitat while on his board. "You notice where the eelgrass grows because it hooks your fin," he says. "I knew where most beds were in the Central Bay, and I knew some of those conditions were right in our harbor."

Scientists Katharyn Boyer and Sarah Hughes, from the Romberg Tiburon Center, measure eelgrass extent on Keller Beach near Richmond. (Jude Stalker)

McGrath's find dovetailed nicely with other happenings at the port. The port hoped to dredge the main shipping channel to accommodate larger ships. The project would produce an estimated 14 million cubic yards of sediment. Most would consist of fine sand, an ideal substrate for eelgrass. "I thought that, after damaging habitat for dredging, wouldn't it be cool to fill it with sediment for restoration purposes? Filling this area back up to historic depths would be real restoration," McGrath says.

Coastal charts from the 1890s show that Middle Harbor was originally shallow enough to support eelgrass meadows, but it has since been deepened to allow the huge hulls of navy battleships and port vessels to nose into dock without grounding. McGrath's team began scrutinizing present-day harbor conditions closely to see if they would sustain an eelgrass bed after construction. They found that fill from the transbay BART tunnel project now blocked the original path of the waves. They worried that altered currents might rob the area of the newly placed dredged material, or smother the new beds with silt, or pour sand right back into the shipping channel. For this reason, the team carefully modeled tidal circulation, bottom elevations, and how far the waves penetrated into the harbor before designing the new meadow. To hold in the sand, the team proposed a jetty extending across the mouth of Middle Harbor.

Years of permitting negotiations later, the bay commission gave its blessing to the project. McGrath's construction team first lined the fill area with fine-grained silts and clays to provide a stable base, then gradually began adding sand. Monitoring stations tracked when each batch of additional sediment had settled enough to add the next. About 5.2 million cubic yards of material were added to the harbor—enough to fill San Francisco's War Memorial building 28 times. By 2010, the bottom of Middle Harbor averaged about six feet deep.

Since then, the nearly 180 acres of shallow-water habitat has gradually come back to life. Least Terns and Brown Pelicans started feeding in the restored area almost immediately, and eelgrass has recolonized the bottom on its own. A new harbor park, operated by the regional parks district, officially opened to the public in 2004. It attracts families, kayakers, and shorebirds, but it also offers an unusual example of state-of-the-art container shipping and underwater restoration occurring side-by-side.

Oysters Back in the Bay?

Hundreds if not thousands of acres of oyster beds once corrugated bay shallows. The 15 thousand tons of oyster shell deposits—all from Olympia Oysters (*Ostrea lurida*) dredged from bay waters each year by mining operations—are a testament to the former abundance of this native bivalve. As part of the effort to restore submerged habitats, scientists are now trying to return native oysters to the bay.

Though an intrinsically important native species, oysters, like coral reefs in tropical seas, are being eyed for the habitat they provide. Their corrugated, tear-shaped shells provide solid three-dimensional structure to a soft, muddy bay floor. Species ranging from tunicates to anemones, and bryozoans to other shellfish, need a hard surface to settle on and grow. Between the loss of bay rocks to navigational blasting and the demise of the oyster beds, such sturdy substrates are in short supply. The nooks and crannies among and between oyster shells offer young crabs and fish places to hide. Because some oyster species grow on top of one another, they form shallow reefs that dampen wave action and reduce shoreline erosion.

Olympia Oysters once played a major role in keeping bay waters clear and filled with the light eelgrass needs to grow. One oyster can filter 30 liters of water per hour. Scientists are analyzing oyster restoration opportunities in the bay by experimenting with hanging various substrates in the water and building new reefs, then observing how many settle down and grow. (Jude Stalker)

In 2001, groups such as Save the Bay began assessing whether enough wild oysters remained in the bay to replenish themselves, given the opportunity. They began by hanging out strings of clean Pacific Oyster shells off bay piers, to see whether oyster spawn drawn to the chemical signal of the shells might settle down. Resembling marine-themed Christmas tree decor, these shell strings attracted a strong showing of infant Olympias in places like Marin's Richardson Bay. Other efforts—ranging from stakes topped with oyster shell clusters to bags of clean oyster shells stacked in mounds and linear reefs—all drew baby oysters but proved very labor-intensive.

Now scientists are exploring the idea of building temporary oyster reefs. One idea is to coat squares of burlap with a mixture dubbed "seament"—pulverized fossil oyster shells mixed with bay sediments and small amounts of Portland cement. The shells might help attract oyster spawn, while the cement will hold the briquettes together just long enough for young oysters to make it on their own. Seament can also be used to build "reef balls," resembling hollow, table-sized wiffle balls. Reef balls have been used around the world to attract corals and establish mangrove stands. Both techniques could provide oysters with a settling surface without adding permanent fill to the bay.

All of these techniques have been used at the Marin Rod and Gun Club restoration site since 2004—attracting thousands of baby oysters and doubling the native Olympia Oyster population present in the estuary. The oysters are also providing a hoped-for side benefit: eelgrass from an adjacent restoration project is growing better between the shell reefs than on its own. In 2010, local experts began similar experiments on the opposite shore, near the Berkeley marina.

Building a Healthy Ethic

Though the ecological well-being of the bay and its watershed may be the primary goal of restoring eelgrass beds and tidal wetlands, and of giving endangered species the habitat they need to thrive, the well-being of the human populace is also important. People—what they do, how they live, and the choices they make—are essential in any restoration package. If people care about the bay, they'll fight for it. Those who walk their dog on the beach, bike along levee-top trails, see Marsh Hawks and Great Blue Herons hunting along the shore, or kayak or boogie board across the water will come to value the bay's contribution to their quality of life.

Over the years, the San Francisco Bay Conservation and Development Commission has made it easier for the region to get down to the bay and touch the water. Four decades ago, when citizens "saved the bay" and created BCDC, there were only a handful of tiny parks and piers along the shoreline. Indeed, one of the mandates of the new commission was to provide more public access to the bay's coastline. By 1989, the commission had helped open more than 100 miles of shoreline for recreation. Today, the public can visit over 300 miles of bayshore, the centerpieces of 135 shoreline parks. In all, these bayside parklands encompass 57,000 acres of open space—an area roughly twice the size of the city of San Francisco.

Residents of some of the densest, most urbanized quarters of the Bay Area can now walk their dogs beneath the signature red bridge at San Francisco's Crissy Field, stroll through the heart of the busiest container shipping port on the Pacific coast along Oakland's Middle Harbor shore, or marvel at muddy future wetlands from paths skirting Marin's former Hamilton Army Airfield. Some of the region's little league baseball teams now play on decommissioned Treasure Island turf, and rock bands perform atop the old pile of garbage that is now the Shoreline at Mountain View amphitheater. Most of these sites was very much off limits to the public 20 years ago.

All of these public shoreline access points will one day be connected by a 400-mile recreational trail that rings the bay. Activists launched the Bay Trail project in 1989. By 2009, they had secured and marked almost 300 miles of trail with signs depicting a curving path along the shore in green, yellow, and blue.

The Bay Trail also seeks to link land to water by providing access to ferries, public boat launches, and a new "Water Trail." Still in development, this trail was described by journalist Paul McHugh in a July 2008 *New York Times* article as "a frame for travel, more than an actual pathway. When a system is created, paddlers, rowers or sailors can connect the dots in any manner or order they like. Or, in whatever way wind and tide demand." Over 400 water trails already ply coastal and inland waters elsewhere on the continent.

A group called Bay Access came up with the Water Trail idea in 2001. Four years later, the California legislature established the San Francisco Bay Area Water Trail, finding that "with loss of public open space, the public increasingly looks to the Bay, the region's largest open space, for recreational opportunities." By 2009, environmental impact reviews for the proposed network of 112 bay access sites, or trailheads, were under way to accommodate human-powered watercraft.

One potential impact is that small, nonmotorized vessels can sometimes enter shallower areas and get closer to wildlife than those with noisy engines. Such stealth approaches often trigger a strong "startle" response. The more they startle, the more precious energy wildlife may use to get out of the way of inquisitive humans. When birds dive or flush (take flight) in response to disturbance, for example, they may also abandon nests, lose foraging time, expend limited energy reserves, and begin avoiding otherwise suitable habitats. Surprised Harbor Seals may abandon formerly preferred haul-outs; and mothers and pups, or mating pairs, can get separated.

Of course, it's how the human behaves, while out paddling, that's most important in the disturbance equation, not the nature of the watercraft itself. For that matter, wildlife advocates are just as concerned about disturbance caused by all the foot, bike, and dog traffic now visiting the bay's beautified shores. To explore such concerns, a number of government-sponsored scientific studies have assessed the level of disturbance from shoreline recreational use.

A 2007 study by Lynne Trulio of San Jose State University found no negative effects of trail use on the number of birds, species richness, or

Save the Bay's Canoes-in-Sloughs program gets adventurers into inaccessible marshes. (Jude Stalker)

proportion of birds foraging, either overall or by season, compared to use of nontrail sites. However, the number of shorebirds did decrease with increasing trail use. Days with higher trail use averaged 25 percent fewer birds than days with lower use. The study concluded that although some human use of trails adjacent to shorebird foraging areas may be appropriate, alternative foraging opportunities away from trails may also be needed.

Beyond sharing trails and shores with the bay and its wildlife, many Bay Area residents are involved in active stewardship of the bay. People participate in bird counts and creek cleanups. They join canoe trips and work parties to rip out invasive plants and nurture more native flora. Both kids and adults flock to dozens of school and nonprofit activities aimed at engaging residents to care for their watershed (see p. 320, "Learning More, Helping Out").

Rachel Davis, a teacher at San Francisco's Hamlin School, begins teaching her students about the bay in sixth grade. The school perches on one of the city's hills, and views of the bay fill its windows. Davis's environmental science curriculum explores seven bay topics: loss of wetlands, oil spills, mercury, fill, invasive species, overfishing, and trash. "We begin the year studying global environmental issues and then I try to bring it back to them locally, to the bay, to things they can notice, see, and feel a connection to," says the former outdoor educator. "At first they get really sad, but then they want to know what they can do to help, right here where they live, and for the world around them."

Conclusion

Restoration has always had a certain ring to it. It's a word that makes people feel not only active and constructive in a positive way but also considerate of both history and progress. But as humans both invade and attempt to salvage what's left of the ecosystem, "restoration" is becoming more complicated.

If, for example, a big new mudflat is created by breaching a levee, and instantly colonized by non-native cordgrass, was the project worthwhile? Is there a need to accommodate adaptations species have already made to altered bay environs—the favoring of salt ponds by shorebirds or the nesting in hybrid cordgrass by Clapper Rails? If the central tenet of restoration now, as one expert suggests, is to "try to work with nature and let nature do the work," is the human definition of nature still valid? Is a non-native species, or a habitat made of plastic and riprap, worthy of preservation? The answer to some of these problems may lie in considering the bay as a dynamic, changing system, and in trying to sustain ecosystem processes rather than saving specific places and species.

It may be time, local restoration experts say, to revisit the goals for bay habitats written more than 10 years ago. Any update should embrace both lessons learned over the past 10 years and the challenges ahead presented by climate change. Marilyn Latta thinks planners should be working toward "thoughtfully integrated designs all the way from creeks to tidal marsh and subtidal habitat. It's a more holistic, living shorelines approach to healing bay habitats."

Economics must also play a role in such an equation. The long-term environmental costs of short-term profit will be severe in the Bay Area, where so much of the region's core infrastructure is built on the shaky foundations of quick and dirty fill.

As locals confront the challenges of planning for urban growth in the context of a warming atmosphere, rising bay, and dwindling water supply, the concept of sustainability will become increasingly important. The elephant in the room, according to UC Berkeley scientist Luna Leopold, is "the crushing force emanating from the national pursuit of unlimited growth. . . . The best science and the most useful application . . . may be negated by [our] failure to draw some limits on the exposure of the ecosystem."

Everywhere I've traveled, I've gone for a swim in the ocean. It's like being at home while being away. When I come out of the water I feel like I've touched every living part of the world.

EMMA MACCHIARINI, BAY SWIMMER, SAN FRANCISCO

LIVING ON ROCK, or at least on rebar-reinforced concrete, is second nature to anyone who's felt the earth roll under their feet in a California quake. Those who lived in the Sacramento Valley through all the floods of the twentieth century learned to retreat to higher ground or behind a levee. Those who live up coastal canyons and foothills know the fear of fire—which once renewed California's grasslands and forests—burning through their communities with frightening heat and speed.

"What is this strange quality in humans that makes them court disaster? They build their homes on floodplains and riverbanks, cliff edges, slipping hillsides, brush-choked canyons and on the slopes of volcanoes. . . . All over this planet we [defy] the eternal forces of nature. Then we try to coerce those forces into doing our bidding," wrote columnist Arthur Hoppe in the *San Francisco Chronicle* years ago.

Shoreline edifices such as this South Bay development may soon be susceptible to storm surges and sea level rise. (Francis Parchaso)

Though Californians may be accustomed to living with quakes, fires, and floods, climate change is certain to challenge their tolerance. It may not trigger shifts in the earth's crust, but it will certainly intensify tides, floods, and fires within the next few decades. According to the U.S. Geological Survey (USGS), the current average of three days of temperatures over 120°F in Sacramento each year may well become three weeks by 2020; areas once at risk of flooding once a century may instead flood every year.

As sea level rise accelerates, the bay itself will get much bigger, but this isn't necessarily anything new, according to climate change director Steve Goldbeck of the San Francisco Bay Conservation and Development Commission (BCDC). "If you take the long view, the bay was once a river valley, and then it was invaded by the sea in an earlier warm period and became the bay we know and love. Now the sea is coming in again. Change is a constant in nature, so the bay is going to adapt—it's just a question of how. This isn't to say we can all just go and drive our Hummers; it's to say there's no reason to go into denial and give up."

Climate Change Basics

Scientists have little doubt that sea level rise is coming to the Bay Area, and it's coming soon. "The state of the science today is that sea level will rise by between half a meter and a meter and a half [16–55 inches] by 2100," says Noah Knowles, a hydrologist. Knowles works with a team of USGS scientists that has married global climate change projections with local data on temperature, wind, tides, flows, and other hydrodynamics. Together, they are producing some of the first detailed forecasts of impacts on San Francisco Bay and its watershed. Their work reveals that climate change is not just something that will affect polar bears in Alaska. In the bay region, there will be flooding in low-lying shoreline areas. In the watershed, there'll be less snow in the Sierra, and it will melt sooner and run off earlier than it has in recent centuries, producing water shortages. Diminishing and fast-melting snowpacks were already being documented in the Sierra as early as 1991.

Windmills in the Montezuma hills of the North Bay, generating electricity without emitting greenhouse gases. (Francis Parchaso)

Winter floods will get larger and more frequent, straining already poorly maintained levees. Soils will retain less moisture through the dry summer, making it tougher for farmers to ripen crops, for gardeners to maintain landscaping, and for salmon to compete with human users for increasingly limited freshwater supplies.

According to the USGS team, the hydrological cycle is intensifying. Wet episodes are becoming wetter and dry episodes drier. California may soon return to the long and frequent droughts the state experienced before the more temperate twentieth century.

The team, led by Jim Cloern, launched their project in 2006 and named it "CASCaDE." The acronym stands for Computational Assessments of Scenarios of Change for the Delta Ecosystem, and it evokes the cascade of effects climate change may have on habitats, species, water supply, and ecology. "CASCaDE looks at the atmosphere, at the watershed, at the rivers, the delta, the bay, and the ocean as one, coupled system," says Cloern. "These models link different landscape components with historic data on flows, reservoirs, salinity, and fish habitat. It's one of the first attempts to tackle the complex interactions of the whole system with climate change."

The team is excited about some of its results. In the first layer of computer work, the USGS's Mike Dettinger figured out how to tie coarse outputs from global climate models to local historic weather station data in order to create a finer resolution output. The result of this "downscaling" endeavor is a synthetic weather record for the state over the next hundred years, projecting daily minimum and maximum air temperature, sunlight, wind speed and direction, and relative humidity.

Colleague Noah Knowles modeled impacts of climate change on snow storage and the timing of melt and runoff through the delta, among other things, and linked them to other hydrodynamic processes such as ocean tides. He also delved into the potential for extreme events in the very near future: "This year's 100-year flood is tomorrow's yearly high tide," he says. In other words, water levels Bay Area inhabitants might now experience only once every hundred years will lap at local shores once every year as early as 2050.

These inundations may be a little different from what people might expect. "It's not like a big flood from a storm, in which the river swells and then recedes over a period of days or weeks. It will be more like a peak comes once a day with the high tide," says another USGS member of the team, Dan Cayan. But the amount of time shores may be engulfed in water may well change from tens of hours to hundreds of hours per year within 50 years. Duration of flooding is important—the longer a coast or shore is inundated, the more it will erode. Cayan, who also heads up climate research at the Scripps Institution, examined how ocean and atmospheric events like low-pressure zones, El Niños, and longer term climate oscilla-

Future increases in sea level will inundate the nesting areas of Snowy Plovers.
(Caitlin Nilsen)

tions in the Pacific might collude with climate change to cause flooding. Sea level height, for example, fluctuates depending on whether the region is covered by a high pressure cell (pressing the ocean down) or a low pressure cell (allowing the ocean to rise).

One scenario the CASCaDE team explored is the perfect storm: when low pressure, high tide, heavy rain, and strong winds coincide to create an extreme sea level event. "All these *forcings* in the bay ride on top of mean sea level and climate change, so there's a likelihood of all these effects occurring together," says Cayan.

Other CASCaDE studies are modeling changes in contaminant transfer through the food web, as well as trends in native and invasive species populations, for example. According to Cloern, "Climate change is going to have many different ramifications, not just warming. It's going to affect all the parts of the system, but some things are going to change more than others. So we can be on the lookout for the bigger things that will be happening sooner."

The Bay's Vulnerabilities

Just about everything built or growing on fill around the bay could get flooded by rising sea levels within the next few decades. At first these airports, highways, hayfields, and South Bay residential areas may only be engulfed in water during extreme events. But as sea level rise intensifies, the frequency and duration of flooding will increase. "Sea level rise maps resemble what the bay looked like before the Gold Rush. When they were diking and filling, they didn't bother to raise the new land very high. So in some ways the bay is going back to where it once was, in short order, except instead of the riches of wetlands and tidal flats developed over thousands of years we may have a big reflecting pond," says BCDC's Goldbeck.

To keep pace with a growing bay, Goldbeck's agency has launched a new climate change initiative. In 2009, BCDC published a vulnerability assessment, which suggests that up to 270,000 Bay Area residents could face flooding from the bay within their own lifetimes.

Noah Knowles, who worked up a series of inundation maps for BCDC based on his USGS computer models, was particularly alarmed by the increased risk to built-up areas. Today, about 68 square miles of these developed areas are vulnerable to yearly inundation; by 2099 the vulnerable expanse will more than double to 140 square miles. For all types of lands— from barren soil and cropland to wetlands and urban areas—Knowles calculates that about 367 square miles is now at risk of periodic inundation, and that this amount will increase to 485 square miles by 2099.

Most of the residential areas at risk lie in the South Bay. Here tides swell to higher levels than elsewhere in the bay due to local hydrodynamics and subsided lands. Protecting these areas—by building bigger levees—will be challenging and expensive. A bigger levee is also wider, spreading the impact onto private lands, backyards, and out into the bay. Areas like Foster City may soon qualify for flood insurance.

"If levees fail and your place is inundated every 100 years, you might consider building there; if your place is flooded every month you're not going to," says Knowles. "As the water level rises and peak events get higher, and mean water levels get higher, the old levees are more likely to fail without substantial reinforcement."

Also on the wet list are San Francisco and Oakland airports, the Bay Bridge maze, long stretches of Highways 880 and 101, and the campuses of Silicon Valley Internet giants. Areas where water historically flowed in and out of sloughs or creeks are especially susceptible; for example, in and around San Francisco's AT&T Park and Mission Bay, and Richmond's industrial port zone. Waves and storm surges could even reach into the lobby of BCDC's own downtown headquarters on San Francisco's Embarcadero, which is built on a graveyard of Gold Rush-era ships.

Getting around could become a nightmare. Highways, railroads, and bridge approaches—built as so many are along the shoreline—could also go underwater. Flooding of other key elements of the region's infrastructure could be even more dangerous. Many sewage treatment plants dis-

0   2   4   8 miles

N

Map 19. Shoreline areas vulnerable to sea level rise in the San Francisco Bay
Area. USGS scientists project a local sea level rise, based on global models, of be-
tween 16 inches (dark blue) and 55 inches (turquoise) by 2100. (Noah Knowles,
USGS & S.F. Bay Conservation and Development Commission)

BAY AREA FACILITIES AT RISK*

99–186 miles of major roads and highways
(Highways 880 & 101, bayshore freeway, bridge approaches)

70–105 miles of railroad track
(Southern Pacific, Amtrak, CalTrain)

22 wastewater treatment plants
(Palo Alto, San Jose)

270,000 residents of 82,000 acres
(largely in the South Bay)

72–93 percent of airports
(Oakland, SFO)

57–87 percent public access sites to shoreline
(Crissy Field, Eastshore Park, Shoreline at Mountain View, etc.)

*From inundation or extreme events associated with 16-inch to 55-inch sea level rise.

(*Source*: S.F. Bay Conservation and Development Commission)

charge through outfalls and drains into the bay, and are vulnerable to backing up when sea level rises and storm surges reach higher than ever before. Likewise, the bay's ring of old landfills and industrial sites, capped by clean soil, could release contaminants and garbage if flooded. Indeed, more than 330 U.S. Environmental Protection Agency–regulated hazardous waste facilities are at risk along the California coast, many in Alameda, Santa Clara, and San Mateo counties.

All told, the California Climate Change Center estimates $100 billion worth of buildings and property statewide will be at risk from sea level rise–influenced 100-year flood events associated with the 55-inch scenario. Two-thirds of the buildings and property on this list lies in the San Francisco Bay Area.

Eventually the impacts will spread into the Sacramento–San Joaquin River Delta, much of which lies deeply subsided behind aging levees. Both rising seas and accompanying extreme surge and tidal events are likely to overtop levees and flood crops and homes.

No one really knows how much wave and wind energy the region's current levee system—whether in the delta or around the bay—can withstand. Most weren't built with several feet of sea level rise in mind. One thing that worries climate change planners like Goldbeck is where to obtain material to build levees. In years past, the dirt was borrowed from areas of the bay not so susceptible to inundation. In an estuary that is fast becoming sediment-starved, what little is left is needed to keep wetlands from eroding and disappearing.

"As we learned from Hurricane Katrina, legislators are used to dealing with large-scale environmental challenges only when they become a crisis. Our challenge is to create urgency now, and take action before the problem becomes unmanageable," says BCDC's executive director Will Travis.

Wetlands as Buffers

In the face of sea level rise, the region's wetlands—both existing and restored—attain critical importance. They offer essential buffers for more urbanized zones. A wave entering a wetland from the bay is slowed and dissipated by vegetation, slough meanders, and elevation changes. Larger wetlands like Marin's Hamilton restoration site and the South Bay salt ponds can act like giant sponges, absorbing the brunt of more intense storms and increased runoff driven by sea level rise. Wetlands are especially important in the South Bay because they stand between waves and inland levees, protecting urban areas.

"We have to think about more than just keeping the bay out with levees and sea walls. We need to be thinking about how to build up our

A decaying duck blind in the marshes near China Camp in Marin County. (Jude Stalker)

ecological buffer along the edge," says San Francisco Estuary Institute's historical ecologist Robin Grossinger.

As sea level rises, wetlands either migrate inland or grow in place. The most urbanized estuary in the world, however, offers little space for wetlands to migrate. In most areas, wetlands abut the hard edge of freeways, railroads, and buildings. If wetlands can't grow out, then they have to grow up. By collecting sediment and growing vegetation, which in turn helps them trap more sediment and build up organic matter, wetlands can sustain themselves in place.

"The bottom line is we have to keep as much mud in the system as we can," says wetland builder Michelle Orr. "It helps to have an overall plan for which areas you're going to maintain for some time, and which you're going to let erode, and let those be sources of sediment for the rest of the system."

Orr and others involved in restoring tidal wetlands are now trying to figure out how to maintain what they've created. Researchers are experimenting with wetland-friendly flood-protection methods. But most ecologists and engineers agree that without its ring of wetlands the bay would be in a much more dire position in terms of sea level rise.

"There's a lot we can do to make the wetland landscape more resilient to sea level rise—by ensuring good sediment supply from the local watersheds, restoring wetlands in strategic places, and providing buffer areas for wetland migration," says Grossinger.

Experts are increasingly worried about coastal squeeze conflicts, and calling for the upland edges of the bay not yet filled with commercial, agricultural, or residential developments to be reserved as undeveloped land so that estuarine marshes can migrate upslope. "We need to shift our primary focus from restoration of subsided baylands to conservation of defensible future estuarine-margin space, so that twenty-first-century tidal marsh habitats can survive," says coastal ecologist Peter Baye, formerly of the U.S. Fish and Wildlife Service.

Adaptation

One of the things humans do best is adapt. With hope, some of the historic resilience of estuarine organisms will help the ecosystem adjust as well. However, parts of the ecosystem may be too stressed already to cope with this additional challenge.

The bay region will soon need to decide what to save and what to let go. Planners say that expensive investments like airports, bridge approaches, and urban downtowns will have to be protected. And they say help will have to be provided to low-income residents in the flood zone.

BCDC is shifting its focus from saving a shrinking bay to managing a growing one. The first step is to assess and pinpoint vulnerable areas. Local and regional governments will then have to figure out just how bad it could get. Estimates will need to be made of the risk to life, limb, property, and local ecology.

Instead of just focusing on the reduction of greenhouse gases by curbing emissions, regional agencies hope to spearhead a combination of mitigation and adaptation. In 2008, BCDC began working jointly with the Association of Bay Area Governments (ABAG; cities and counties), the

Urban development surrounds the bay, creating congestion, smog, and greenhouse gases. (Max Eissler)

Sea level rise pole at Crissy Field lagoon, on the San Francisco shore. Colored balls depict different levels of projected rise, from red (19 feet, 8 inches, if the Greenland ice cap melts) through yellow (4 feet, 7 inches, the high end of predicted sea level rise by 2100) and blue (low end of predicted rise). (Ariel Rubissow Okamoto)

Metropolitan Transportation Commission (MTC; regional transit and roads), and the Bay Area Air Quality Management District. "ABAG is building the houses, and MTC the freeways, that are going to get flooded, and the air board is responsible for reducing the greenhouse gases causing the problem. So it's a good idea for us all to work together on climate change," says Will Travis.

As part of estuary planning, CASCaDE scientists hope to model structural changes in the watershed such as the building of a peripheral canal or the flooding of multiple delta islands after an earthquake. "Climate change is not an isolated mechanism of ecosystem alteration. It interacts with land-use change and water management. It's just the outer layer of the onion," says Cloern.

Engineers and ecologists are already talking about three shoreline triage options: to hold the line, retreat, or change the land use. Phased abandonment of low- and medium-density urban areas at high risk is on the table to discuss, as well as banning new development in future flood zones. There's also talk of improving the California coast's "armor" to the tune of $14 billion and 1,100 miles of new or improved levees and sea walls, and of prohibiting development in natural lands adjacent to wetlands, to give them room to retreat from advancing seas.

COOL IDEAS FOR COMBATING RISING TIDES

Starting in 2009, BCDC has held regular design competitions to solicit innovative ideas for how the Bay Area could adapt to climate change. In the first year, over 100 designs and ideas arrived from all over the world. Winning ideas ranged from changing the topography of the urban waterfront and shoreline evolution through recovered wetlands, to grand-scale interventions using everything from a flow-through ventilated levee across the bay to a buoyant membrane under the Golden Gate. For competition results, go to www.bcdc.ca.gov.

Climate change is not just a problem for planners, engineers, and scientists to solve. The ultimate adaptation will have to come from ordinary people deciding that they can and will change to help the quality of the environment. No longer some futuristic specter, climate change will arrive in the lifetimes of people we know and love.

"I'm strangely optimistic in the face of evidence," says Noah Knowles. "Of course we'll adapt; that's what we do. There'll be difficulties along the way, and a lot of expenses, and we're going to have to make choices as to what things we want to save and what things we don't."

Goldbeck is also optimistic. "The Bay Area is full of really smart people. It's a center for innovation and the environmental movement, so people are going to embrace change, once they understand how climate change will affect them, and want to do something about it."

CODA

THE OTHER DAY at dusk I took a walk along San Francisco's Aquatic Park, where the shape of the shore still follows an original cove. Though humans have added piers and breakwaters and a city to the scene, on this evening the activities of people and wildlife blend in the abalone light.

It's an El Niño year, rich in fish food. At this time of day, when the tides are turning, the slack water is so full of sardines and mackerel that fishers have abandoned their rods to dip hoop nets into the water.

A group of sea lions is swimming so close together that each animal looks like it is riding another's back. They chase the fish around the cove. About 20 feet ahead of the lead sea lion hovers a gyre of pelicans. It's almost as if the big birds in the air and the big mammals in the water are working together to make the most of the fish.

Soaring single file through coastal skies like modern pterodactyls, California Brown Pelicans are rebounding from decades of pesticide poisoning. DDT bans and habitat conservation have helped. In November 2009, officials removed the Brown Pelican from the endangered species list. (Max Eissler)

A bystander mentions seeing more sea lions in the bay and more pelicans along the shore this year than in decades. In the air, the brown birds flap their great wings in slow motion—gliding on an updraft, flapping downwind. When they spot the silver backs of fish, they back flap for an awkward moment, choosing their mark. Then they pin back their wings and drop like daggers, their splashes wetting thin air.

Along the shore, cyclists weave through tourists trying to capture a West Coast sunset in the chip of a cell phone. In the water, two white-capped swimmers match laps from buoy to buoy, while a third powers back-and-forth in between. The pelicans dive in and out of the water all around them, but neither humans nor birds ever collide.

In the half-light, the arc of the swimmers' arms merges with the pelican wings taking off from the water. The wet heads of the sea lions soon become indistinguishable from the swimmers' caps. At one point, the sea lions surround a pair of swimmers and the group swells suddenly into a single form. Then the white caps separate from the black caps and the bay wraps them all in cool equanimity. ARO

GLOSSARY
Sources: SFEP, SFEI, USGS.

Acre-foot The amount of water required to cover an acre of land to a depth of one foot, or 43,560 cubic feet.

Anadromous Fish that spend all or part of their adult life in salt water and return to freshwater streams and rivers to spawn.

Anoxia The condition of lacking oxygen.

Assemblage Collection of species typically found together in a given habitat.

Benthos The community of plants and animals that live on or in the seabed and at the bottom of the bay (nonplanktonic).

Biomagnification The progressive increase in concentration of a contaminant as it moves up the food chain, such that each animal has a higher concentration in its tissues than its food did.

Bryozoan A type of filter-feeding aquatic invertebrate that generally lives in colonies of interconnected individuals; they often grow on rocks, shells, and algae, as well as on ship bottoms, pier pilings, and other surfaces.

Byssal thread The threadlike fibers mussels secrete to attach themselves to rocks and other hard substrates.

Climate forcing A disruption in the amount of energy stored in earth's climate system, such as an increase in the amount of heat trapped in the atmosphere, which causes shifts in ocean temperatures, rainfall patterns, and other aspects of climate.

Cryptogenic A species of uncertain origin, which may be either native or introduced.

Cubic feet per second A flow rate, typically used to describe the quantity and speed of flow in rivers and streams.

Culvert A pipelike drain that passes beneath a road, embankment, or path.

Dabble A feeding behavior shown by certain species of ducks that use their beaks to filter food particles from the water.

Demersal Species that spend most of their lives on or near the seabed.

Epiphytic Species that grow on top of other organisms but are not usually parasitic.

Estuary A place where fresh water and salt water mix, such as a bay draining rivers or streams, a salt marsh, or where a river enters an ocean. In an estuary, salt water is measurably diluted by fresh water.

Euryhaline Species capable of tolerating a wide range of salinities.

Gyre A major circular moving body of water created as currents are deflected by winds and the rotation of the earth.

Halophytes Plants that tolerate or require high concentrations of salt in surrounding soil and/or water.

Hydrodynamics The motion or action of water, which is influenced by winds, tides, currents, topography, and other factors.

Hydrograph Changes in the volume or rate of stream discharge reaching a particular location over time, as depicted in a graph.

Larva The newly hatched, earliest stage of various animals that undergo metamorphosis.

Managed marsh Wetland where water levels are regulated to achieve specific goals such as growing food plants for waterfowl or providing habitat for target species.

MLLW Mean lower low water, or the average of the lowest tide level observed for each day. One of several similar acronyms including MHHW, mean higher high water; MHW, mean high water; and MLW, mean low water.

Osmoregulation Control of water and ion concentrations within the body of a living organism.

Otter trawl A type of fishing net with two rectangular doors that keep the mouth of the net open as it is towed behind a ship.

Pacific Flyway A major bird migration route along the Pacific coast of the Americas stretching from Alaska south to Patagonia.

Parts per A measure of concentration expressed as the relative abundance of pollutants or other minerals in a solvent; water with two parts per billion of mercury would contain two micrograms of mercury per kilogram of water.

Pelagic Species that live in the open ocean.

Rafting Resting together on the water, as done by groups of Sea Otters or ducks.

Redd Depression dug into the gravel of a river bottom by an egg-laying female salmon.

Regime change A shift in a prevailing ocean cycle or pattern that marks the start of a new set of conditions.

Riffle A shallow stretch of stream where rocks break the flow of water.

Riprap A layer of stone or rubble designed to protect and stabilize stream banks, shorelines, and other areas subject to erosion.

Salt panne An area that traps marine waters during the highest tides; evaporation increases the salt concentration of the remaining water or leaves hypersaline soils and a crust of salt behind.

Shoals Sandbars and other linear forms of sediment build-up in a body of water.

Smolt An anadromous fish physiologically ready to make the transition from fresh water to salt water; age varies with environmental conditions.

Spawn To produce or deposit eggs, sperm, or young.

Trophic level The position an organism occupies in the food chain.

Turbidity The amount of solid particles suspended in water that cause light rays shining through the water to scatter.

Upwelling A current of cold, nutrient-rich water rising to the surface; occurs when strong seasonal winds push surface water away from a coast to be replaced by deeper waters.

Water column The water in a lake, estuary, or ocean that extends from the bottom sediment to the water surface.

HISTORICAL TIMELINE

1769	Spanish explorer Gaspar de Portola is first European to see San Francisco Bay.
1772	Father Juan Crespi and Pedro Farges see the delta for the first time.
1848	Italian colony begins fishing full time in San Francisco.
1849–1884	Hydraulic gold mining.
1852	First California salmon law, prohibiting weirs or obstructions in streams, and establishing a no-fishing season.
	Californians begin channelizing waterways and reclaiming wetlands.
1861	State Reclamation District Act allows drainage of delta lands and levee construction to prevent flooding.
1863	First Pacific coast fish cannery established on Sacramento River.
1871–1908	Early introductions of Striped Bass, oysters, and other nonnative species.
1872	First fish hatchery built on the McCloud River near Mt. Shasta.
1878	Creation of California Fish and Game Commission.
1887	Fishing licenses required for commercial boats.
1890	First West Coast sardine cannery, on San Francisco Bay.
1915	State starts keeping systematic records of commercial fish landings.
1940	Contra Costa Canal begins diverting water from the estuary.
1940s	Reber plan proposes dams in the upper estuary to prevent salt water intrusion into drinking supplies, and creates new freshwater lakes.
1942	Shasta Dam completed on Sacramento River.
1948	Friant Dam completed on San Joaquin River.
1950s	Bay Model built in Sausalito by U.S. Army Corps to test effects of various salinity barriers and physical modifications to the estuary.

1951	Central Valley Project begins pumping at Tracy Plant.
1961	Save the Bay formed—first major environmental group focused on a body of water.
1963+	Rapid invasions of non-native copepods (small crustaceans).
1963–1969	State Water Project begins pumping at Banks Plant.
1965	State legislation establishes regional commission to protect the Bay, the San Francisco Bay Conservation and Development Commission (BCDC).
1966–1972	Major federal and state environmental legislation (Porter Cologne, Clean Water Act, and endangered species) changes management of bay and delta. Environmental impact reports required for developments. "No-net-loss" policy for wetland development.
	Wetland restoration focuses on dredged material disposal sites.
1968	Oroville Dam on Feather River completed.
1969	First notable wetland restoration experiment on 32 acres at Palo Alto's Faber Tract, including first planting of California cordgrass (*Spartina foliosa*).
1973	First "designed" restoration project in the East Bay's Pond 3, in the Alameda Flood Control Channel.
1976	First large (130 acres) bayland restoration without planting at Muzzi Marsh, Marin County, as mitigation for Larkspur Ferry Terminal.
1978	State Board issues Water Rights Decision 1485 requiring federal and state water projects to meet delta water-quality standards.
1980s	Age of restoration for mitigation (70 percent of 34 projects next two decades). Push for "instant" wetlands.
	Conflicts among government agencies, ports, and fishing community result in a "mudlock" over the impacts of bay dredging.
1982	First design guidelines for restoration published by BCDC.
1983	University of California's Margaret Race completes first scientific critique of wetland mitigation banking and restoration success.
1986	Invasive Overbite Clam appears in San Francisco Bay.
	State supreme court strengthens water board's power to protect all uses of delta water, including fish and wildlife (Racanelli).
1988	State approves $120 million over 10 years for levee maintenance.
	Suisun Marsh salinity-control gates begin operation.
	Shell oil tank leaks 420,000 gallons into wetlands near Martinez.

1989	Sacramento River winter-run Chinook Salmon listed as endangered species, requiring operational changes in federal and state water projects.
1992	Passage of the Central Valley Project Improvement Act allocating 800,000 acre-feet of water annually to the environment.
1993	Delta Smelt declared a threatened species by federal and state governments.
	Diverse interests, led by San Francisco Estuary Project, complete first comprehensive environmental management plan for Bay–Delta (CCMP).
	Regional monitoring program established to monitor compliance with water-quality standards by San Francisco Estuary Institute.
1994	Bay–Delta Accord signed, and CALFED Bay–Delta Program begins work to balance competing beneficial uses of freshwater and estuarine resources.
	First major allocation of state's limited freshwater supply to restore ecosystem function (estuarine salinity standard, "x2").
	Shell oil spill mitigation fund purchases 11,800 acres North Bay salt ponds, first large landscape secured for restoration.
1995	Region creates San Francisco Bay Joint Venture to coordinate wetlands planning and funding baywide.
1996	Voters approve millions of dollars for Delta restoration with Proposition 204.
	A cooperative effort between government agencies and stakeholders develops a long-term management strategy for dredged material disposal in the bay.
	First "beneficial reuse" of dredged material for wetland restoration at Sonoma Baylands.
	First big fights over conversion of seasonal to tidal wetlands.
	Ship dry-docked in San Francisco leaks 80,000 gallons fuel into bay.
1998	San Francisco Estuary Institute completes first comprehensive maps of historic and current wetlands in San Francisco Bay *EcoAtlas*.
	Cooperative CALFED program completes programmatic environmental impact report offering three alternatives for fixing the delta, and launches ambitious restoration for rivers, delta, and estuary.
	Accidental levee breach creates hundreds of acres of new tule marsh on Liberty Island (largest unplanned restoration in the delta).

1999	A hundred top scientists set acreage goals for baywide habitat mix necessary to sustain endangered and important species ("Habitat Goals").
2000	CALFED (Record of Decision) calls for restoration of 7,000–9,000 acres of tidal marsh in Suisun Marsh, and in 2001 agencies sign Suisun Marsh Charter to develop a balanced regional plan.
	Salmon migrate more freely up Butte Creek after four dams removed and 11 fish ladders added.
	Voters endorse large-scale bay restoration with Propositions 12, 13, 40, and 84.
	Coastal Conservancy recognizes tidal restorations becoming invaded with non-native spartina and launches eradication program.
2001	First experiment with subtidal restoration of eelgrass beds in bay.
	Long-term management plan for bay dredging completed.
2002	Populations of key pelagic organisms in delta, including native Delta and Longfin Smelt, and introduced shad and Striped Bass, dramatically decline.
2003	Region undertakes second large, landscape-scale, purchase, and restoration of 15,100 acres of salt ponds, most in the South Bay.
2004	Design guidelines published by Coastal Conservancy incorporate restoration lessons and layout a rigorous planning and design process.
2006	Green Sturgeon's Sacramento River/San Francisco Bay estuary population listed as threatened.
2007	Vessel *Cosco Busan* crashes into Bay Bridge and spills 53,000 gallons of bunker oil.
2008	Salmon fishery closed due to low populations.
	Delta Vision Strategic Plan establishes as coequal goals to restore the delta ecosystem and create a more reliable water supply for California.
	Bay Delta Conservation Plan developed in which water contractors seek to obtain 50-year permits for water exports, and region adopts a Natural Communities Conservation Plan and Habitat Conservation Plans.
2009	Federal government issues biological opinions on Delta Smelt and salmonids with wide-reaching implications for ecosystem restoration and water management.

2010   Subtidal goals project reaches agreement on how to restore ecosystem functions underwater in bay.

State Water Resources Control Board announces delta ecosystem needs 75 percent of unimpaired flows to be viable, and works on new flow criteria. State fish and game department proposes complementary biological and species-specific objectives.

Region begins planning for sea level rise impacts on bayshore and delta levees.

2011   New scorecard on bay–delta health, an updated "state of the estuary," released by The Bay Institute and the San Francisco Estuary Partnership.

REFERENCES

Primary Materials

Anderson, M. Kat. 2005. *Tending the Wild: Native American Knowledge and the Management of California's Natural Resources.* Berkeley: University of California Press.

Bay Institute. 1998. *From the Sierra to the Sea: The Ecological History of the San Francisco Bay–Delta Watershed.* San Francisco: Author.

CALFED Bay–Delta Program. 1999–2007. *Science Actions* (delta, mercury, rivers, Delta Cross Channel, organic matter, shallow-water habitat, native grasslands). Sacramento, CA: Author.

CALFED Science Program. 2008. *The State of Bay-Delta Science.* Sacramento, CA: Author.

California Department of Fish and Game. 2001. *California's Living Marine Resources: A Status Report (Pacific Herring, Dungeness Crab, Starry Flounder and other species).* Sacramento, CA: Author.

California Department of Fish and Game. 2008. *California Aquatic Invasive Species Plan.* Sacramento, CA: Author.

California Department of Fish and Game. 2009. *State and Federally Listed Endangered and Threatened Animals of California.* Sacramento, CA: Author.

California Department of Fish and Game. 2009. *State and Federally Listed Endangered and Threatened Plants of California.* Sacramento, CA: Author.

Carle, David. 2004. *An Introduction to Water in California.* Berkeley: University of California Press.

Cohen, Andrew. 2000. *An Introduction to the San Francisco Estuary.* Oakland, CA: San Francisco Estuary Project.

Conomos, John T. 1979. *San Francisco Bay. The Urbanized Estuary.* Ashland, OR: American Association for the Advancement of Science, Pacific Division.

Davis, William Heath. 1967. *Seventy Five Years in California.* San Francisco: John Howell Books.

Ebert, David, and Matthew Squillante. 2003. *Sharks, Rays and Chimaeras of California.* Berkeley: University of California Press.

EDAW, et al. 2007. *South Bay Salt Pond Restoration Project, Final Environmental Impact Statement/Report, Executive Summary.* San Francisco: EDAW.

Evens, Jules. 2005. *An Introduction to California Bird Life*. Berkeley: University of California Press.

Gilliam, Harold. 1957. *San Francisco Bay*. New York: Doubleday.

Gilliam, Harold. 2002. *Weather of the San Francisco Bay Region*. Berkeley: University of California Press.

Goals Project. 1999. *Baylands Ecosystem Habitat Goals*. Oakland, CA.

Goals Project. 2000. *Baylands Ecosystem Species and Community Profiles*. Oakland, CA.

Hart, John, and David Sanger. 2003. *San Francisco Bay, Portrait of an Estuary*. Berkeley: University of California Press.

Hedgpeth, Joel W. 1979. *San Francisco Bay, the Unsuspected Estuary*. Ashland, OR: American Association for the Advancement of Science, Pacific Division.

Holland, Elise. 2001. *The State of California Rivers*. San Francisco: Trust for Public Land.

Kelley, Robert. 1989. *Battling the Inland Sea*. Berkeley: University of California Press.

Leidy, Robert. 2007. *Ecology, Assemblage Structure, Distribution, and Status of Fishes in Streams Tributary to the San Francisco Estuary, California*. San Francisco Estuary Institute, April 2007, Contribution no. 530.

Lightfoot, Kent G., and Otis Parrish. 2009. *California Indians and their Environment*. Berkeley: University of California Press.

Lund, Jay et al. 2010. *Comparing Futures for the Sacramento–San Joaquin Delta*. Berkeley: University of California Press and Public Policy Institute of California.

Margolin, Malcolm. 1978. *The Ohlone Way: Indian Life in the San Francisco–Monterey Bay Area*. Berkeley: Heyday.

Reisner, Marc. 1986. *Cadillac Desert*. New York: Penguin

San Francisco Bay Conservation and Development Commission. 2009. *Living with a Rising Bay: Vulnerability and Adaptation in San Francisco Bay and on the Shoreline*. San Francisco: Author.

San Francisco Estuary Institute. 1998–2009. *The Pulse of the Estuary* reports. Oakland, CA: Author.*

San Francisco Estuary Project. 1990–1992, *Status & Trends* reports. Oakland, CA: Author.

San Francisco Estuary Project. 1992–2008. *State of the Estuary* reports. Oakland, CA: Author.

San Francisco Estuary Project. 1993–2009. *ESTUARY* newsletter. Oakland, CA: Author.

Save San Francisco Bay Association. 1961–1986. An oral history by Malca Chall, the Bancroft Library, University of California, Berkeley, 1987.

Skinner, John E. 1962. *A Historical Review of the Fish and Wildlife Resources of the San Francisco Bay Area*. California Department of Fish and Game,

*Note: *Pulse* reports (www.sfei.org) include many papers relevant to this book, some authored by the individual scientists quoted in these pages.

Water Projects Branch Report no. l. Sacramento, CA: California Department of Fish and Game.

Sloan, Doris. 2006. *Geology of the San Francisco Bay Region.* Berkeley: University of California Press

Steere, J. T., and N. Schaefer. 2001. *Restoring the Estuary: Implementation Strategy of the San Francisco Bay Joint Venture.* Oakland, CA: San Francisco Bay Joint Venture.

Subtidal Goals Project. 2010. *San Francisco Bay Subtidal Habitat Goals Report.* Oakland, CA: California State Coastal Conservancy.

Walker, Richard A. 2007. *The Country in the City: The Greening of the San Francisco Bay Area.* Seattle: University of Washington Press.

Water Education Foundation. Layperson's Guides. Sacramento, CA: Author.

Articles and Other Publications

Bartholomew, George A. Jr. 1943. The daily movements of cormorants on San Francisco Bay. *The Condor* 45(1): 3–18.

Baxter, Randy, et al. 2008. *Pelagic Organism Decline Progress Report: 2007 Synthesis of Results.* Interagency Ecological Program. Sacramento: California Department of Water Resources.

Baye, Peter. 2007. *Selected Tidal Marsh Plant Species of the San Francisco Estuary: A Field Identification Guide.* Berkeley, CA: San Francisco Estuary Invasive Spartina Project.

Chin, John L., et al. 2004. *Shifting Shoals and Shattered Rocks: How Man Has Transformed the Floor of West-Central San Francisco Bay.* USGS & US DOI Circular 1259.

Cloern, James E., et al. 2007. A cold phase of the East Pacific triggers new phytoplankton blooms in San Francisco Bay. *Proceedings of the National Academy of Sciences* 104(47): 18561–18565.

Cloern, James E., et al. 2010. Biological communities in San Francisco Bay track large-scale climate forcing over the North Pacific. *Geophysical Research Letters* 37: L21602, doi: 10.1029/2010GL044774.

Cohen, N. Andrew, and James T. Carlton. 1998. Accelerating invasion rate in a highly invaded estuary. *Science* 279: 555–558.

Collins, J., et al. 2007. *Ecological Connections between Baylands and Uplands: Examples from Marin County.* Oakland, CA: San Francisco Estuary Institute, report no. 521.

Fregosa, Theresa, et al. 2008. *Sediment Deposition, Erosion and Bathymetric Change in Central San Francisco Bay: 1855–1979.* USGS Open File Report 2008-1312.

Grigg, Emma K., Sarah G. Allen, et al. 2004. Harbor seal, *Phoca vitulina richardii*: Population trends in the San Francisco Bay Estuary, 1970–2002. *California Fish and Game Scientific Journal* 90(2): 51–70.

Haltiner, J., and C. Beeman. 2003. *Restoring Floodplain and Channel Functions to Incised and Leveed Stream Systems.* San Francisco: Philip Williams & Associates, Ltd.

Higgins, S. A., Bruce Jaffe, et al. 2007. Reconstructing sediment age profiles from historical bathymetry changes in San Pablo Bay, California. *Estuarine, Coastal and Shelf Science* 73: 165–174.

Jaffe, Bruce, et al. 2007. Anthropogenic influence on sedimentation and intertidal mudflat change in San Pablo Bay, California: 1856–1983. *Estuarine, Coastal and Shelf Science* 73(1–2, June): 175–187.

Kelly, J. P. et al. 2007. Status, trends, and implications for the conservation of heron and egret nesting colonies in the San Francisco Bay area. *Waterbirds* 30: 455–478.

Kimmerer, W. J. 2004. Open water processes of the San Francisco Estuary: From physical forcing to biological responses. *San Francisco Estuary and Watershed Science*, February 2004, Article 1. Available at scholarship.org/uc/item/9bp499mv#page-1.

Klimley, Peter, Josh Israel, et al. 2006. The green sturgeon and its environment: Past, present and future. *Environmental Biology of Fishes* 79(3–4): 187–90.

Knowles, Noah. 2009. *Potential Inundation Due to Rising Sea Levels in the San Francisco Bay Region*. Sacramento: California Climate Change Center.

Luoma, S. N., and J. E. Cloern. 1982. *The Impact of Wastewater Discharge on Biological Communities in San Francisco Bay*, pp. 137–160. Ashland, OR: American Association for the Advancement of Science, Pacific Division.

Malamud-Roam, Frances, et al. 2007. Holocene climates and connections between the San Francisco Bay Estuary and its watershed: A review. *San Francisco Estuary and Watershed Science* 5(1), February 2007, Article 3. Available at scholarship.org/uc/item/61j10tw.

Martin, Maureen, et al., 2007. Seasonal chlorophyll A fluxes between the coastal Pacific Ocean and San Francisco Bay. *Marine Ecology Progress Series* 337: 51–61.

Miller, Jeremy. 2009. Rebooting urban watersheds: Activists restore blighted Bay Area creeks—and impoverished communities. *High Country News*, June 1.

Mitchell, David. 2007. *The Importance of Recycled Water to the San Francisco Bay Area*. Oakland, CA: M Cubed.

Peterson, David, et al., 1995. The role of climate in estuarine variability. *American Scientist* 83: 58–67.

Pritchard, Donald. 1967. *What Is an Estuary? Physical Viewpoint*. Washington D.C.: American Association for the Advancement of Science.

RMC Water and Environment. 2004. *Innovative Approaches: Water Management for the Bay Area*. Oakland, CA: Bay Area Clean Water Agencies.

Schoellhamer, David et al. 2007. Suspended sediment and sediment-associated contaminants in San Francisco Bay. *Environmental Research* 105(1): 119–131.

Sommer, Ted, et al. 2007. The collapse of pelagic fishes in the upper San Francisco estuary. *FISHERIES* 32(6): 270–277.

South Bay Challenge: Reclaiming the salt ponds for people and nature [special insert]. 2004. *Bay Nature* 4(4): 17–32.

Stenzel, Lynne, et al. 1995. Breeding success of double-crested cormorants in the San Francisco Bay Area, California. *Colonial Waterbirds* 18: 216–224.

Stenzel, Lynne, et al. 2002. Abundance and distribution of shorebirds in San Francisco Bay Area. *Western Birds* 33: 69–98.

Vollestad, L. A., et al. 2004. Effects of freshwater and marine growth rates on early maturity in male coho and Chinook salmon. *Transactions of the American Fisheries Society* 133: 495–503.

Warnock, Nils, Mary Anne Bishop, and John Y. Takekawa. *Spring Shorebird Migration from Mexico to Alaska: Final Report 2002.* Unpublished Progress Report, Point Reyes Bird Observatory, Stinson Beach, CA, and U.S. Geological Survey, Vallejo, CA.

Individuals Interviewed

CALIFORNIA DEPARTMENT OF FISH AND GAME

Randy Baxter, 8/07
Mike Donnellan, 7/07
Kathy Hieb, 7/07, 8/07, & 9/07
Ken Oda, 8/07
Becky Ota, 8/07
Larry Wycoff, 7/09

SAN FRANCISCO ESTUARY INSTITUTE

Josh Collins, 7/09
Ben Greenfield, 11/07
Robin Grossinger, 7/09
Rainer Hoenicke, 3/08

U.S. GEOLOGICAL SURVEY

Jon Burau, 4/10
Jim Cloern, 4/07, 9/07, & 5/09
Bruce Jaffe, 4/07
Noah Knowles, 6/09
Jim Kuwabara, 1/11
Sam Luoma, 4/08
Cory Overton, 4/09
Dave Peterson, 4/07
Dave Schoellhamer, 4/07 & 5/09
Jan Thompson, 7/07

OTHER

Sarah Allen, National Park Service, 9/07
Peter Baye, plant ecologist, 8/09
Ode Bernstein, Invasive Spartina Project, 6/09
Gary Bobker, The Bay Institute, 6/07
Warner Chabot, League of Conservation Voters, 10/09
Andy Cohen, Center for Research on Aquatic Bioinvasions, 4/09
Laurel Collins, Watershed Sciences, 7/09
Jules Evens, Avocet Research Group, 9/07

David Freyburg, Stanford University, 6/09

Harold Gilliam, Writer, 5/09

Steve Goldbeck, S.F. Bay Conservation and Development, 3/08 & 5/09

Jeffrey Haltiner, Philip Williams & Associates, 7/09

Bruce Herbold, U.S. Environmental Protection Agency, 7/07, 9/07, 2/08, & 12/09

Ingrid Hogle, Invasive Spartina Project, 6/09

Beth Huning, San Francisco Bay Joint Venture, 6/09

Amy Hutzel, San Francisco Bay Area Conservancy, 5/09

Josh Israel, University of California Davis/U.S. Bureau of Reclamation, 7/07

Ed Keller, U.S. Army Corps of Engineers, 5/08

John Kelly, Audubon Canyon Ranch, 9/09

Wim Kimmerer, Romberg Tiburon Center for Environmental Studies, 12/07

John Largier, University of California Davis, 4/10

Marilyn Latta, California Coastal Conservancy, 7/09

David Lewis, Save the Bay, 3/08

Jim McGrath, retired, Port of Oakland, 7/09

Sylvia McLaughlin, Save the Bay, 4/09

Jeff Miller, Alameda Creek Alliance, 8/09

Peter Moyle, University of California Davis, 12/09 & 3/10

Peggy Olofson, Invasive Spartina Project, 2/10

Michelle Orr, Philip Williams & Associates, 5/09

Eric Polson, Polson Engineering, 3/08

Randy Raines, RMC Water and Environment, 1/10

Tim Ramirez, San Francisco Public Utilities Commission, 11/09

Christopher Richard, Oakland Museum of California, 8/09

A. L. Riley, San Francisco Bay Regional Water Quality Control Board, 7/09

Steve Ritchie, San Francisco Public Utilities Commission, 5/09

Barbara Salzman, Marin Audubon, 5/09

Stuart Siegel, Wetlands and Water Resources, 3/10

Christy Smith, U.S. Fish and Wildlife Service, 7/09

Phil Stevens, Urban Creeks Council, 5/09

Tina Swanson, The Bay Institute, 6/09

Will Travis, S.F. Bay Conservation and Development Commission, 10/09

Lisa Owens Viani, San Francisco Estuary Partnership, 6/09

Rachel Wark, RMC Water and Environment, 1/10

Sarah Warnock, avian biologist, 10/09

Phil Williams, Philip Williams & Associates, 5/07 & 7/09

ONLINE RESEARCH MATERIALS

CALFED Science Program, Sacramento
   www.calwater.ca.gov/science

California Water Atlas, Online Version 2010
   www.archive.org/details/The_California_Water_Atlas

CASCaDE (climate change/delta)
   cascade.wr.usgs.gov

Pacific Institute
  pacinst.org
San Francisco Estuary Institute
  www.sfei.org
San Francisco Estuary Partnership
  www.sfestuary.org
San Francisco Estuary & Watershed Science, online journal
  www.estuaryarchive.org
U.S. Geological Survey, San Francisco Bay and Delta
Water Resources Program, Menlo Park
  sfbay.wr.usgs.gov/
Water Resources Center Archives
  wrca.library.ucr.edu/

LEARNING MORE, HELPING OUT: A FEW PLACES TO START

SAN FRANCISCO ESTUARY PARTNERSHIP
www.sfestuary.org

BAY-ORIENTED NGOS
BayKeeper & Deltakeeper
www.baykeeper.org/
The Bay Institute
www.bay.org
Save the Bay
www.savesfbay.org

BAY REGION GOVERNMENT AGENCIES
San Francisco Bay Conservation and Development Commission
www.bcdc.ca.gov
San Francisco Bay Regional Water Quality Control Board
www.swrcb.ca.gov/rwqcb2

GOOD READING
Bay Nature Magazine
www.baynature.org
ESTUARY NEWS
www.sfestuary.org
San Francisco Bay: Portrait of an Estuary, by John Hart and David Sanger.
University of California Press, 2003
San Francisco Bay Shoreline Guide, by Jerry Emory. University of California Press, 1995

FILMS AND ONLINE PRESENTATIONS
San Francisco Estuary Partnership Podcasts and Film Gallery
www.sfestuary.org/podcast
www.sfestuary.org/gallery
Saving the Bay
A two-part documentary film produced by Ron Blatman
www.savingthebay.org
Sierra to the Sea overview
sierratosea.ucdavis.edu

ENVIRONMENTAL EDUCATION
Aquarium of the Bay, Pier 39, San Francisco
www.aquariumofthebay.com
Canoes-in-Sloughs, Save the Bay
www.savesfbay.org/learn-and-explore
LHS MARE
lawrencehallofscience.org/mare

(continued)

Literacy in Environmental Justice
www.lejyouth.org
River of Words
www.riverofwords.org
STRAW, The Bay Institute
www.bay.org/watershed-education

Things You Can Do

11 Simple Ways to Help
www.sfestuary.org/pages/index.php?ID=2
Pesticide Management
www.ourwaterourworld.org
Pollution Prevention: Baywise
(waste disposal tips, pharmaceuticals, motor oil, etc.)
www.baywise.org
Water Conservation
East Bay: www.ebmud.com/resource-center/water-conservation-
resources
San Francisco: conserve.sfwater.org

Restoration and Landscaping Guides

Bay Friendly Landscaping & Gardening Coalition
www.bayfriendlycoalition.org
Design Guidelines for Tidal Wetland Restoration in San Francisco, produced by The Bay Institute, Philip Williams & Associates, and
Phyllis M. Faber
www.wrmp.org/design/
Green Streets & Rain Gardens
www.flowstobay.org
www.sfestuary.org/pages/index.php?ID=7
Shoreline Plants: A Landscape Guide to San Francisco Bay, BCDC
www.bcdc.ca.gov

Note to Readers

For more information and links related to this book, go to:
bayariel.com/ARO-baybook.html
or
www.ucpress.edu/series.php?isbn=9780520268261
Send feedback and corrections, so the next edition will be even better!

ART CREDITS

The authors wish to express their immense appreciation for the stunning images contributed so generously by all the photographers credited in this guide.

Thank you also to Afsoon Razavi for expert technical support on the cover photography.

Special thanks to the San Francisco Bay Joint Venture for supporting quality professional work on maps and wetland graphics for this book.

PAGE I	Avocet being banded on the eastern levee of Pond A8, near Alviso, as part of South Bay salt pond mercury contamination studies. Pond A8 is being carefully monitored due to its location downstream of the New Almaden mercury mine. (Scott Demers)
PAGE III	A decaying duck blind in the marshes near China Camp in Marin County. (Jude Stalker)
PAGE VI	Shorebirds at the Coyote Hills Regional Shoreline. (Kathleen M. Wong)
PAGE 1	Crissy Field on the San Francisco shore of the Golden Gate National Recreation Area. (Ariel Rubissow Okamoto)
PAGE 13	Bay waters. (Francis Parchaso)
PAGE 53	Brown Pelican in breeding plumage. (Richard Bohnet)
PAGE 105	An early railroad bridge, visible from the Dumbarton Bridge, that once swung open to permit ships to pass, but is now welded in this position. (Francis Parchaso)
PAGE 149	Container ships berthed at the Port of Oakland. (Courtesy of the Port of Oakland)
PAGE 209	Snow Geese flying over Central Valley wetlands. (Jim Morris, California Rice Commission)
PAGE 237	South Bay salt pond restoration project. Pond "SF2" with newly created bird islands in 2010. (Cris Benton)
PAGE 285	Marsh and creek at Bay Bridge maze in Emeryville. (Drew Kerr)
PAGE 299	Fading light on the bay. (Francis Parchaso)

INDEX

Note: Page numbers in bold indicate the main discussion of a species.

underwater, subtidal, 274–281
   wetlands, 213, 239–273
Richard, Christopher, 112, 199, 214
Richards, Byron, 34
Riley, Ann, 272
Rio Vista, 24
Ritchie, Steve, 170, 245, 262
river(s), 15, 23–25
   confluence, 24
   Cosumnes River, 24, 217
   Guadalupe River, 24, 268
   Merced River, 23
   Mokelumne River, 142
   Napa River, 30, 260
   Petaluma River, 249, 253
   Sacramento River, 22, 217
   San Joaquin River, 23, 142, 217
   Tuolumne River, 139, 142, 210
RMC Water and Environment, 233–234
Rock Crab. *See* Red Rock Crab
Rockefeller, David, 155, 157
Romberg Tiburon Center, 278
Rowlandson, Thomas, 106
runoff. *See* storm-water management
Rust, James, 111

Sacramento River, 22, 217
Sacramento–San Joaquin River Delta, sub-
   bays and rivers, 16 (map)
Sacramento River Flood Control Project,
   120, 138, 142
salinity, 21–23, 38, 56, 196
   plant adaptations to, 67–69
salmon, 78, 79 (photo), **83–85**, 89, 93, 110,
   228
   cannery, 123
   Chinook Salmon, 79 (photo), **83–85, 184–
      185,** 194, 231
   Coho Salmon, 103
   hatchery, 126, 223–225
   protection, 129, 192–196
   runs, 195, 217
   tracking, 84
salt grass, 67–68, 71
Salt Marsh Harvest Mouse, 181–182, 186–
   187
salt ponds. *See* pond, salt; restoration
salt production, 132–133, 262
saltwater intrusion, 144
Salzman, Barbara, 180–181
San Francisco Bay Area Conservancy, 245
San Francisco Bay Conservation and
   Development Commission, 7, 8, 10,
   155–156, 179–180, 240, 281, 287–288,
   291–294, 296–297

San Francisco Bay Joint Venture, 188–189,
   245, 258 (sidebar)
San Francisco Bay Regional Water Quality
   Control Board, 8, 170, 188–189, 227,
   243
San Francisco Estuary Institute, 89, 140–141,
   159, 161–162, 167, 198, 212, 251, 268,
   294
San Francisco Estuary Project/Partnership,
   205, 222 (sidebar)
San Francisco Public Utilities Commission,
   210, 231
San Francisco State University, 240, 283
San Francisquito Creek, 151
San Joaquin River, 23, 142, 217
San Joaquin Valley, 165
San Jose State University, 282
San Pablo Bay, 31–32, 41, 77
   Wildlife Refuge, 256–262
sand dunes, underwater, 31
sand mining, 134
sandbars, 44
sanderling(s)s, 55, 99
sandpipers, 95–96, **98–101,** 103 (fig.)
   Least Sandpiper, 99
   Western Sandpiper, **99–101,** 103
Santa Clara Valley Water District, 268
Sarcocornia pacifica, **71–72**
sardine, 48, 102
   canneries, 132
Save San Francisco Bay Association, 6–7,
   152–157, 176, 208, 280
   Save the Bay, history documentary, 154
      (photo)
   Save the Bay's Canoes-in-Sloughs, 282
      (photo), 319
Schemmerling, Carole, 225
Schoellhamer, David, 14, 41–42, 44, 249–250
Schoeneoplectus californicus, 67, **74**
scorecard, 207–208
Scripps Institution, 289
sea level rise, 19–21, 49, 199, 285–298
   areas vulnerable to, 292 (sidebar)
Sea Lion, California, 65, 79, **92–93**
seafood processing, 131–132
Seals, Harbor, 72, 92, **94–95,** 103, 170
Sears Point, 259
seasonal wildlife events, 103
sediment, 41–45, 167
   cores, 49, 158–159
   dredge disposal, 179
   restoration needs, 248–251, 255, 295
   sea level rise adaptation, 295
selenium, 165
Sevengill Shark, 79

ABOUT THE AUTHORS

Kathleen M. Wong (left) and Ariel Rubissow Okamoto (right). (Max Eissler)

Ariel Rubissow Okamoto, journalist and essayist, has been writing about San Francisco Bay's watershed for over 25 years. She lives overlooking the water in North Beach, San Francisco. She specializes in bringing the work of leading local scientists, natural resource managers, and environmental activists to life on the page. Her writing has appeared in *Bay Nature* magazine, the *San Francisco Chronicle*, *Estuary*, and numerous government and nonprofit publications.

Kathleen M. Wong is a Bay Area native and science journalist specializing in California ecology. She has written for numerous national and regional magazines, newspapers, textbooks, and other publications. The former editor of *California Wild* magazine, she is now a science writer for the University of California Natural Reserve System.

Series Design:	Barbara Haines
Design Enhancements:	Beth Hansen
Design Development:	Jane Tenenbaum
Composition:	Bytheway Publishing Services
Text:	9/10.5 Minion
Display	ITC Franklin Gothic Book and Demi:
Prepress:	Embassy Graphics
Printer and Binder:	CS Graphics

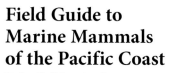

Field Guide to Marine Mammals of the Pacific Coast

Baja, California, Oregon, Wahington, British Columbia

Sarah G. Allen, Joe Mortenson, and Sophie Webb

California Natural History Guides, 100
$24.95 paper   978-0-520-26545-5
$60.00 cloth   978-0-520-26544-8

Natural History of the Point Reyes Peninsula

Jules G. Evens

Fully Revised and Expanded Edition
California Natural History Guides, 94
$24.95 paper   978-0-520-25467-1
$60.00 cloth   978-0-520-25465-7

Weather of the San Francisco Bay Region

Harold Gilliam

Second Edition
California Natural History Guides, 63
$14.95 paper   978-0-520-22990-7
$29.95 cloth   978-0-520-22989-1

Introduction to California's Beaches and Coast

Gary Griggs

California Natural History Guides, 99
$50.00 cloth   978-0-520-26289-8
$19.95 paper   978-0-520-26290-4

For other CNHG titles
visit www.ucpress.edu/go/cnhg